Modern Times, Ancient Hours

Working Lives in the Twenty-first Century

PIETRO BASSO

Edited and translated
by Giacomo Donis

VERSO

London · New York

First published as *Tempi moderni, orari antichi* by FrancoAngeli 1998
© Pietro Basso 1998
Updated and expanded edition first published by Verso 2003
© Verso 2003

Verso
UK: 6 Meard Street, London W1F OEG
USA: 180 Varick Street, New York, NY 10014–4606

Verso is the imprint of New Left Books

ISBN 1–85984–565–7

British Library Cataloguing in Publication Data
A catalogue record for this book is available from the British Library

Library of Congress Cataloging-in-Publication Data
A catalog record for this book is available from the Library of Congress

Designed and typeset in Monotype Bembo by Illuminati, Grosmont
Printed by R.R. Donnelley & Sons, USA

Contents

Acknowledgements

I wish to express my fraternal thanks to Charles-André Udry, whose help and support was decisive in bringing this edition to light. I thank him for his invaluable encouragement and advice; for his constancy in focusing attention and criticism on the conditions of existence of the working class; and, as editor of *Page 2* (a magazine we greatly miss) and leading spirit of *Raisons d'agir sur le lieu de travail*, for the opportunities he gave me to discuss the issues presented here with other researchers and activists. This English edition of my book is dedicated to him.

My special thanks go to the editor and translator Giacomo Donis. All books are transformed and reshaped in translation, which always involves interpreting and rewriting. Fortunately, this translation has made my work clearer and more incisive, and thus more accessible to the men and women who experience, every day, just how hard the life of workers in this new century is.

I also wish to thank Guido Mandarino for his assistance in gathering and analysing the material relating to the present-day situation in Germany.

And, finally, my thanks to Ines Andreetta, librarian of the Philosophy Department at Venice University, for the great job she did tracking down documentation from all over the world.

Introduction

Many say that the sickness of our society is unemployment. It is self-evident. The International Labor Organization speaks of one billion unemployed and underemployed persons in the world today. Few, however, see that this society suffering from unemployment is, at the same time, suffering from overwork. And fewer still are aware that in this capitalist market society the two diseases, unemployment and overwork, feed off one another, while furiously attacking the very same part of the 'social body' – namely, the working class (or working classes). This shall be my theme: the intensive and extensive exploitation of wage labour – an old theme, but one of enormous importance today.

This book maintains that in Western society, for at least the past twenty-five years, the average working time of wage labourers has become increasingly burdensome and invasive – more intense, fast-paced, 'flexible' and long. This is true not only in industry and agriculture, but in all branches of social organization – and is particularly true in that very world of 'services' which has been so aggressively presented as the postmodern El Dorado of light, clean, satisfying work, with short working hours.

Such a thesis may be surprising. As for the intensification and speeding up of working time – the reader may admit that this is so. But as for its getting longer – now *that*, you say, just cannot be true. Yet, as we shall see, it is perfectly true; and I have come to such a conclusion entirely on the basis of a scrupulous critical examination of hard facts.

Let me say, however, that the road we have to follow will be tortuous, for a number of reasons. First, because the official sources and methods of investigation are almost always unreliable. They do not take into account an incredible amount of the paid and unpaid working time of common working humanity. So, from the beginning to the end of this examination, we have to bear in mind the fact that 'men and women work *much more* than the usual statistical estimates lead us to believe.'[1] And it is not fortuitous that this warning comes from an expert on female labour, who has experience of that macroscopic distortion which makes the daily household labour of women vanish from the official statistics. But the falsifications such statistics contain, and socialize, do not stop here. The sloth of the official statistics, and their covert *ideological* criteria, also permit them to overlook the greatly expanding area of nondomestic 'shadow' work,[2] of casual work, as well as the substantial amount of time that, in an epoch of generalized 'Toyotaism', wage workers 'voluntarily' give their companies just to prove their loyalty. I have, accordingly, made limited, and necessarily critical, use of the 'official figures', even though I knew I could only partially replace them with data capable of fully reflecting the real state of affairs.

But the obstacles to a truthful analysis of working time are not limited to the sphere of statistics. A second kind of difficulty stems from the customary way of looking at working time. Normally, the point of view is narrowly national, empirical, reduced to the present moment, and permeated by the conviction that technological progress has more or less automatically cut working time in the past and will do so in the future. I see things differently. My constant point of reference is the international context and its massive conditioning of *all* national contexts. I have systematically adopted the historical-comparative method – the only method capable of giving a unitary account of social processes that have deep roots and far-ranging consequences. Finally, I have kept my distance from any form of technological triumphalism. Technology, which today claims to be absolute lord and master of social life (but this is mystification!), is neither free from social relations nor superordinate to them; it is in fact nothing other than a potentiality that can be used (also where working time is concerned) for opposing social ends by opposing social forces.

The investigation of *real* working hours is further complicated by contradictory situations and trends in the world – and specifically in the 'West', that part of the world on which we shall focus our attention. So, in our case, the investigator is called upon to draw careful distinctions between the rule and the exception; to determine what works for, and what against, the consolidation of the rule; and, finally, to identify what links rule and exceptions together. The whole question may be summed up in the following terms. On the question of working hours, who today best represents the fundamental trend of globalized capitalism: the United States (as Japan did earlier) or France? I am convinced it is the 'American' trend that is gaining the upper hand – the trend towards heavier and longer working time. Of course most of my European colleagues – especially the French speakers among them – heartily disagree.

I have in front of me a special issue of the French magazine *Croissance*, the theme of which is 'a thousand and one ways of employing time'; it is an exemplary expression of a certain way of thinking. There is one article with the highly explicit title 'The Americans are Tired Workaholics', which concisely and cuttingly sums up the less than brilliant US record on the question of working hours. As the article points out, in 1997 the average US working man spent about 50 hours per week on the job, with 10 per cent regularly working as many as 60 hours. Working women got by with 44 hours – not counting their household work of course, which brings their weekly workload up to between 65 and 80 hours, slightly less than 10 or slightly more than 11 hours per day. Vacations? Not more than two weeks a year. And if you want to make a good impression on your bosses, you'd better work extra hours *and* with a smile on your face, *and*, if necessary, give them plenty of your weekends too! The article concludes that 'the notion of totally free time, time for oneself, which can be dedicated to reading, music, family, friends, or to just doing nothing is a luxury that only a few North Americans can enjoy.'[3] So, the Americans are suffering from workaholism, to the point where their 'mental balance' and personal relationships are devastatingly impaired. But where does this disease come from? What has caused it? Is it transient or not? What has been its role in the sharp recovery of competitiveness of the US economy? What has been and will be its impact on the rest of the West and on the entire world? And are the conditions that brought about a lengthening of hours in the United States not to be found in Europe, or are they looming on the European horizon too?

There is not a word about any of these questions in our article from *Croissance*. I mention it not just to catch out a superficial journalist, but to point the finger at a superficial way of dealing with this issue that is not created by journalism itself, but in fact absorbed from 'social science' – and in particular from a sociology that, clearly hallucinating, is convinced 'we have already entered a society in which free time exceeds working time',[4] and that leads us to believe that sooner or later the US-Americans will certainly 'change their minds', illuminated by that beacon of civilization which is Europe. 'The 35-hour week in the United States? It won't come tomorrow but the idea is in the offing – the Americans want free time', we are assured. The idea that having more time for oneself may be the new American dream – now, that's not hard to believe. But that is not my point. It is this: *why*, in the country that is the engine and the model of our (dark) present, are working hours for working men and even more for working women, for the entire working class, getting heavier and longer? *Why*, there, right in the middle of a new technological revolution, has the majority of the proletariat been dragged into the experience of 'working longer for less'?[5] For a properly historical-theoretical analysis of these questions I refer the reader to the last chapter of this book; for now I can offer no more than a careful, if essentially descriptive, comparison of the US and the European situations.

At the bottom of the workaholism in the United States there is, first of all, the creeping reduction of the purchasing power of wages, which has been advancing for two decades. This phenomenon is so serious that one now speaks of a 'general crisis of wages'. And as for the US labour force, which just a quarter of a century ago was by far the best paid in the world, as one pundit recently put it: 'American labour is cheap.'[6] The deterioration of wages has involved 80 per cent of the working men and 60 per cent of the women, and contrary to popular opinion it has not been limited to the less educated. If the heavy-handed pressure of US companies to wrest hours and hours of overtime work from their employees (turning living time into working time) has met with little more than lukewarm opposition, this has been due in part to the general decline of wages – including the minimum wage itself, which has reversed the trend and risen slightly only in the past two years. And this decline has been helped – not hindered! – by the low pay and high insecurity of the much-acclaimed millions of 'new jobs' created in the services sector, whose crowning glory is the casual and ultraflexible McJob.[7]

Low wages are not the only cause of long hours, of course. There are other, strongly interacting factors at work. There is the climate of social insecurity created by the endless sequence of mass firings of 'guaranteed' workers inaugurated in 1981 by Reagan, and continued under the Clinton administration with the mass downsizing of corporations.[8] And the continual erosion of company benefits and of the degree and range of health and pension coverage ensured by the state. And the resumption of massive immigration from Latin America and Asia that puts at the disposal of US capitalism a huge amount of labour power disposed – of necessity – to accept working conditions and hours heavier than 'normal'. And, in the other direction, there is the wave of manufacturers, including segments of avant-garde production, that are moving to the Third World, with many others threatening to follow them. And, finally, there is the long-standing decline of the unionization of US workers, caused both by the ruinous policy of the AFL–CIO (ruinous from the standpoint of the permanent interests of the workers), and by specifically union-busting policies pursued by Republicans and Democrats alike.[9]

Our question now is this: are the conditions that have made working time heavier and longer in the United States producing the same effect throughout Europe? I think the answer is clearly yes. What we can observe is, at most, a certain delay due to the fact that Europe made great gains in competitiveness on the United States from 1945 to 1975 – since, in the long run, a monopoly tends to hamper the monopolist, while at least for a certain period the ruins of war benefit the losing side; and also due to the fact that the European proletariat has (until now) been more combative and better organized than its American counterpart – more capable of resisting the globalizing course of 'neoliberalism'. However, if we take off our rose-coloured glasses we cannot help but see that the 'law of the wolves'[10] – the supreme law of globalized capitalism – is progressively imposing itself in Europe too, even if Europeans still like to think they are different.

What has first curbed and then diminished the average level of wages has been, in this order: the violent attacks of Thatcherism; the policy of 'necessary sacrifices' imposed on and self-imposed by the major European unions (necessary for reinflating profits and return on capital, financial and otherwise); and finally the increasingly strict anti-inflationistic policies of the European central banks and now of *the* European Central Bank, whose social target is wage labour. The goals that Thatcher, Chirac and Kohl were not able to attain at one blow have been slowly but surely attained by Blair, Schröder and Jospin (and now Raffarin) – with the bankers pulling the strings. True, Europe creates fewer jobs than the United States. But that does not stop it from following the United States wholeheartedly in the casualization of employment, with the result that from two-thirds to three-quarters of the new jobs that are created are without the 'old' safeguards. And this, as any child can see, weakens the position of workers who continue to enjoy those safeguards and are now faced with pressures for new, and worse, conditions of wages and hours. So in Europe too we now have our own swelling legions of the working poor.

And – as if the general process of the globalization of poverty, with its mouth-watering opportunities for outsourcing production all over the world, had not been enough for European capitalists – then came the manna of 1989! With the collapse of so-called 'real socialism' a huge area for the construction of a European system of thousands upon thousands of *maquiladoras* with Third World wages and hours opened up on the very patio of Europe. Poland, Slovenia, Croatia, Romania, the Czech Republic, Slovakia, Albania, Bulgaria, Ukraine... Then, as the crowning event of that semi-spontaneous collapse, methodically organized and directed, jointly, by the United States and Europe, we had the war in Yugoslavia and against Yugoslavia. Regarding our theme: in Eastern Europe in the course of ten years *millions of jobs, the 8-hour day, and the relative moderation of the work pace were all swept away.* You won't find much about it in the official statistics, which record practically nothing in real time – especially when it comes to the torment of labour imposed upon the working class. But it is common knowledge that working days of 10 to 12 hours and more are spreading throughout Eastern Europe. It is downright foolish to fool oneself or others. This tidal wave against workers in the East will also hit, has already hit, the working and living conditions of Western European wage labour, beginning with wages and working time – indirectly, or also directly, with the new wave of immigration we are seeing today.

So *all* the conditions are present – except, in part, for the complete disorganization of the proletarian movement – for Europe to follow the United
States also in the direction of heavier and longer working hours and of
workaholism. Workaholism is not a genetic disease that only strikes the Japanese and the US-Americans; no respecter of nations, it is just one of the
pathological results of the capitalist market economy, never sated with profits
and possessed by the pursuit of unpaid labour time.

It is up to the reader to decide whether my examination of working time
in Europe is adequate and convincing. My basic thesis is already clear, and
thus may be tested. I only wish to add that the intensification, 'flexibilization'
and lengthening of working hours that, nonhomogeneously, has been taking
place in Europe since 1975 has been divided unequally between genders,
generations, races and nationalities. Between genders, because the heavier
burden has fallen upon women, who have entered the labour market in
increasingly greater numbers, both on their own initiative and because the
market and the state have had great need of fresh, low-cost labour power that
is flexible and, for the most part, specializes in demanding and delicate service
jobs. And for these newly employed women the burden of nondomestic labour
has, very often, been almost entirely *added to* the household work they did
before, since the division of domestic tasks between men and women has
varied very little. By the same token, young people have had to accept a
percentage of casual work, dangerous work, atypical work, night work, intense and repetitive work, work 'à la carte', as well as a lengthening of working hours, that is disproportionately high – at least as high as the corresponding
rate of unemployment.[11]

The division of these additional burdens between races and nationalities
has been no less unequal. The heavier and harder hours and tasks have fallen
to the immigrant workers – almost 'naturally' – that is, according to the
hierarchized and neocolonial nature of the relations existing on the world
market.[12] These workers have also been subjected to a policy of immigration
restrictions, oppressive controls and indiscriminate stigmatization on the part
of European governments and 'public opinions', which has globally lowered
their concrete possibilities of self-defence in the face of the impersonal (but
pure white, and pure Western) mechanisms of differentiated super-exploitation.

What place does the new French legislation on the 35-hour week have in this picture? Is it an exception? A bluff? An alternative? Is it a model that Europe, and even the United States, may be prepared to copy? Or is it a partial exception that can be functionally combined with an opposite trend, buttressing it? For now, I shall leave my answer in abeyance. After all, we are only in the preface and I have already given my reader too many clues about the crime and the culprit. Let us at least have some suspense over the role of the butler! And then, this question will be addressed in the whole of Chapter 5.

On the other hand, I must ask my reader to have no doubt about the fact that this book is the exact opposite of a *De profundis* for the working class. The trend towards a comprehensive worsening of working and living conditions for the mass of working people – the tendency to institute 'ancient' hours in modern times – is *inherent* in mature capitalism and in its cultural and political institutions. But it is not, for me, an *ineluctable* tendency to which the working class must bow down as before an inescapable destiny. What is inescapable, and certain, for whoever has eyes to see and ears to hear, is only the fact that capitalism – even the capitalism of the 'new economy' – is incapable of freeing labour and of freeing *from* labour as gruelling, as an experience of estrangement, as physical and psychical emptying performed for others; from labour as something the worker is forced to do, just to survive, or to consume commodities.

Contrary to the spirit of the times, here we shall not celebrate the progressiveness and omnipotence of capital – nor, *à la* Foucault, that of political power. The best we can do for now is to recall, to evoke, the only social force that is capable of reducing working time in the service of profit and contesting its laws – the force of the working class. This force alone, which has fought for centuries for the reduction of the working day, has a vital interest in renewing the struggle with heightened intensity and greater scope, in order to make it a truly world struggle that includes all sectors of social activity – together with, not in opposition to, the struggle against the sickness of unemployment. I am convinced that on a worldwide scale all the conditions are slowly coming together for this renewal of the struggle. True, we don't hear much about it today, especially not from the professional fabulists. And it is no less true that the first steps were quite timid. Think of the first European strike for the 35-hour week in April 1992, or the first international company strikes (such as the UPS strike in 1997), or the Renault strikes all over Europe in 1998, followed by the (less timid) Seattle demonstrations in the autumn of 1999, and the rise of the antiglobalization movement, the World March of Women in 2000, the general strikes in Europe in 2002, and so on. But the tradition of working-class struggle, and the millennial human aspiration to work that does not break the body and the spirit, to work worthy of free men and women in free association, engaged in satisfying, with solidarity, the most genuine human needs as these needs have matured in the course of the history of societies – this tradition and this aspiration are still alive beneath the ashes.

Technology itself, far from being the hateful threat that many people fear, seems to address working men and women with the following invitation: 'Here I am, ready to help you satisfy your profoundest aspiration. But I cannot do it all by myself; first you will have to free me from the clutches of capital. Free me, and I will help you free yourselves. I have been waiting for you to take the initiative. When the devil do we start?' A very good question: when the devil do we start again?

I

The Question of Working Hours

The art of keeping slaves is being progressively refined.
Anton Chekhov

I

At the beginning of the twenty-first century – after the century of the second and the third industrial revolutions, of Taylorism and Toyotaism, of the conquest of the eight-hour day and mass 'free' time – what has become of the length, intensity and quality of working time? Current socio-economic literature answers this question in two different ways.

One part of the literature, concerned with depicting epochal scenarios, treats the question with a presumptuousness that borders on derision, as if it were a non-issue. The overall quantity of living time that is absorbed by working time, it asserts, is being continually reduced. In less than a hundred years, working hours have been cut in half. And, momentary disturbances notwithstanding, it is destined to decrease substantially even more and, at the same time, to be filled with 'contents', according to a line of evolution presented as natural and necessary. The only condition to be respected is that robotic-informatic technology and the capitalist market economy have to be given free rein. It sounds like the good news we've all been waiting for! The ancient torment of labour, and of labour time, spent 'for others', gruelling, long, dull, subject to iron-fisted regimentation, is about to disappear! Along with the era of industry, the era of work as 'hard labour' is drawing to a close, and the magic oyster of the 'postindustrial' epoch opening up. The epoch of light, many-sided, intelligent activity, flush with personal independence and universal creativity. The end of alienated labour and its torments. The beginning of free social activity, and of happiness (or not?), for everyone (or *almost* everyone). If not right away, well, it won't be long now! So say Toffler, Gershuny, Sue, and company.[1]

The tone with which this is pronounced brooks no reply – it expresses self-evidence, indisputability. But, may I ask, do we find in these 'futurologists' (or in their more modest 'presentologist' colleagues) any serious examination of what a normal working day or working week really is today for workers in general, and for factory workers in particular? And if they happen to come up against *facts* that darken the brilliance of their forecasts, just look at the rabbits they pull out of their hats!

Another faction of 'experts' circle around the question, so to speak; they give us low-profile analysis. Instead of sketching epochal scenarios they do case studies of particular aspects and situations. They 'stick to the facts' and aim to be 'concrete'. But in a period of transition like the one we are in today, what they see as 'concrete' can take no other form than an infinite variety of disconnected things, a to-and-fro of social splinters without rhyme or reason. For them there are no general trends of working hours; one can only speak of a vast plurality of different hours that move in contradictory directions. Here hours rise, and there they fall. Here, in fact, they get heavier; but there they get lighter – as many different hours as there are different kinds of work. There is no longer an 'average' working condition, but only an extremely diversified gamut of working conditions not comparable with one another. And what is more, there are as many different hours as there are different kinds of capitalism. We no longer have just one capitalism, but many nonhomogeneous and alternative capitalisms! And within each capitalism we have two, three, seven, twenty-seven sub-capitalisms, each one with a series of unique particularities. As for working times and conditions, nothing remains but universal fragmentation.

The studies produced by this empirical school give us a heap of useful information[2] but have nothing to say about the fundamental question, which is this: as a whole and on a worldwide scale, in what direction is working time going, and why? And often, despite their surface agnosticism, with some hesitation and no little inconsistency, these 'empiricists' end up by exalting stereotypes of the socio-economics of the status quo. They do so, for example, when they present the restructuring, diversification and flexibility of hours as ineluctable processes that are beneficial to all sides of society – to companies and to workers – when it is simply not true.

The real state of affairs, for the growing mass of unskilled labour but for higher echelons of workers too,[3] is a far cry from this sort of dreamwork. Capitalist progress, the capitalist market economy, has no intention of freeing wage labour from the burden of toil it has had to bear up to now. It is simply preparing more sophisticated, and even more totalitarian, forms and methods of squeezing out work than those used in the past, without by any means forgoing its time-honoured tried-and-true methods and forms.

At the beginning of the twenty-first century, working time – still long, but now obsessively fast-paced and 'flexible' – remains the pivot (and the despot) of living time for hundreds of millions of workers all over the world, the centre of their existence, their number-one problem – when it is not an out-and-out nightmare. Working hours, especially after the crisis of 1974, far from decreasing day after day, have manifested a growing resistance to reduction, and for years have tended to increase while also growing more intense and variable. And the full extension of the so-called process of 'globalization' cannot but heighten these trends – even if at the same time, dialectically, it lays the groundwork for a renewal of the movement of world struggle for the drastic and general reduction of working hours.

The aim of this book is to describe, even if summarily, the characteristics of this situation made up, more than one may think, of ancient hours in modern times; to analyse its effects on the overall condition of the life of workers, while at the same time attempting to indicate, at least in general terms, its causes and possible solutions.[4]

II

I speak, with a dash of metaphor, of 'ancient' hours to highlight the fact that social dynamics are following a course different from the one most people expect of modernity. I do not mean to assert, however, that financial globalization and corporate reorganization according to the criteria of the 'Toyota production system' are about to bring us back the 15- or 16-hour day. The history of society never retraces its steps (and, to be sure, globalization cannot be represented as a road going backwards), neither can it be harnessed in facile linear schemata. Indeed, it is not fortuitous that my investigation begins with the critique of a facile linear schema – originally drawn up by Keynes and embraced by official social science ever since.

Keynes was convinced that the work time of working people would be reduced and lightened *automatically* with the progress of science, technology, and the growth rates of the economy and productivity. But the basic trends of the world system of working hours and the changes in the work organization that took place in the course of the twentieth century give the lie to that conviction and to any sort of technological or technocratic triumphalism. The long-term evolution of industrial hours demonstrates, on the contrary, that the average length of working time decreased more in precisely the historical phase in which production and labour productivity increased relatively less. In sum, if there is a rule to be discovered in this matter, it is the following: in the twentieth century the reduction of working hours in industry has been, and is, *inversely proportional* to the growth of investment, to technological progress and to the growth of productivity. The more these factors advanced, the more problematic it became for workers to obtain new reductions of working hours. It is a genuine paradox, which we may call the paradox of labour productivity (under capitalism).

The paradox is confirmed in the current situation of Western industry where, despite the very latest technological revolutions, companies and states are more, not less, reluctant to reduce working hours. This reluctance now concerns all the dimensions of working time: daily, weekly, yearly, lifetime. And, since the mid 1970s, it has resonated with an increasingly stronger drive to liberalize working time and lengthen it anew, both in fact and in law – together with, not as an alternative to, its intensification.

This, primarily, is what I am referring to when I speak of 'ancient' hours. But I also refer to the fact, ignored in every Western study on working hours, that today the vast majority of industrial workers are to be found in the newly industrialized countries of the Third World, where they have to come to grips with nineteenth-century working hours at the service of twenty-first-century productivity. This is the other aspect of our question, which it is becoming less and less possible to conceal. In fact the globalization of financial flows, which has locked the liquid capital of the planet into a single (firmly hierarchized) unitary circuit, proceeds on the same scale to the functional reorganization of industrial, agricultural and 'services' production. This process continually brings the two poles of world production – the 'centre' and the 'periphery' – closer together, while increasingly putting the two different conditions of wage labour that correspond to them in direct and systematic competition. The consequences, which in part are already tangible, are two-fold. On one hand, hours we thought were dead and gone are now being imported to the West (think of the growing diffusion of night work, Saturday work, Sunday work); on the other, the burden of heavier working conditions in the advanced capitalist countries is loaded onto the shoulders of workers in the Third World, hindering every effort they make to improve their lot. The result – both in the 'centre' and on the 'periphery' – has been to make working time longer and more burdensome than it was in the 1960s and 1970s (a process that, in the long run, cannot but create a strong social resistance, which has already begun to stir).

An evolution of worldwide working time in such sharp contradiction to general expectations surely deserves to be closely investigated and to have its enigma explained. Instead, it has received frightfully little attention. To the best of my knowledge, there is only one study that has unambiguously acknowledged just how substantial the phenomenon is: namely, *The Over-worked American* by Juliet B. Schor,[5] which – parallel to and independently of my investigation (and vice versa) – has come to the same analytical conclusion. I make reference to Schor's book, however, not only because of this agreement, but also because it concerns the leader, engine and model of the 'developed' world – the country that, in capitalist terms, is ahead of all the others and farthest from that mythical nineteenth century to which the 'experts' relegate the extensive exploitation of the working class, as if it were an archaeological find. And let me observe in passing how, while in Europe almost everything that comes from America is sacrosanct, this interesting text has been either totally ignored by our experts, or else discussed only for what is insubstantial in it and not for its notable substance, which is analytical and accusatory.[6] Only our practical and pragmatic entrepreneurs see things differently (but, according to a well-known principle of the division of labour, they are not 'scientists'!); they make no bones about saying that we need to follow the example of America, where working hours get longer!

III

'Beginning in the late 1960s', Juliet Schor tells us, 'the United States had entered an era of rising worktime.'[7] 'Blinded by the power of technology – seduced by futurist visions of automated factories effortlessly churning out products', the experts 'were unable to predict or even see these trends.'[8] But 'these trends' are all the more surprising if one considers the fact that labour productivity has doubled since 1948. Workers in the US now produce in less than six months as much as they could produce in a year in 1948 – which means that, abstractly speaking, their working time could have been halved without altering that standard of production (and consumption) which half a century ago was taken as a point of reference by the entire world. And instead not a single drop of this rise in productivity has trickled down (so to speak) to diminish working hours. On the contrary, between 1969 and 1989 the average annual working hours of full-time employees rose 158 hours (an increase of half an hour per day, or one month per year).[9] It should be noted, moreover, that the gender distribution of this added burden of toil has been unequal, with 161 more hours for employed women (287 more annual hours for nondomestic work, offset by a 126-hour reduction in domestic work), 139 for men. But the sacred principle of equality is safe if we look at the statistics on leisure time – which has fallen about 15 per cent for both women and men. If things go on like this and at this rate, by the year 2010 Americans will achieve the glorious goal of 3,000 working hours a year.[10]

Schor indicates the host of anti-social consequences of this 'irrational' course of working time: from the growth of the unemployment rate to the diffusion of workaholism; from the lack of time for sleeping and eating, for family and friends, to the rising stress due to the impossibility of satisfactorily reconciling work and family life; to the increase in problems of both physical and mental health – the latter being particularly acute in the case of workers on assembly lines and (another slap in the face of facile 'evidence'!) in the electronic sweatshops. All this leads Schor to conclude that 'time poverty is straining the social fabric'. The American worker is increasingly overworked.[11]

But this global exasperation of the onus of work, reconstructed with precision and cogency by Schor, still has to be explained. And the explanation can only be found in the nature of the production process typical of the market economy. This is the problem with *The Overworked American*. Its explanation in fact proves to be both limited and partial. Limited, because it looks to certain traits peculiar to the socio-cultural situation of the United States for the origins of a phenomenon that first came to light in the USA, but is by no means exclusively American property. And partial, if not evasive, because Schor thinks she finds the cause of the overwork that manifests itself in the processes of production and the reproduction of labour power *outside* these processes themselves, in the moment of distribution, in the compulsive consumeristic craving typical of American society (that is, in 'the insidious cycle of work-and-spend').[12] Note well: what she has to say about the historical-social (and by no means natural-eternal) character of consumerism is unquestionably cogent, as are the passages in which she demonstrates (polemically, against the neoclassical economists) that US workers did not in fact 'choose' this mode of the social use of labour productivity – if anything they adapted to it. It must also be said that Schor correctly identifies the 'entrepreneurial class' as the social force most avidly opposed (yesterday and today) to the reduction of working hours. And nonetheless she is convinced that such behaviour is not coerced behaviour, dictated by the *laws* of the production and exchange of commodities, but rather is the inevitable result of a series of subjective misjudgements made by the entrepreneurial class, which at the end of the day will prove counterproductive for the competitiveness of the American economy.[13]

But here Schor is making a big mistake – also and above all where social theory is concerned. Disliking the direction that capitalism and US-American society have taken, she imagines that an 'alternative' – philanthropical and ecological – capitalism is possible (and desirable), when in fact there is no such thing; she fails to take adequately into account, or 'misjudges', what *real* capitalism really is. Like any other form of social organization, capitalism cannot be indifferently this and that. It has its proper rules of operation. And its first and fundamental rule is the *law of profit*, since capitalism is not generic production of goods, but production whose purpose is profit. These rules, even if tempered, restrained, obstructed, and even provisionally neutralized by a combination of circumstances, reassert themselves nonetheless; and the greater the obstacles on their path, the greater the force with which they counter them. This is why it is deviant, for social science, to refuse to recognize that which is the real supporting structure of capitalist economy – dreaming, instead, of a capitalism that at least a little, and for a little, is capable of renouncing profit and money.

'In the international market', Schor claims, 'what matters in the long run is not how many hours a person works, but how productively he or she works them.'[14] It is just not so. And such opposition between the length and the quality of working time is not justified. Abstracting from any other historical, political or military factor, for over a century and a half the international market has been ruled by the optimum combination between the greatest possible length and the greatest possible production intensity of working time. The worldwide success of Japan since World War II, with its 'model' organization of production and work – call it 'Toyota production system', 'Toyotaism', or 'lean production' as you will – is nothing other than the most recent demonstration of this 'optimum combination'. And as the 'West' (the term, here, includes Japan), for the first time in its history, finds itself competing with the most dynamic nations of the Third World in a growing number of production sectors with a high intensity of living labour, the 'optimum combination' becomes even more important. And its importance is made even greater by the acceleration of financial globalization now in progress, which is boosting the global volume of world production, and 'wants' to do so by stiffening competition between nations, corporations and workers. So it is not a question of either long hours or maximally productive hours, but – within the not-rigidly-defined limits of the possible – both the one and the other.

What is more, when Ms Schor is confronted with the contemporaneous growth of unemployment and working hours, like other liberal authors she just cannot understand why companies have not even taken the only 'rational' and 'human' solution into consideration – namely, the reduction of working hours. Well, even the coarsest of those experts she takes to task with such finesse could answer her, quite rightly, that the market and the corporation are not charitable institutions; that for them the infallible yardstick of rationality is profit, a good return on one's capital; and that from their point of view this is also the most human of the criteria of social regulation since the 'open (market) society' is, as Popper tells us, the best of all societies that has ever existed and can ever exist. And our coarse expert, as proof of the rationality of the behaviour of US multinationals (rational with respect to the market and to the interests of US capitalism), could point to the recovery of competitiveness in the USA over the past ten to twenty years. A recovery, moreover, that has owed a very great deal to the lessons learned from the 'Japanese model' – not the least of which consists in lengthening hours to the outer limits of human endurance.

By the same token, we cannot expect to find any great concern for the absolutely legitimate alarm about the pathogenic, anti-egalitarian, anti-ecological character both of long and heavy hours (an American woman with a full-time job works, outside and inside the home, between 65 and 80 hours a week) and of neurotic consumerism. Indeed, in the logic of the market everything is decided by the growth rates of quantities produced and profits made, independently of what goods and services are produced, how they are produced, and for whom they are produced. If those key figures add up, any cost paid by man and nature will appear to be as light as a feather.

As long as one remains, materially and ideally, within the sphere of commodity production, there is no escape – either material or ideal – from the 'inexorable necessities' of competition and profit. And if one invokes, as Schor does, a yardstick for judging time (and working time) that, at last, will be able to release it from the money that is oozing out of its pores – well, if taken seriously, this would mean calling into question not just certain exacerbations or exaggerations of commodity production but rather commodity production as such, shaking its very foundations. If our social critic fails to do this, then even the most obtuse of economists (or sociologists) – better versed in the workings of capitalist production and its substantial immutability – will come closer than she does to the real heart of the question. After all, in the 1970s and 1980s it was the United States that followed Japan, just as now it is Europe that, plodding along, follows the two rich countries with the 'abnormally' long hours – not the other way around. As long as the match is played on the field of the competition between profit-making concerns, the winner can only be Japanese and American 'irrationality', not European 'rationality'.

IV

But Schor does deserve credit for having indicated all the problems contained in the question of working time. Dealing with working time means, in fact, dealing with the *capitalist social system* as a whole. The trend towards a freeze, if not an increase, in the length of the working time of industrial (and services) employees, coupled with its intensification and diversification, goes back to the basic regulatory principles of current social organization. So, indeed, to get to the bottom of this trend, in theory as in social practice, one has to go back to 'old' questions that are reputed, vainly, to have had their day. Questions such as the nature of the process of capitalist production as production for profit; the commodity-character of labour power and its peculiarity of being the only commodity that adds value; surplus value (yes, that too!); the curious double-dealing of science, a power of labour that acts as a power of capital, against labour; the no less 'curious' contradictions between technical–scientific progress and profit, between the saving of work and its dissipation, between the forced intensification of labour and equally forced mass unemployment; and, finally, the class struggle over working time, which is an aspect and moment of the historic alternative between two systems of production.

These questions must be faced. The labour time of workers is not just a detail of social life; despite the extraordinary development of machinery and science, it continues to provide the energy for the entire social edifice of capitalism. The relations between classes, nations, genders and individuals are inscribed in the buying and selling of labour time, in its internal composition (first and foremost in the relation between necessary, paid labour and surplus, unpaid labour), in its connection with comprehensive social time. In the recent – and the less recent – history of the length of working time we can find the kernel of the whole story of the struggle between capital and labour, the whole of modern political and social history.

Moreover, anyone possessed of even the slightest sense of history can see that in no previous epoch and form of society has there ever been a greater social and personal centrality of work and working time. Working time is the hub of the complex unitary mechanism of social times, of so-called 'free' time, of reproduction time – and, all the more, of individual times. As such, it structures the totality of expressions of social life, affecting even the most intimate feelings of the inner world. Indeed, it is working time, especially for and with the characteristics it has assumed with capitalist industry, that shapes the notion of time, the representation of time, the ideology of time, not only in industry but in society as a whole.[15] This is why the study of the length of working hours in the present and in the foreseeable future, while in appearance only sectorial and quantitative, in reality encompasses a tangled mass of questions that go far beyond working conditions, the work organization and the labour market, to take in the living condition of workers, and the existence of society, as a whole.

If, in general, in the analysis of social and human phenomena it is meaningless to oppose quantity and quality, this clearly must be true of our present analysis as well. By which I mean, if some 30 per cent of Japanese workers are so completely swamped by the habitual quantity of work to be done that they worry about dying of *karoshi* (death from overwork), can we imagine that outside the workplace these same people are able to weave rich tapestries of personal relationships? Can we imagine them intent on painting, sculpting, composing music, writing poetry, or even 'just' enjoying art? Can we expect them to be on the front line in the political life of society? Well, I don't think so. As a matter of fact, these workers are (how could it be otherwise?) the greatest consumers of television (or the most consumed by television) in the world, shoulder to shoulder with their 'overworked American' colleagues.[16] The long, exasperating coercion to perform the fragmented, banal tasks of the factory produces 'coerced' workers ready to swallow, in king-sized doses, the slop[17] dished out by the industry of mass media banality. It is not hard to imagine the consequences of all this for their personalities, their knowledge of the world, their *joie de vivre*, their capacity to react to the way they are treated in the workplace and in social life. But aren't these extreme cases, and far from home? Not at all. For example, if and when someone decides to take a closer look at the celebrated economic boom of the Italian northeast, what will be discovered is not only a workload far above the national average, but also rates of alcoholism, drug consumption, gratuitous violence, automobile accidents, and mental health problems that are just as far above average, along with an 'astonishing' (why astonishing?) direct and indirect correlation between the two series of national records.

Considering its depth and extension, I certainly cannot claim to have exhausted the question of the length of present-day working time in these few pages. I do hope, however, that I have managed to *formulate* the question adequately, and to have indicated its main causes and implications – without, of course, claiming to have grasped the underlying socio-historical situation in all its richness.

V

But even determining the 'facts' of the matter is no simple task. In an age in which every 'thing' is calculated with a precision that borders on perfection and in which production time is sliced up and computed right down to the smallest fraction of a second (informatics technicians now work with nano-seconds, billionths of a second), there is no (public) computation as question-able as the calculation of working time, or as neglected as the calculation of unpaid working time.

The official estimates of working hours are among the least reliable products of a discipline – statistics – which richly deserves its reputation for being the ideological science par excellence. In Italy (I know whereof I speak!) the state of the art is even worse than in most other places, not only for the scarcity and dispersion of its sources, but also for its failure to produce the surveys that interest us most. And I am not just referring to specific data on working hours – it is the entire statistical picture regarding the labour market that is woefully incomplete, to say the least. Recently, ISTAT (the Italian Central Statistics Office) itself estimated that 22.3 per cent of all employment is un-documented,[18] and thus not accounted for in the official surveys. And since this 'shadow' sector evidently consists of employees, craftsmen (often sub-contracted), 'independent consultants' who are actually company employees, or very small businesses with hours almost always longer than the average, it is clear that any 'rigorous' ISTAT estimate of actual working hours – if such a thing existed – would be far lower than the truth.

But the fact is that the existence of such a vast 'shadow economy' (of production and hours) is no longer a peculiarly Italian phenomenon (nor was it ever exclusive to Italy). In the other European OECD countries, too, the shadow economy is growing fast, along with its 'shadow' working hours. A study by the University of Linz[19] estimates that the slice of the entire economy represented by this 'sector', which was less than 5 per cent on average in 1970, surged to over 15 per cent in 1994. The greatest extension of the shadow economy was, indeed, in Italy (25.8 per cent, over against the 10.7 per cent of 1970), in Spain (22.3 per cent) and in Belgium (21.4 per cent, from the 10.4 per cent of 1970), but in the OECD nations on the whole, including the more 'virtuous' members of the club, in twenty-five years the 'shadow' area doubled, or even tripled. This area, clearly, is highly labour-intensive, composed for the most part of small businesses, in which there are frequent violations of the provisions of collective agreements in all fields, including working hours.

There is at least one other reason why official working hours are generally shorter than real ones: namely, the official statistics are mainly compiled on the basis of company sources – and the companies are almost always large companies.[20] Unfortunately I have had to make considerable use of these incomplete and reticent[21] sources, since field research in which workers are called upon to speak for themselves is both limited and very rare. Whenever possible, however, I have also had recourse to unofficial sources, which as a rule give real hours different from and longer than the official ones. But even these hours are not necessarily quite true, since it often occurs that companies and employees (fearing that a survey will end up in the hands of revenue authorities) make common cause in not declaring overtime that has effectively been worked.

Another difficulty arises from the fact that, today, a social question such as that of working hours has to be analysed on a *world scale*. This has induced me to make generalizations that are inevitably coarse-grained. Especially with regard to working times and conditions in the Third World, where official statistics are even less reliable than those for the 'developed' countries, I can give no more than a bare introduction to the theme. I have attempted to control the damage by taking a few countries that we do know somewhat more about as representative of a more comprehensive socio-economical course; but, clearly, what is needed in this area is a host of new, adequately researched studies.

My study is essentially concerned with working hours in industry.[22] Now, I know that to followers of the religion of the 'postindustrial' or the 'end of work' this will appear to be a lingering over a world and a time that are past, while neglecting to examine what is and will be. Since this is not the place for a full-scale reply to such simplifications, let me begin with the most superficial aspect of the question and just say this. The mass and the rate of industrial employment have never been as great, in the world, as they are today. The mass of workers employed in industry in the strict sense amounted to approximately five hundred million people in 1995, three and a half times more, in absolute terms, than in 1950; and the increase is considerable also in relative terms, since in the same period the world population only doubled. This means that *today*, at the very moment of history in which the industrial proletariat is supposed to be extinct, there is a social working *day* in world industry that amounts to no fewer than four and a half billion hours of work, and which probably exceeds five billion hours, most of them supplied by the proletariat. Not bad, for the phantom work of a phantom class! And if it is true that since the 1960s in the USA, since the 1970s in Europe, and since the 1980s in Japan industrial employment has been falling, first in percentage and then in absolute terms, this is not because industry has become outmoded but, on the contrary, because it has reached exceptional levels of productivity (on average more than double the levels in 'services'), which means that it is capable of producing ever greater quantities of commodities with a decreasing comprehensive volume of labour. Furthermore, in the rest of the world, home to four-fifths of humanity, industrial employment is on the rise. It is there, today, that we find 80 per cent of all the industrial workers in the world; it is there that over the next thirty years 99 per cent of the estimated one billion new workers will be concentrated – with at least 20 per cent of them employed in industry.[23]

But, beyond the raw numerical data, there is also the fact that the time of the factory, the system of industrial hours, continues to be the central organizational point of reference for the whole society in the very countries now called 'postindustrial'. While it cannot be denied that finance, the stock exchange and the banks are dominating industry more all the time, it is the 'new' model of work organization proper to industry that is transmigrating towards the variegated world of services (banking, information, wholesale and retail trade, health care),[24] of transportation, and even of 'civil' service – and not the other way around. This transmigration concerns working time as well. And the more penetrating studies on 'free' time have shown how even that time which by its very definition ought to be diametrically opposed to working time is progressively shaping up as a 'job' (a 'free-time job' we might call it) modelled on the 'full', fast and organized time of material production.[25] Facts such as these are what have led me to take the working time proper to industry as representative of trends that broadly apply also to extra-industrial working time, and even to nonworking time.

But beyond the numerical and organizational factors, the decisive factor for our question is *structural* – namely, the role of industrial production in the comprehensive accumulation of capital.[26] This will be hard to understand for those who think we are living in an age of the production of words by means of words, or for those who dream that the production of money by means of money can go on indefinitely without ever going through the process of material production; but not for those who recall that to this day the greatest political, military and financial powers in the world are none other than the greatest *industrial* powers, and that the *industry* of information and communication, the greatest symbol of 'postmodernity', would never have flowered and prospered without the degree of development attained by the traditional manufacturing industry.

VI

This book observes, recounts and critiques the condition of labour from the side of labour, not from the side of the market. And it does so from the 'point of view' of a future organization of social life that is no longer founded on the exploitation of one class by another, of one human being by another, but rather on the genuine social cooperation of all concerned. I reject the conservative and antihistorical point of view that sees humankind as destined by nature, if not by divine will, to live within social relations made up of exploitation and oppression.

So, to the objection that this is a book that takes sides, my answer is this: what text on working time, what product of the social sciences in general does not take sides? In a society such as ours, divided into classes, and then into races, nations and states – divided between dominators and dominated – how could social science, which is a fruit of this divided society, be neutral – 'objective' – with respect to social forces and interests in conflict with one another? How could it be truly 'pure', impartial, disinterested? Is not such a claim an outright mystification?

After all, a demonstration of the impossibility of this hypothesized neutrality has been given us by no less an authority than Max Weber, the maximum theorist of the 'value-neutrality' of the socio-historical sciences, who categorically denied it from the beginning to the end of his career – from his inaugural lecture in Freiburg (an emblem of ultra-'one-sided' socio-economics) right up to the last conferences (no less socially and politically 'one-sided'). It was Max Weber who, as if to justify his by no means 'value-neutral' way of doing socio-economics, said: Everyone follows their demon. Right. And if this demon, which is not personal but rather socially and historically determined, is hated by the gods – or fetishes – of the moment; if, then, following this demon will not win us the applause of the crowd – never mind! 'O gentlemen, the time of life is very short! ... And if we live, we live to tread on kings.'[27]

2

Long-term Trends 1945–89

Keynes's Prophecy

In our investigation of working hours in Western industry it may be useful to begin with one of the most famous of Keynes's *Essays in Persuasion*,[1] which, while couched as a forecast, is in fact the cogent expression of a point of view that is still current today.

It is the day after the financial and production crash of 1929, and Keynes sees a sense of 'economic pessimism' spreading both among 'the revolutionaries' and, with an opposite spin, among 'the reactionaries'. He is concerned about it, and this concern induces him to enter the fray in defence of the full vitality of capitalism. To this end he decides to 'take wings into the future' and sketches an exceedingly rosy picture of the 'economic possibilities for our grandchildren'. 'We are suffering, not from the rheumatics of old age, but from the growing-pains of over-rapid changes, from the painfulness of re-adjustment between one economic period and another.'[2] We can understand this if we look at 'what is going on under the surface', at 'the true interpretation of the trend' of the economic process of capitalism, at the way in which the 'accumulation [of capital] by compound interest' has progressed, and at the magnificent chain of scientific inventions and technical improvements to which that accumulation has given rise. If we do this with a sufficient sense of history, says Keynes, we have to conclude that the union between technical–scientific progress and 'compound interest' – that is, the capitalist form of social production – has now brought humanity just a step away from the solution of its 'economic problem'.

So, Keynes assures us that despite the turbulence of the present there is absolutely no justification for a pessimistic vision of the future. On the contrary, we can rest assured that 'within a hundred years' those very economic and technological forces which, since 1700, have broken the age-old stagnation of 'the standard of life of the average man', will bring us into 'the age of leisure and of abundance'. Having reached that point, for humanity there will be only one problem: 'To make what work there is still to be done to be as widely shared as possible' through a drastic reduction of working hours. Keynes sees no insurmountable structural difficulties in bringing about such a radical innovation in the organization of production and of social life. And as for opposing interests – not even a shadow. He foresees that the most serious obstacle, then, will be constituted by the psychological reluctance of our 'old Adam', who, accustomed from the dawn of time 'to strive and not to enjoy', will be loath to forgo his generous daily ration of sweat. But the hurdle will be cleared 'gradually'. One will just have to be flexible, especially at the beginning, making some concession, without excessive condescension, to this stubborn enslaver of himself: 'Three-hour shifts or a fifteen-hour week may put off the problem for a great while. For three hours a day is quite enough to satisfy the old Adam in most of us!' So, Keynes concludes, let us set off with vigour and with unswerving confidence on our way down the road of profit; 'avarice and usury and precaution must be our gods for a little longer still'; but in this way the attainment (via capitalism) of 'our destination of economic bliss' will take care of itself.

In Keynes's wake, at the apex of the cycle of post-war development, Fourastié calculated that by the year 2000 in the most industrialized countries working hours could be no more than 30 hours a week (for 40 weeks a year), which amounts to 1,200 hours a year. As recently as 1968 H. Kahn and A.J. Wiener, again with reference to the year 2000, believed it would be possible to cross the limit of the 1,000 hours of work per year, as long as the increase in productivity is reabsorbed by an increase in leisure time.[3] And the prophet of this historic enterprise is, of course, capitalism – the combined power of technical–scientific progress and what Keynes called 'compound interest', also known as profit.

Even if these due dates have come and gone, verification of Keynes's prophesy and Fourastié's and Kahn's hypotheses appears no longer to be of interest. No one puts them explicitly into question; indeed, they are generally accepted. A further reduction of working hours continues to be taken for granted, especially by experts on 'long-term' social evolution. Still, quite a few economists and sociologists have been feeling a twinge of embarrassment on the subject, which has induced them to desert the analysis of the length (to say nothing of the intensity!) of *daily* and *weekly* working hours and focus all their attention on the sum of *yearly* hours. As Dahrendorf and Sylos Labini, Gorz and Valli insist,[4] in just over a century – but this time they are looking *backwards*, to the economic possibilities for our... grandparents – the average yearly length of the labour time of a worker has been cut in half. And from this we are to conclude that, thank goodness, we are working a lot less today than we did yesterday, and the natural course of working hours in capitalism will continue to follow this trend.

But if the truth be told, history has responded harshly both to Keynes's prophesy and Fourastié's and Kahn's hypotheses. The course of events since 1930 and the most reasonable forecasts for the future give the lie to the conviction that capitalist development necessarily entails a continuous, systematic reduction of working hours in industry. The past half-century confronts us with an altogether different trend. While there has been an enormous rise in labour productivity (from a minimum of around 150 per cent in the United States and in Great Britain to a sensational maximum of over 1,500 per cent in Japan), the average length of daily and weekly individual working time has remained practically unchanged, or has dipped but just barely (France holds the record with a decrease of 13 per cent), *usually only as a result of relentless labour struggles*. What is more, beginning with the crisis of 1974–75, a reduction of the labour force employed in industry together with an increase in structural unemployment produced a trend (sharper in the 1980s) towards a de facto increase in the length and flexibility of working hours, which quantitatively and qualitatively augmented the weight of working time within the comprehensive living time of workers.

The notes that follow aim to shed light upon this state of affairs. While this preliminary exposition has many limits, there is one in particular that deserves special notice. Since the world economy is an organic unity characterized by very close interdependence between its (very unequal) parts, any investigation of the trend of working hours in the contemporary world that wishes to be complete must necessarily be conducted on a worldwide scale. Since the present study is limited to the principal countries of the West, it can be no more than partial. But, I must add, this 'partiality' by no means favours my thesis. On the contrary, it is clear that if the considerable mass of wage labour in the Third World were taken into account, the worldwide average for the length of the working day (or week or year) of the industrial proletariat would rise by no small amount. In a future study I hope to examine this not-secondary question, and in particular the relation between working hours in dominating and dominated countries.[5]

The Harsh Response of History

In the West the customary working day in industry is still 8 hours. It has been that way, at least in Europe, since 1919. In many countries, and in the Old World in particular, the conquest of the 8-hour day became the norm between 1917 and 1919, in the wake of the revolutions in Russia and in Germany.[6] For what it is worth, the last important international agreement on the question of working hours approved by the Bureau International du Travail also dates from 1919.[7]

The conquest, as is well known, was not definitive. First the reaction of the industrialists to the crisis of 1929, then the preparation for and outbreak of World War II, played havoc with it – not only in the countries under the yoke of Nazi and fascist regimes, but in the ultra-democratic America of Franklin Delano Roosevelt as well. Roediger and Foner write:

> Pearl Harbor had hardly been bombed before many industrialists launched a drive to abandon the forty-hour week. Linking the fall of France to the shortening of working hours there, World War I aviation hero Captain Eddie Rickenbacker, by the second war an aviation executive, toured the nation speaking against forty hours. Senator Harry F. Byrd of Virginia even held, in late 1942, that shorter hours had contributed to American military defeats. This came despite a 1942 rise in the average working week in the manufacturing industries from 40.6 to 43.1 hours, the second biggest annual increase in the twentieth century. Indeed, by February 1942, more than half of all war materiel plants worked over 48 hours weekly; in machine shops, the average was 55 hours, with 70 hours per worker per week not uncommon.[8]

So a formal abolition of the 8-hour day was not indispensable; its universal de facto suppression was quite sufficient.

Once Keynes's 'growing-pains of over-rapid changes' caused by the war had been overcome, there was a (neither immediate nor automatic) return to more 'normal' working times and paces. In the course of reconstruction, and afterwards, plants were progressively modernized, the mechanization of production went forward by leaps and bounds; and yet – despite the enticing promises of political economy – there was no sign, in industry or in government, of a spontaneous tendency to reduce working hours. On the contrary! In the 1950s working time swelled to the point of grazing, and often of breaking through, the ceiling of 50 hours per week in peacetime (in de-Nazified Germany in 1950 it amounted to 2,316 hours a year!) – longer hours than in the first half of the 1920s.

The only significant reduction of working time since World War II was due to the militancy of the working class itself in the late 1960s. Unlike the case of 1917–19 however, this time the mobilization of workers was only able to reduce the length of *weekly* hours, leading to the transition – neither instantaneous nor generalized (think of Japan, or of the enormous 'gulag archipelago' of small businesses) – to a 5-day week of 8 hours a day.

But a comprehensive look at the entire post-war period and at all the major industrial powers (not limiting ourselves to Europe) cuts this latest 'conquest' down to size. Where, in fact, the 5-day 40-hour week was already in place (the United States), or where there was a low degree of labour conflict (Japan), the situation remained almost unchanged for forty years. The comparison in Table 2.1 between the situation of 1948, when the business cycle was already in full expansion, and that of 1987, at the height of the recovery under Reagan, makes this perfectly clear.

After three-fifths of the time ('within a hundred years') indicated by Keynes as a bridge towards 'the age of leisure and of abundance', the vast majority of the 60 million industrial workers of the greatest Western powers are still toiling 8 (or more) hours a day for a total of 40 (or more) hours a week. Our incorrigible old Adam has nothing to complain about – the workload is not so very far from what it was in the 1930s;[9] and it is not at all likely that the international diffusion of the 'Japanese model' and of so-called 'flexibility' will change things for the better – as far as workers are concerned.

Table 2.1 Average hours of manufacturing production workers, 1948 and 1987

	Period	1948	1987	Variation (%)
United States	weekly	40.0	41.0	+2.5
Great Britain	weekly	46.7	43.5	−7.0
Japan	monthly	184.1	178.2[a]	−3.2
Germany	weekly	44.6	40.1	−10.0
France	weekly	44.6	38.7	−13.0
Italy	daily	7.95	7.77[b]	−2.3
	weekly	43.4[c]	41.0[d]	−5.6

[a] 1986.
[b] 1984.
[c] Estimate from A. Iovane and G. Pala, *Lavoro salariato e tempo libero*, Milan: Angeli, 1977, p. 101, n. 117.
[d] Union estimate of de facto weekly hours for 1987.[10]

Source: *One Hundred Years of Economic Statistics*, ed. T. Liesner, London: The Economist Publications, 1989, pp. 44–5, 98–9, 192–3, 216–7, 242–3, 266–7.[11]

But our discussion of the historical dynamics of nominal working hours will remain abstract unless they are put in relation to the corresponding dynamics of labour productivity and intensity. This alone will permit us to discern the exponential increase in the extraction of unpaid labour time and the enormous profusion of psychophysical energy that are concealed behind the stagnation, or limited reduction, of the hours of an industrial worker.

Labor productivity – the quantity of value produced by a given quantity of labour in a given period of time – has grown without respite, in pace with the 'degree of development of the conditions of production' (Marx). But that is an old story, and the figures in Table 2.2 speak for themselves. They also have a surprise in store, however, for anyone who believes there is an automatic connection between the perfection of technical means of production and a reduction in the working time of the producers themselves (i.e. the

Table 2.2   Growth rate of labour productivity in industry,
1870–1981

	Annual variation in GDP/employee (%)		
	1870–1950	1950–73	1973–81
United States	1.6	2.4	−0.2
Great Britain	1.2	2.9	1.8
Japan	1.7	9.5	4.7
Germany	1.3	5.6	2.6
France	1.4	5.2	3.2
	Overall variation in GDP/employee (%)		
	1870–1950	1870–1981	1950–81
United States	256.0	504.6	69.8[a]
Great Britain	159.7	478.1	122.6
Japan	285.2	4,385.1	1,064.0[b]
Germany	181.0	1,108.4	330.0
France	204.1	1,155.6	312.9

[a] Data furnished by the Bureau of Labor Statistics (see *The Economist*, 17 February 1990) for the period
    1973–89 give a different result: for 1950–81 we have a 100.1 per cent increase for productivity in
    industry, and a 158 per cent increase for 1950–89. It is this estimate that is referred to in the text.
[b] Expanding the calculation to 1988 (see R.W. Bednarzik and C.R. Shiells, 'Labor Market Changes
    and Adjustments: How Do the US and Japan Compare?', *Monthly Labor Review*, February 1989, p.
    33), the growth of productivity in Japan between 1950 and 1988 amounts to 1,549 per cent!

Source: A. Maddison, 'Comparative Analysis of the Productivity Situation in the Advanced Capitalist
Countries', in *International Comparisons of Productivity and Causes of the Slowdown*, ed. J.W. Kendrick,
Cambridge MA: Ballinger, 1984, p. 73.

workers). In point of fact, the working time of industrial employees fell more
sharply precisely in the historical phase (1870–1950) in which the growth of
productivity was (relatively) less; and, vice versa, it has remained semi-stagnant
in the period (1950–81 and beyond) in which the growth of labour productivity has been greatest (even if at a certain point it did slow down).

The mechanization and automation of the production processes and the unremitting 'rationalization' of the methods of utilizing labour power have greatly contributed to the *intensity* of working time. The modern factory has indeed come a long way, from the pioneering studies of Taylor and the Gilbreths to Henry Ford's assembly lines (with the time needed for production calculated down to the second), on to the exportation to Europe of this 'scientific organization' of work, right up to Toyotaism on the one hand and robotics on the other. And if along the way a sea of time has been put at the disposal of one part of society, the way has also led towards the totalitarian domination of the time of the machine (increasingly continuous and dense, yet analysed and fractionalized into thousandths of a second) over the natural time of the worker – and with that, to the methodical elimination of 'dead time' from living labour.

The intensity of labour has increased in proportion to the quantity of machinery that industrial workers have to set in motion, coordinate, follow and control. It is unquestionable that in the course of the cycle of post-war development there was a sharp increase in the quantity of fixed capital per employee. A study by Confindustria, the Italian Manufacturers' Association, estimated that, for Italy, from 1950 to 1983 the comprehensive value of fixed capital increased more than fivefold, rising at an average rate of 5.01 per cent annually, against a growth of industrial employment for the entire period of less than 80 per cent.[12] As regards fixed capital, over this period we note the gradual narrowing of the gap between sectors that were highly capital-intensive from the outset and sectors of lower technical composition, and the increase in capital with respect to labour also in smaller firms. In the course of the 1980s the share of investment in 'labour saving' technologies rose progressively, as firms aimed less at augmenting production and more at increasing productivity and the intensity of labour. We must not forget, then, that the statistical comparison is made here between entities that are only formally homogeneous, since an hour of work in 1990 has a specific weight far greater than an hour of work in 1948. These are the general trends, from 1945 to 1989, in the variation of the length, productivity and density of working time throughout the advanced capitalist world. We shall now turn our attention to some particularities of the individual countries.

The Situation in the United States and Japan

Let us begin with the United States, which accounts on its own for about a quarter of the industrial workers in the OECD countries. Unlike Europe, in the US there is no controversy about the almost 'absolute stability' of daily and weekly working hours over the past half-century (and longer). W. Leontief,[13] among others, has recognized the phenomenon, while B.K. Hunnicut spoke of it in the following terms:

> But the shorter-hour process stopped after the Great Depression. After World War II, the working week stabilized at around 40 hours. A broadly based economic and social trend that had existed for over a century reached some sort of historical plateau nearly fifty years ago.

After noting that in the United States economists 'have written dissertations and books with such titles as "The Age of the Constant Workweek"' and 'have made the claim that there has been *no* increase in leisure time since World War II', Hunnicut goes on to say that 'in fact, if anything, a good case may be made that Americans have increased their work time'. Indeed, with the huge influx of women into the labour force, 'as a percentage of the total population, more people are at work today than ever before'. The result does not change if we examine the question in terms of the length of working time over the full span of a worker's life, since 'the years added to the life span in this century have been divided between work and leisure; and most of those extra years have been devoted to work'. Hunnicut concludes:

> Added to these trends, the last few years of Reaganomics have seen weekly hours of work increase to above 40, and some observers, with a degree of satisfaction, see this as a process that is likely to continue.[14]

D. Owen, in his studies of long-term trends in working hours, fully concurs with this picture. In the United States, Owen says, for about one hundred years working hours decreased; then they began to rise or fall, with a mean of about forty hours, according to the upturns and downturns of the economic conjuncture (not, then, as the automatic effect of technical progress or 'compound interest'). Certainly, if one takes the entire US economy as a point of reference, it may seem that weekly hours have continued to decline also since World War II. But this would be highly misleading, since such a decline depends entirely upon working hours in the retail trade or in other non-production sectors of service industries[15] – sectors, moreover, in which a reduction of hours (when it is really the case) signifies lower wages and greater casualization of labour.

By the same token, the official figures for 1989 confirm that the average working week in the US manufacturing industry is 41 hours, and that the level of overtime in the late 1980s is higher than it was in the 1950s and 1960s. It is not true, however, that the situation is completely immobile – there have been some noteworthy transformations. In the first place, in the period from 1957 to 1978 working hours had already begun to grow longer overall; the percentage of employees working more than 49 hours a week rose from 14.3 to 20.6 per cent of all workers (+6.3 per cent), while the percentage of employees working less than 40 hours only increased from 7.5 to 9.4 per cent (+1.9).

Second, as a specific study by the Bureau of Labor Statistics of May 1985 ascertained, two phenomena took shape over the long term that contributed to the rise in real working hours: namely, the spread of multiple jobholding and the (notable) decrease of absenteeism.[16] This study also gives the lie to the facile identification of the 40-hour week with the 5-day 9-to-5 week. In the United States working on Saturdays is routine for 20 per cent of all employees, and 12 per cent routinely work on Sundays. Working outside the canonical '9 to 5' proved to be regular practice for one sixth of full-time employees, and for no less than half the people working part-time.[17]

In this area too, then, the advent of Reaganism did nothing other than strengthen inclinations already proper to capitalism in the USA (and elsewhere). Far from stopping at the social items in the state budget, Reagan's crusade against the welfare state struck deep into the working conditions of the proletariat. His campaign against the power of organized labour, the impulse given to the liberalization of the labour market and, in another respect, to the restructuring of manufacturing industry (with the creation of sweatshops based on more overwork, more underpay, and more female labour), could not but worsen working conditions in all respects, including the length of working hours. But the situation is paradoxical. In the very country that in the twentieth century has been the prototype of that 'combined power' Keynes considered the decisive factor for the reduction of working hours, not only have hours not decreased for half a century but, as *Business Week* reports, the 'sweat factor' is on the rise.[18] To combat the stagnation or the fall in real wages, to cope with family debts (the rate is now the highest in the OECD countries), to drive out the unexpected spectre of downward mobility, an ever greater number of US workers are forced to bear an increase in the sweat, weight and length of working time. At the other end of the social structure, the 'exceptionally strong business opposition' to any reduction of the working day or working week to less than 8 or 40 hours respectively has prevailed to the point that the word 'leisure' itself now appears 'often in pejorative quotes'.[19]

The situation in Japan clearly shows that the difficulties we have seen in the USA are not limited to an economy reacting to a loss of competitiveness. The facts of the Japanese manufacturing industry contrast even more sharply with the perspective of an automatic and vertiginous fall in working hours in pace with the advance of profits and technology.

Working more than 8 hours a day is common practice in Japan due to the permanency of overtime (among other things). Weekly hours commonly exceed 40, due both to the length of the working day and to the fact that for employees in small businesses, who make up nearly two-thirds of the 15 million industrial employees, working on Saturdays is practically the norm (even in large firms 72 per cent of the employees work at least one Saturday a month). In 1989 real annual hours were from 15 to 35 per cent longer (Maddison's estimate for 1984 was 32 per cent) than the (by no means short) US hours; while, close as we are to 'the age of leisure and of abundance', the paid vacations of a Japanese worker amounted, on average, to 7.5 days a year.[20] In short, the nation that for more than a decade had been universally considered to be a symbol of the super-efficient market economy of the future was the nation that squeezed its workforce more than any other and that had by far the longest working hours in the First World.

One of the mainstays of the Japanese 'prodigy' is its 'peculiar' (including the 'peculiarity' of long hours) form of organization of the immediate production process, commonly known as 'Toyotaism'. To understand the genesis of the 'Toyota Production System' I do not think it suffices simply to go back to the defeat of the labour movement in the 1950s, as Jürgens and others do.[21] For sure, the present-day situation in Japanese factories is the result of a capitalist power 'exceptionally free from conditioning', and from the conditioning of a militant unionism in particular; but the roots of this 'exceptional freedom' of company management take hold, apart from the events after World War II, in the particular mode of formation of Japanese capitalism itself. A transition from feudalism to capitalism that was substantially 'painless', accomplished by means of a revolution from above (as Barrington Moore, Jr maintained); the generally smooth integration between the landed aristocracy and the merchant classes; the recycling of the samurai and the recasting of their military attitudes in the constitution and government of the dawning industry; Japan's almost total isolation (until the early 1930s) both from the world market and from the repercussions of the socio-political upheavals in Asia and in Europe; the constitutional programmatic and organizational fragility of its working class, still hampered by the conditioning of the past and already constrained in the vice of the new social order, which (as Taira put it) had gone from serfdom to serfdom[22] – these, in broad outline, are the main characteristics of the phase of formation and incipient consolidation of Japanese capitalism, which also explain how it managed to bridge its historical gap with respect to Europe and the United States, while the conditions of its working class fell even farther behind.

It was not until the end of World War II that the 8-hour day made its way timidly into Japan. What enabled it – it goes without saying – was not the 'true trend' of capitalism praised by Keynes, Fourastié, Dahrendorf and company, but rather the brief experience of self-management by the workers in a number of mines and factories after the war.[23] The liberal democratic government, for its part, refused for decades even to consider the possibility of signing the 1919 international convention on the 8-hour working day.

So Toyotaism flowered on a ground that had been cultivated for more than a century – the last step being the crushing of the new-born Japanese labour movement in the early 1950s. It has often been emphasized that other specifically Japanese factors contributed to its success, such as the still-very-much-alive pre-bourgeois traditions of 'faithfulness' and attachment to the 'community' one belongs to, which in the past was the *buraka* or the *mura* and today is the firm, the company; or the strongly nationalistic tone of Shintoism, and so forth. This is no doubt true. But the local socio-historical conditions rooted in a more or less distant past that favoured the rise of Toyotaism is one thing, while the *substance* of Toyotaism is quite another. In substance Toyotaism is by no means an exclusively Japanese phenomenon, but 'simply puts in practice the organizational principles of Fordism in a condition of unlimited managerial prerogatives.'[24] Japanese entrepreneurs imported, thoroughly studied and assimilated the technical and socio-political lesson of Taylorism and of 'human relations' – and then re-exported to the rest of the industrialized world a 'new' product that derives from the artistic perfecting and the merger of those very 'models'.

By the same token, the 'just-in-time' system, which is the cardinal organizational practice of Japanese industry, is nothing other than the fundamental principle of the Taylorist system pushed to the extreme, saving time, space and labour to minimize the costs of production and maximize the productivity of labour. But the disciples proved even more radical than their master, laying down the rule that the amount of labour power employed in production has to be slightly less than what is strictly necessary, in order to guarantee the company the greatest possible intensification of labour, as well as structural overtime.

The case is similar with the general principle of 'zero inventories', which stitches together the various sources of the optimization of profit – on the one hand by reducing the inventories of materials and products, and on the other by reducing the 'inventories' of labour and unsaturated working time ('zero "dead" time'). Its manifold consequences all have the effect of making the working day heavier and longer. In the first place, in Japanese industry the workload is estimated to be 15 per cent heavier than in the United States. The amount of work that is paid but not worked (unproductive, wasted, 'dead' time) has been cut down practically to the bone (to around 5 per cent, or three minutes per hour!). And, finally, there is the permanent recourse to overtime – 20 per cent is considered to be the norm, and not only in the smaller firms (the so-called circuit of the 'mercenary market'). In the largest automotive plants, for example, average monthly overtime between 1972 and 1981 (except for the recession year of 1975) never dipped below 16.5 hours, with about 25 hours as a rule and peaks close to 30, which is to say around 1 hour – sometimes more, sometimes (slightly) less – per day.[25]

But Japanese company managers openly claim that longer working hours, apart from lowering the costs of production, also help instil in their workers a 'sense of belonging to the firm'. Workers also show their loyalty by participating in the 'quality circles' or other activities organized by the company, such as the vocational training 'offered', frequently, outside working hours, to say nothing of the generalized sacrifice of part of one's vacation time, and so on. These are all ways, and methods,[26] by which Japanese firms extract a share of 'their' workers' already limited free (from work) time.

In this light, it is no exaggeration to say that 'abnormally' long working hours are as essential a component of Toyotaism as the equally 'abnormal' intensity of work or the exorbitant concern for product 'quality'. This picture presents us with an (apparently) paradoxical contradiction between Taylorism and Toyotaism. Despite a later muddying of the waters, it is a fact that the original form of Taylorism considered a certain nominal reduction of daily working hours to be a useful – and sometimes indispensable – means to the growth of productivity and profits and to the increase in unpaid working time that is a precondition of such growth. We find nothing of the sort in Toyotaism, which in a world-historical context very different from the one at the turn of the century tends, rather, to prolong the workers' stay in the factory as much as possible, even beyond the hours of production, precisely in order to attain the objective that remained Taylor's bugbear: to wring out of the workforce a real, 'sincere' cooperation with company management, while snatching not only their muscular and mental energy but also their soul.

The Situation in Europe

As for the major European countries, they can be schematically divided into two groups. On one hand Great Britain, Greece, Portugal, and to a lesser extent Spain, tending towards the Japanese standard; on the other Germany, France, Italy, Belgium, Holland and the Scandinavian countries, where since World War II the industrial proletariat has secured reductions of working hours not limited to an increase in paid vacations.

It is a cruel irony that Great Britain, which had been the cradle of the trade-union movement and of the first struggles for a regulated working day, has become one of the countries with the longest working hours in the West. The fact is denounced (not exactly to the unions' credit) by a document of the TUC itself,[27] which notes that in Britain in the 1980s the gap between 'basic'[28] and actual hours grew wider. Basic hours have fallen generally, for male manual workers from the 39.9 weekly hours of 1979 to the 39.1 hours of 1988, and for female manual workers from 38.5 to 38 hours. But actual hours have gone in the opposite direction; after falling between 1979 and 1981 due to the recession, they began to rise with the new conjuncture, thanks to the general increase of overtime hours, reaching record levels not seen since the 1950s (when, however, the unemployment rate was around 1 to 1.5 per cent, compared to the 10 to 11 per cent of the 1980s). At the end of the 1980s 56.8 per cent of male and 26.8 per cent of female workers regularly worked overtime, with a weekly average of 10.1 and 6.3 hours respectively (from not less than one hour up to about two hours a day). Taking into account the fixed overtime that – as we see – is not such a peculiarly Japanese phenomenon after all, the average weekly hours of male workers in British industry amounted in 1988 to 45 hours. And this means that if slightly less than one half of male British workers put in forty hours a week, then more than 50 per cent of them work close to if not more than 50 hours, while more than a quarter of female workers habitually work more than 45 hours.

Looking at long-term trends, we may note that the 47-hour week was introduced in the British metalworking and shipbuilding industries in 1919, and that the average working week in the manufacturing industry was 46 hours in 1924 and 46.3 in 1938.[29] We should also bear in mind the fact that the longest hours are often to be found in the most tiring and harmful branches of work (coal mining, cement working, transportation, metal working). And as for Keynes's making 'what work there is still to be done to be as widely shared as possible', suffice it to say that in Margaret Thatcher's decade employment in industry was slashed by 30 per cent, while productivity rose considerably (by about 4 per cent annually between 1979 and 1987), almost exclusively (given the small amount of investment) in virtue of the greater efficiency of labour.

The situation in Germany (in 1983) is cogently described in the document issued by Industriegewerkschaft Metall demanding a 35-hour week. It reports that as of 1983 Germany was 'one of the countries with the longest weekly hours' (41.6 hours on average) and that in the years between 1967 and 1983, despite exorbitant restructuring, contractual hours in the metalworking industry had not been reduced 'by a single minute.'[30]

Both the IG Metall document and the analysis of sociologists close to the labour movement underline a problem that is usually neglected (if not cancelled) – namely, that the workload in industry is very heavy and is not, as many believe, diminishing. Oskar Negt wrote:

> For more than a century it has commonly been maintained that the increased complexity of the processes of production and the intensification of labour call for longer rest periods for workers. In the event, despite the apparent reduction of working hours, the heightening of exploitation and the greater 'scientificity' of the production processes have augmented the workers' degree of fatigue, ailments both psychical and physical, the predisposition to disease, etc.[31]

The evidence regarding the harmfulness of factory work in Germany presented by IG Metall is impressive and shocking. German industrialists did not even contest it, preferring to avoid the question and concentrating their own propaganda against the 35-hour week (defined as a 'stab in the back for German industry') on the argument that the reduction of working hours does nothing to boost employment.

As for workers' 'free' time, IG Metall maintains that 'the free time we are left with once we have taken care of everything we have to do has not increased, but in fact has diminished', at least if the increase of traffic and, generally, of mobility and distance from the workplace are taken into account, in addition to the greater profusion of 'time and nervous energy demanded of workers to resolve practical and bureaucratic problems, find housing, go to public offices, and also to look for work'.[32] Keeping these contradictions in mind, it is not hard to understand why the 'campaign' for the 35-hour week was heatedly supported by workers; combined with the no less heated resistance of the German industrialists, it led to the hardest and longest strike in the last fifty years in Germany (more than five and a half million hours 'lost', with 537,000 workers participating in the strikes).

Even after the improvements attained by the metalworkers, the printers, and by other unions, the average working week in German industry was still 40.1 hours in 1987 (compared to 44.6 hours in 1948). Not before 1989 did it fall, in the metalworking sector, to slightly less than 40 hours – underscoring, however, a mechanism of partial compensation between the reduction of contractual hours and the growth of overtime.[33]

Between 1918 and 1990 the productivity of industrial labour in Germany took a great leap forward, amounting to some 900 per cent. In relation to this figure, the distance dividing the 48-hour week won by the German proletariat in December 1918 and the 40 (39.9 to be exact) hours of 1989 is not exactly an abyss (we are speaking here, of course, in abstract quantitative terms – on the socio-political level the question is far more complex, and indeed would have to be turned upside down). Not by a long shot. And neither is the distance dividing the 40 (or slightly less) hours of 1989 from the average hours of the 'peacetime' years of the Nazi regime. But then how are we to explain the fact that democratic legislation in Germany on the question of working hours has continued to be based, for over half a century, on a decree of 1938 signed by Hermann Göring?

Italy is part of that group of countries where there has been a certain reduction of weekly working hours since World War II – though not as great a reduction as the official statistics indicate. When the Italian Central Statistics Office (ISTAT) talks about a working week of 37.1 hours in Italian industry in 1987, the figure is not to be – and is not – taken seriously.[34] Estimates by the trade unions for the same year are 4 to 6 hours higher – no small difference! Furthermore, according to ISTAT, average hours are shorter in Italy than in Germany, but a precise comparison of hours in two key firms shows just the opposite.[35] In point of fact, on the question of working hours the progress made by industrial workers in Italy since 1920 can be summed up, essentially, in Saturdays off and summer vacations. There has been no significant progress, however, where the length of the working day is concerned (at least not since World War II; according to *The Economist*, Italians worked 7.95 hours a day in 1948 and 7.77 in 1984).

The conquest of the 40-hour week after the mass strikes in the *autunno caldo* of 1969 was less significant than the reduction of the working day that was won between 1917 and 1919. Its limits and contradictions were already discussed in Quaderno 26/1970 of *Rassegna Sindacale*, which continues to be one of the labour movement's most important statements on the question to this day. Indeed, there was no lack of triumphalism and, vice versa, of concern about the excessively 'advanced' position taken up by the Italian labour movement. But a more critical analysis of the attainment of the 40-hour week presented the 5-day week as 'the point of least resistance of the capitalist front'. Recognizing Saturday as a nonworking day in fact signifies, for companies, 'giving up to the workers in the first place their least productive hours, i.e., the last hours worked after an entire week of exertion and before their weekly day off' while successfully 'keeping the production flow during the week unchanged', without upsetting the company's organization of the time worked.

Furthermore – the Quaderno continues – the transformation of Italy into a 'serious consumer society' in the late 1960s called for a certain increase of 'free time', which was absolutely indispensable for the expansion of mass consumerism and of so-called 'services'. This led to a contradiction between the 'individual capitalist who is opposed, as such, to any reduction of hours', and the 'collective capitalist' who does have some interest in reducing working time, in order to leave workers more time for consumption. Forced by the strength of the workers' mobilization to make concessions, the capitalist class found in the 5-day week or in the lengthening of vacations 'a shrewd way of getting around the contradiction'. On the other hand, 'the workers' giving up their traditional demand for the reduction of the working day in favor of the 5-day week' was seen, realistically, also as an aspect of the adaptation of the working class to the 'society in which it operates'. A sign of this adaptation is the fact that workers 'were by no means opposed to the possibility of a solution to the problem of hours that permits them an entire day or several days of freedom, even if this in fact saddles them with a heavier daily workload'.[36]

Since 1975, however, not only individual firms but also all their associations have been adamantly opposed to any further reductions of hours, heatedly resisting even minimal nominal reductions of annual hours (as in the *bagarre* over the reduction of 16 hours per year – less than 1 per cent – in the 1988 metalworkers' contract) while gaining 'a notable increase in de facto hours, attributable to a massive recourse to overtime and a reduction of absenteeism'.[37] Between 1976 and 1988 overtime rose, in fact, from 2.8 to 4.7 per cent of total hours worked in industry, and the lengthening of de facto weekly hours amounted, in 1989, to 42–44 hours at Fiat Mirafiori and 47–48 hours at Alfa–Lancia in Pomigliano. The ISTAT tables themselves record the phenomenon (the index of real hours per worker rose from 100.6 in 1976 to 103.3 in 1988), and there is no doubt that, if they took the situation in smaller businesses fully into account, where a working day of more than 8 hours is the rule (and whose weight in the comprehensive structure of industrial employment increased in the 1980s), the extent of the phenomenon would be even greater.[38]

France is the European and Western country which has had the greatest reduction of working hours. But the French originality is rife with shadings and accents. Beneath the small numerical variations, however, the basic trends are the same as in the rest of the industrialized world. Indeed, if we take as our point of reference not post-1945 but rather 1936, when Léon Blum's Popular Front government introduced the 40-hour week, the reduction shrinks to a trifle – in 1988 the official average working week in French industry was, precisely, 38.8 hours.[39]

The most conspicuous feature of the French situation is represented by state intervention in support of the reduction of hours. But this propulsive action was short-lived, with the impetus of Mauroy's decision to introduce the 39-hour week being left to peter out by Mitterrand. The 35-hour week, which was supposed to reign by the mid 1980s, remained a myth until 2001, while the Delabarre law, the Séguin law and the measures of January 1990 giving tax credits to companies that keep their plants operating at maximum capacity, made it abundantly clear that legislative incentives for the (official) reduction of hours are, rather, an instrument in support of a greater utilization of facilities and a greater flexibility of working time.[40]

In France too, then, the rather irregular course of the historical dynamics of daily and weekly hours in industry owes more to the vicissitudes of the national and international class struggle than it does to technical innovation and increased labour productivity; if, indeed, working hours were strictly (and inversely) related to these factors, they would have had to decline almost continuously. As for the capitalist – that personification of 'compound interest' – he obstinately continues to see eye to eye with Lambert-Ribot, one of the key opponents of the original introduction of the 40-hour week: 'Pretending to live in abundance while working less' is a 'genuine aberration'.[41] Words of wisdom of a genuine rentier, living in great abundance without working at all!

The Lengthening and Restructuring of Hours, after the Crisis of 1974–75

Since the end of World War II, then, in the most 'advanced' countries of the West the daily and weekly working time of industrial workers (the case is slightly different only for annual hours) either has been substantially stationary, as in the United States, Japan and Great Britain (which together account for 70 per cent of the employment we are considering), or, as in France, Germany and Italy, has decreased to a limited extent. An extent, moreover, that would shrink even more if the statistical surveys were capable of reflecting the expansion of the 'shadow economy' (and of 'shadow hours') and the increase in multiple jobholding. And, as we have seen, all this has taken place in the context of a comprehensive growth in labour productivity and intensity that, while sharply differentiated, is unequaled in the history of capitalism.

Mainstream socio-economic literature paints us a totally different picture of the state and 'genuine' historical trends of working hours. According to Sylos Labini, for example, 'in the past hundred years weekly hours have been *systematically* decreasing in all the developed capitalist countries', in virtue of the partial transferral to these hours of the increase in productivity. (The transferral is partial but continuous, in his opinion). 'Taking longer vacations into account', Sylos Labini states, 'working time has been reduced by about a half; the decrease is even greater if we make reference to the entire life span and take into account the longer scholastic period and lower retirement age.' Certainly, if we look at the question over a shorter term ('the past thirty years'), and just look at the Italian manufacturing industry, 'it may seem that this trend has made no great progress, since the fall in contractual hours has been slight.' But the appearance is deceiving: 'in Italy, … – but the case is analogous in the other industrialized countries – the average number of hours effectively worked every year by each employee in the manufacturing industry from 1954 to 1982 decreased by approximately 25 to 30 per cent.'[42] These statements call for careful analysis, precisely because they express the consensus of the 'scientific community' on the question we are examining.

To begin with, it should be noted that the decrease in weekly hours over the course of the twentieth century was not the least bit systematic – that is, linear. Even if (just for a moment) we prescind from the processes induced in the 'new' continents by the domination of the 'developed capitalist countries', to obliterate any image of linearity we need only think back to the two periods of forced universal lengthening of working time – namely, 1914–18 and 1939–45. Even prescinding from the two world wars (which is common, if quite curious practice, since their historical reality is hard to deny),[43] the existence of an automatic relation between growth of labour productivity and reduction of individual working hours still cannot be demonstrated. As a matter of fact, over the last hundred years the greatest reduction of industrial working hours in the principal countries of the West (apart from the precocious Great Britain and the tardy – in this case – Japan) was won by the working class between 1880 and 1920 with the cutting down of the working day from between 11 and 12 hours to 8 hours, while the objectively slight progress from the 48-hour working week of 1919–20 to the 40 (or more) hours of today boils down to the attainment (not everywhere) of the short 5-day week. Therefore the only rigorously historical thesis is as follows: there is no mechanical relation between the expansion of productivity and the contraction of individual working time, especially now that the transition from extensive to intensive capitalist development has been accomplished. On the contrary, it is a fact that *greater* development of labour productivity means *less* reduction of working hours in industry 'in all the developed capitalist countries'. Furthermore, it is not true that 'if we make reference to the entire life span' of a worker of a hundred years ago and compare it with that of a present-day worker, the latter works less than half as long overall as the former. A century ago life expectancy was less than half what it is today, so an industrial worker was 'compensated' for the torments of his or her labour with a premature death, 'ammò de bella età' (cut down in my youth), as the spinner from Cremona sang in Mandelli's song. The present-day worker – though only in the 'North' of the world – enjoys far shorter nominal hours; but the more than doubling of life expectancy also means for him or her a considerable increase in the number of years worked – and between the two processes, as a simple calculation shows, in absolute terms there is substantial compensation.[44]

What is more, the amounts of time being compared here are not homogeneous in terms of quality and density. The 12 hours of work of a century ago, in a factory that had not yet been 'rationally' organized and in which machinery had not yet become absolute despot of the working process, while physically exhausting still conserved a porosity far greater than the practically nonexistent porosity of 8 hours in today's automated factory (conceived of as an integrated system). Even if in a certain number of tasks less muscular effort is required, the density of working time has (in general) increased, so that the lessening of fatigue is often offset by the comprehensive increase of the workload. Neither is it tenable to affirm that the reduction of hours in Italy has been 'analogous in the other industrialized countries' – as we have seen, the evolution of the situation in the United States, Japan and Great Britain has been quite different; and it is rather arbitrary to discuss the post-World War II period not in its 'entire span', but choosing as points of comparison on the one hand 1954, when production was surging and hours were particularly long, and on the other 1982, a recession year with particularly reduced hours.

Finally, we come to the 'genuine trends' operating 'over a shorter term' – here, the periodization I propose is quite different from Sylos Labini's. His division, in fact, consists of two periods. We have already spoken of the first (1954–82); the distinctive feature of the second (1983–87), in his view, is the novelty that 'the overall number of hours worked rises, while employment falls'. A novelty that is seen to be 'perverse' and – so it seems – wholly contingent, attributable to an excessive rigidity of the labour market and, at the same time, 'to the weakness of the unions and the workers' fear of losing their jobs'; a novelty, moreover, destined 'in the long run' to give way to a recovery of the 'natural' inclination of working hours to shrink through the effect of technological innovation.[45]

A more logical subdivision of the post-war period is one that takes as its watershed the crisis of 1974–75, which, as is very well known, was the point of departure for the full-scale campaign launched by companies against wage labour, designed to reverse the fall of profit margins and productivity ratios. Now, it is the entire phase stretching from 1975 to 1989 and not just a part of the 1980s (1983–87) that is distinguished by an attack on the reduction of working hours won by the labour struggles of the 1960s and 1970s. And this attack, which is not due to transitory 'perversions' but rather to fundamental contradictions of capitalist society, found expression not only in the renewed lengthening of de facto hours, but also in other processes that are usually reputed – quite wrongly – to be 'neutral', such as the restructuring and maximum flexibilization of working hours.

The increase in real working hours over the fifteen years between 1975 and 1989 was due to such general factors as the compression (or, at least, containment) of wages and the rise in unemployment, and to more specific factors such as:

1. the measures taken against absenteeism (wage incentives, disciplinary sanctions, anti-malingering campaigns, etc.);
2. the general increase in overtime;
3. the strengthening of pressures and procedures aimed at limiting and sub-ordinating the action of unions to company and national 'compatibilities' and keeping labour conflict in check, to ensure the greatest possible con-tinuity and regularity of the production process;
4. the heightening of the intensity of work and the methodical shortening of breaks, in line with that which Taddei and Boulin called the 'explicit or implicit substitution of the notion of the real length for that of the declared length' of working hours;[46]
5. the elimination of public holidays, as occurred in Italy in 1977;
6. the growth of the 'underground' economy and of small businesses in general, in which it is normal that daily and weekly working time exceed legal and contractual limits;[47]
7. the increased use of migrant workers who can be easily blackmailed (think of the mass of Chicanos and of displaced Asians who migrated to the USA in the 1980s, or of the new migration flows from the 'South' to the Mediterranean countries of Europe).

There is also the fact that the outsourcing of mature labour-intensive production to the dominated continents, which reproduces on the 'periphery' of the world market the working conditions the industrial proletariat has endured for centuries in the West, has increasingly negative repercussions for workers of the 'centre' – also in the area of working hours.

As we see in Table 2.3, even the official statistics – which, for the most part, manage to overlook these processes – do reflect the trend we are talking about.

But the renewed lengthening of de facto hours (noted also by Sylos Labini) is only *one* aspect of the recent changes that have increased the weight of working time for the industrial proletariat. Another aspect – in itself no less

Table 2.3 Average hours in the manufacturing industry, 1975 and 1987

	Period	1975	1987	Variation (%)
United States	weekly	39.5	41.0	+ 3.5
Great Britain	weekly	43.6	43.5	− 0.2
Japan	monthly	167.8	178.2[a]	+ 7.0
Germany	weekly	40.4	40.1	− 0.8
France	weekly	41.7	38.7	− 7.5
Italy	daily	7.68	7.77[b]	+ 1.3
	weekly	40.6	41.0[d]	+ 1.0

[a] 1986.
[b] 1984 (last year recorded).
[c] Commission des Communautés Européennes, *La répartition du travail. Objectifs et effets. Annexe statistique*, Brussels, 1978, table 2.
[d] Minimum union estimate.

Source: Liesner, *One Hundred Years of Economic Statistics*.

weighty – is the restructuring of hours designed for maximum saturation of the potentialities of industrial facilities and maximum efficiency in their utilization.[48] Since for a certain period the restructuring of hours went hand in hand with measures for their reduction, it is practically taken for granted that the major changes in the organization of hours now under way represent an exchange that is equally advantageous for both labour and management. But even a glance at the European experience in this area (especially in France) cannot but give rise to legitimate doubts about the nature and the effects of this 'equal' exchange.

The report prepared in the mid 1980s by D. Taddei for the Fabius administration[49] clearly illustrated the positive effects for companies of utilizing their plants more hours per day, per week, per year:

1. An *effet de capacité*, since 'keeping the existing machinery "running" for twice as long' has the same effect on the production capacities of the firm as 'doubling the stock of machines' – but with an evident saving of capital,

which is particularly useful given the decline in investment that took place 'after the first oil shock';

2. An *effet de compétitivité* due to the fact that 'the costs of utilization of [fixed] capital, which are in general fixed costs, can be spread over a larger number of units produced and sold', which is vital especially in 'an epoch of great technical progress and therefore of rapid obsolescence' of plants like the one we are in today;

3. An *effet de rentabilité* that derives from the first two effects, since the expansion of production capacities and markets linked to the reduction of production costs cannot but improve company profitability.

Taddei argues that it is basically a question of increasing the rotation rate of capital by reducing the rotation time of fixed capital, which is particularly profitable in periods of technological innovation, when new machinery is introduced that has not yet been fully perfected and that it is thus opportune productively to 'wear out' as soon as possible. The increase in production without the need to increase the advance of capital ensures companies' greater profitability. But, besides the individual firms, it is also the nation as a whole that profits from a lengthening of the utilization time of plants. In fact the *effet de cannibalisme* between firms of the same sector is more than offset, for the nation, by other advantages such as the renewal of plants, the reduction of production costs, the rise in productivity and the … *effet de cannibalisme* on non-French firms[50] – which, *mutatis mutandis*, also holds for the capitalisms and the companies of other 'nationalities'.

But what are the consequences for industrial workers of this increase in the utilization time of plants? As Taddei admits, it unquestionably leads to an 'essential sacrifice' consisting in the 'change of habits affecting the personal life of the interested parties' caused by the diversification of hours. For the workers there is, however, a sort of 'negotiable recompense' consisting in an exchange between diversified hours and reduced hours, which could give rise to a 'positive-sum solution'[51] – positive both for companies and for workers. But what has actual experience shown?

The diversification (or restructuring) of hours has meant, concretely:

• A generalized increase in shiftwork, a system of hours that is totally or partially asynchronous with respect to the rhythms of the natural functions of the 'interested parties' (a human being is a diurnal animal) and to the rhythms of social life.[52]

- An extension of work to Saturdays in particular. In Italy, since the early 1970s, the '6 × 6' system has been widespread (6 hours a day × 6 days a week), especially in the textile industry. But that which is called, with a horrible neologism, the 'banalization' of Saturdays goes far beyond that sector of industry, as is shown – to gave just one example – by the explosion of obligatory Saturdays at Fiat towards the end of the 1980s. Even in Germany, 'despite the law against it', the number of workers who regularly work on Saturdays rose, between 1982 and 1987, from 18 to 32 per cent; IG Metall, commenting on the agreement reached with BMW in Regensburg, pressed the charge that 'the entrepreneurs want to bring back Saturdays as regular working days in industry'.[53]

- A further extension of work to Sundays. The percentage, while low at the moment, is on the rise (in Germany it rose from 7 to 10 per cent between 1982 and 1987); and highly indicative of the impetus in this direction is the fact that even within unions of Christian orientation the resistance on principle to Sunday working is waning.[54]

- The introduction of shifts that structurally exceed 8 hours per day. Common practice in weekend jobs, shifts of this kind are also beginning to take root beyond these 'abnormal' situations. In its new plant at Avezzano, for example, Texas Instruments intends to introduce regular (day- and night-) shifts of 12 hours with an average working week of 42 hours (in Dallas, they say, it brought 'excellent results'); and Peugeot, at its Poissy plant, has organized a working week of 41 hours with shifts of 10¼ hours for four days.

- An increase in nightwork, with frequent agreements of 'non-compliance' with the prohibition of nightwork for women (in Italy alone the number of such agreements rose from 199 in 1983 to 399 in 1987). The Bureau International du Travail – which is not given to painting the world in black and white – considers this type of work a cause of 'progressively greater stress' due to the 'alteration of the natural biorhythm', and, in social terms, of 'disorganization' of personal and family life.[55]

- There are, finally, the forms of elasticity of hours in the strict sense, such as elasticity of the beginning or end of the working day, or the so-called 'annualization' of working time that, according to a study by C. Tuchszirer, 'permits firms in Belgium and West Germany [and not only there] to link the working time of their employees to the conjunctural variations of production, without having recourse to overtime or temporary un-employment.'[56]

What, meanwhile, has become of the 'negotiable recompense' of reduced hours? In their detailed report on the agreements of *réduction–réorganisation* of working hours stipulated in France in the 1980s, Taddei and Boulin claim that in some cases workers have been rewarded with a reduction of hours in exchange for increased 'flexibility' (with hours, in any case, becoming 'more unpleasant'; recompense is not compensation, and negotiable is not equivalent to automatic). In other cases this has not occurred. But in point of fact it is Taddei and Boulin themselves who make their own harmonious formula ('reduction–reorganization' of working hours) meaningless, when they note that in the course of the 1980s 'the question of the regulation of working time has prevailed over the question of its reduction'.

Not only are these two processes not identical; they are not inseparable either. The shift from one priority (reduction) to the other (restructuring), 'visible in the national statistics' (while the length of the working week fell from 40.3 to 39.2 hours between January 1982 and January 1983, it was still at 38.9 hours six years later), is also 'visible' in the results of bargaining between labour and management. The theme of the reduction of working hours is, in fact, 'in decline in company agreements (375 in 1984; 251 in 1987) and is almost completely absent from sector agreements, while the theme of *aménagement* is more present all the time, with 1,225 company agreements in 1984 and 2,272 in 1987', and the trend continued in 1988.[57]

As far as companies are concerned, while it is difficult to appraise the consequences of the above-mentioned innovations on their competitiveness, it is certain that the consequences on their 'financial profitability' have been 'very positive'.[58] Equally positive, for them, has been the shifting of bargaining (when there really was bargaining) to the company level. In this way, through the 'multiplication of schemas of organization' (as many as five different types of shift in the same plant), the firm manages to bypass 'union mediation'

(Japanese style), establishing 'direct communication with the workers' and trying to satisfy their 'latent aspirations' (as individuals, consumers, student-workers, mothers, fathers – but never as members of the working class).

The shifting of emphasis from the reduction to the reorganization of working hours discussed, for France, by Taddei and Boulin, in fact concerns Europe as a whole. Apart from the change in the composition of capital, the shift reflects a change in the balance of forces between labour and capital, produced also by the increased flexibility of the workforce. In Germany, too, where a contractual agreement was reached on the 35-hour week in the metalworking industry, beginning in 1996, the toll the working class has already paid for this uncertain future benefit is no small one. As a result of the *Lebercompromise*, 87 per cent of the workers in the metalworkers' sector were affected by measures regarding the restructuring of working hours – measures which the German industrialists manoeuvred to bypass and rescind reductions of hours that had nominally been granted.[59] So Negt is not mistaken when he considers the strategy of flexibility in the use of the workforce (which entails the reorganization of working time) 'unequivocally political' – a weapon used by companies to 'shatter the foundations of solidarity between workers', suppressing the 'common moments' between them on the one hand, and on the other appealing 'astutely to their partial human needs' through a 'person-alized' use of non-working time, to legitimate themselves as 'good fathers' to 'their' (dependent) employees.[60]

So the 'perverse' novelty Sylos Labini noted over the 'short term' possesses far greater body and depth than he was willing to admit: (1) because it concerns the entire period from 1975 to 1989, in which time – belying his basic theoretical assumptions – not one iota of the rise in productivity has been transferred to a reduction of working hours; (2) because the lengthening of de facto hours came not by itself but entangled with their restructuring, inexorably intensifying the burden of labour and the overall fatigue of the working class;[61] (3) because there are *structural* reasons for these (not exactly ephemeral) processes, regarding the composition of capital, the mechanisms of accumulation and, at bottom, precisely those 'genuine trends' of capitalist production that ought to have brought humanity – and in a sense have brought humanity – to the brink of 'the age of leisure and of abundance'.

Technical Progress, Profit, Working Time

It is time to draw some conclusions. Observing what has occurred in the last half century, the period of the most intensive and extensive economic growth in the history of capitalism, we see that the union between the power of 'compound interest' (capital) and technical–scientific progress *has not* produced a spontaneous tendency to reduce nominal (to say nothing of real) working time in industry. And certainly not to reduce it drastically and in general! Indeed, belying the prophecies of Keynes and his ilk, exactly the opposite has occurred. While the increase in the productivity and density of labour has multiplied the surplus working time alienated from the industrial proletariat, the length of the working day and working week has remained (almost) completely unchanged in the United States and Japan, and has diminished only slightly in Europe. What is more, while companies did make some concessions to organized labour in the late 1960s and early 1970s, after the crisis of 1974 they did everything possible to take back what they had given with... compound interest, through wage reductions and the de facto lengthening and reorganization of working hours. Both Reaganism (in political economy) and Toyotaism (in the area of company organization) did nothing other than voice – and heighten – the contradiction between the increase in the productivity and intensity of labour and the capitalist resistance to reducing working time.

So, especially from a certain moment in capitalist development onward, there has been no prospect of 'easy' (albeit conflictual) reduction of individual working hours in keeping with the advance of technology and profits. In the long run, it has been the other way around. In the developed capitalist countries the productive force of social labour continues to rise, but there is no trend towards a fall in working hours.

This increase in the rigidity of nominal working hours in Western industry is destined to remain an enigma (repressed, but certainly not resolved) as long as people refuse to take the real (contradictory) nature of the capitalist form of production for now. Since the theme is too complex to develop fully here, I shall limit myself, in conclusion, to examining just one of the many strands that compose it.

Contrary to the harmonistic vision of capitalism, in the real space of history technical progress and profit tend to *diverge*.[62] Their combination contains and prepares, on new levels, their opposition. Raising the organic composition of capital, in fact, may incidentally guarantee surplus profit to *individual* capitalists who are 'ahead' of their competitors; but in the final analysis it entails greater difficulties in the creation of surplus value for the *totality* of social capital. This has negative repercussions on the possibility of reducing customary working time. The greater the incorporation of science in the immediate production process, the greater the reduction of the part of the working day that corresponds to the worker's wages, which means that an ever greater increase in productivity is needed to give continuity to the process of accumulation. All this can only lead to *greater structural impediments* to further cuts in individual working hours.

As the upward spiral of the accumulation of value compressed necessary working time, it became more difficult for companies (especially once big modern industry, around the turn of the century, underwent its first comprehensive 'rational' reorganization) to offset with the heightened intensity and productivity of labour what they had been forced to lose in the extension of nominal working time. The part of the working day composed of necessary labour can, of course, be compressed; but the more it has already been compressed (in Europe, in 1972, it amounted on average to about 2 hours per day per worker, based on the work year, and to 1½ hours, based on the calendar year),[63] the more complicated it becomes to compress it further. For this reason, in mature capitalism, there is a substantial risk (for companies) that every contraction of the working day (especially if a large one) may translate directly into a proportionate expansion of necessary working time − or, which comes down to the same thing, into a proportionate reduction of surplus working time. Abstracting from every other element, we see in the struggle between capital and labour an indisputable historical shift from the time of the working *day* to the time of the working *week*, with capital's recent attempt to define working hours exclusively in terms of the working *year*. This phenomenon, together with the flexibilization and restructuring (if not *lengthening*) of working hours over the fifteen years from 1975 to 1989, reflect an organic aversion of the capitalism most 'advanced' towards the 'age of leisure and of abundance' to the reduction of nominal (to say nothing of *real*) working hours.

Calling attention to this contradiction does not mean absolutely ruling out the possibility of future reductions of hours in Western industry (such a thing has only become much more complicated). Neither does it mean that company management is about to reintroduce the working day of a hundred years ago, since this (except in special cases – but even then it would not simply be a return to the past) is not compatible with the technical and social conditions currently existing in the West (do not forget, however, that it has been reproduced on a large scale in the 'periphery'). Nor that a return of the crisis will not entail the usual (for crises) 'reductions' of hours in the form of mass dismissals and the like. Nor, finally, that in any case longer hours (8 or 9 hours a day, or 45 hours a week) are more profitable for capitalists than 'reduced' hours (say, without going too far, the 7-hour day and 35-hour week), even if as a rule – as the 'Japanese miracle' teaches – this is precisely the case.

But it has been a while now since Denison, one of the greatest experts on the questions of growth and productivity, formulated the hypothesis that above the threshold of 2,500 hours of work per year (50 hours a week) reductions of hours can be 'fully compensated' with an increased intensity of labour, while below the limit of 1,762 annual hours (approximately the current European average) this 'compensation effect' must be ruled out. This is a hypothesis that is gaining ground today – albeit on an almost entirely empirical basis – also in circles 'uncontaminated' by the critique of political economy.[64]

3

The Confirmation of the 1990s

As we have seen, the trend towards a reduction of working hours came to an end in the mid 1970s (in the mid 1960s in the United States); working time began to stagnate or to grow longer, and in any event to become heavier. This reverse trend, which continued throughout the 1980s, has confirmed and consolidated itself in the 1990s.

There have been three crucial elements in the ongoing process of consolidation. First, the diffusion of the 'Toyota system'; second, the diffusion of variable (or 'flexible') hours; third, the diffusion of neoliberal policies regarding the labour market. International in scale, intersecting and superimposed in time, these three elements express the effort of world capitalism as a whole to overcome its own crisis by transforming it into a crisis of wage labour.[1]

The Diffusion of Toyotaism

It may seem strange to give prominence to the international diffusion of the Toyota Production System precisely when Japan, apparently past its heyday, is going through a phase of economic and social uncertainty. But we must bear the causes of Japan's recent 'day of reckoning' in mind; namely, reckless financial and building speculation and heightened inter-Asian competition, coupled with a first impasse in the Asian boom, inadequate technological dynamism in several key sectors, as well as, perhaps, the employment structure itself. It is also true, however, that Japan's hard core of resistance to the blows

of the crisis and of international competition is precisely its automotive industry and its 'model' of workforce organization, which continue to be firm
points of reference for advanced industry all over the world.

This is so because over the past twenty years Toyotaism has proved to be
the system of organization of production and work best suited to cycles of
slow growth such as the ones that followed the recession of 1974–75. Its
worldwide success stems from its ability to reduce production costs in a period
when this was, and is, absolutely necessary for guaranteeing high levels of
profit. In fact, the merit of 'lean production' is – as Womack, Jones and Roos
affirm – that it

> uses less of everything compared with mass production – half the human effort
> in the factory, half the manufacturing space, half the investment in tools, half the
> engineering hours to develop a new product in half the time. Also, it requires
> keeping far less than half the needed inventory on site, results in many fewer
> defects, and produces a greater and ever growing variety of products.[2]

The superiority of 'lean production' compared to 'mass production' (Taylorism and Fordism) and 'neo-craft production' (the Volvo of Karmal or Udevalla)
is to be found, then, in its ability to 'halve' the costs, which means *the time*
(not the hours!) of commodity production. The heart of lean production is
the 'zeroing' of all idle, unproductive, 'dead' time, both in the individual
production processes and in the complicated business of fitting these processes
together, within each factory and between different factories, both at the
moment of production in order to create an uninterrupted flow, and in the
connection between design, production and distribution. But a system of
organization of industrial production and of the lives of workers that is so
closely tied to the synchronism of 'just-in-time', so intent upon continually
new productivity goals, and at the same time so devoid of 'buffers and safety
nets', is a 'fragile' mechanism because its jamming in just one point immediately unleashes a chain reaction right down the line. The system works well
only if it can count on the workers' total devotion to and cooperation with
the firm. For this 'machine that changed the world' to run smoothly, as our
MIT analysts observe, '*it is essential that every worker try very hard*. Simply going
through the motions of mass production with one's head down and mind
elsewhere quickly leads to disaster with lean production.'[3]

It is no longer sufficient that a worker 'does just what he's told to do, and no back talk', as Taylor prescribed.[4] Now something more than supine obedience is demanded – namely, a continuous 'creative tension' for responding to the ever-greater 'challenges' (for which read 'productivity schedules') posed by the company. In the final analysis, the whole secret of Toyotaism boils down to having each and every worker sink every last drop of his or her physical and mental capacities into the performance of the task; that the 'autonomated' or 'auto-activated' worker help management correct 'in progress' defects both of the production process and of the product as they occur;[5] that workers give the best of them*selves* (not just the best of their abilities) to the company, which is their second and superior self.

This is something more than what Taylor demanded of his man Schmidt – not something different from or opposed to it. Because in Toyotaism, too, it is still management that gives the orders, still management that checks to see that its orders have been applied correctly; except that, now, the 'self'-control of workers expands the horizon of the usual centralized control – workers checking and controlling *themselves*. The canons and objectives of this 'auto-control', which are no different from those of centralized control, are established unilaterally by the company – dictated by the impersonal power of the market (certainly not by the customer, as the Toyotaist vulgate would have it). In short, the Toyota production system aims at the maximum productivity of labour by means of the most systematic[6] squeezing and 'auto-squeezing' of labour power, pursued also through the activation (for the 'company good') of those 'intellectual' resources of labour that Taylorist methods – or their overly reductive application – had failed to exploit.

This active involvement, this auto-activation of the workforce in increasing the productivity of its own labour (a genuine masterpiece of company policy) depends less upon the genius of an Ohno or a Shingo than it does, as we have seen, upon the peculiar mode of formation of Japanese capitalism, together with the total disorganization of 'organized labour', which was violently annihilated during the period of Allied occupation. But it also has to be attributed to the ability of firms to give industrial workers something tangible in return. The vast majority of workers have had a significant increase in real wages and enjoy a sort of 'company welfare' system; a considerable part (around 30 per cent) also enjoy prolonged job stability; and, for a certain number of workers, there is upward social mobility, both in the union ranks and in technical and organizational positions. This is why Toyotaism, and the 'Japanese' system of work organization in general, have been able to come such a long way with (relatively) so few problems.

To achieve 'auto-activation' of the workforce, the Toyotaist method goes so far as to grant workers an 'ideal' recognition of their 'importance' for the life and success of the company. To put it bluntly, nineteenth-century capitalism treated workers like beasts of burden, and made them *feel* like beasts of burden. In the course of the twentieth century, which was a century of both proletarian and popular revolutions (even if no one remembers them today), the capitalist class had to learn to deal with the question somewhat differently. It has also learned, when need be, to praise the usefulness, the 'dignity' and even the 'beauty' not just of labour in general, but of manual labour in particular. And it has done so with particular propagandistic efficacy precisely in the most openly totalitarian of its political expressions – Fascism, Nazism and, on the scale of company organization, Toyotaism, which does something more in this sense than Fordism itself. If Fordism in fact promoted the wage-earning slave of the assembly line to the rank of 'consumer', Toyotaism promotes him to nothing less than 'citizen' of the company, almost on a par with the white-collar worker. On condition, however, that he make 'his' company into his family, community, homeland and city-state, to be defended against everything and everyone in a relentless (and, for wage labour, fratricidal) battle. On condition that he behave like a model slave, not simply like an 'ox-man'. On condition – and this is what the whole 'system' is really driving at – that he participate heart and soul in the struggle to cut production costs and production time in half, and to raise company profits.

Taiichi Ohno – who built, or at least perfected, the Toyota production system – states more explicitly than most of his interpreters that this is indeed its real substance, and in particular that a certain density and quality of working time is at its core. He wrote that the supreme goal of his managerial activity had always been the reduction of production costs, and that he pursued this goal by keeping to one simple basic idea: the total elimination of wasted time (and labour). His fundamental operative criterion was production with the least possible manpower. And to this end he brought the 'eye' of management as close to his 'manpower' as possible (bureaucratization had taken it too far away), in order to make every motion of every worker transparent.[7] In short, lean production aims at stripping workers of the means and methods of defending and saving the working energy they have acquired over long decades of experience in mechanized production (just as the Taylorist work organization aimed at depriving them of the know-how accumulated over centuries of artisanal production). At the same time, it makes them 'freely' cooperate in their own disempowerment in order to organize the most efficient possible use of their labour and of their time (which is the same thing), in the name of company profitability.

As for the specific issue of working time, Ohno sums it up, and gives us the essence of Toyotaism, in these terms: 'Manpower reduction means raising the ratio of value-added work. The ideal is to have 100 per cent value-added work. This has been my greatest concern ["my obsession"] while developing the Toyota production system.'[8] This is the system: cut working time until you attain the ideal goal of sixty seconds worked every minute, sixty minutes worked every hour, and overall yields of 100 per cent − which means a production line that practically never stops, or that stops only to correct the 'waste' that prevents it from being in fast and perpetual motion.

This 'obsession' with reducing the quantity of labour used in the production process to a minimum entails a limitless raising of the density of working time. Working time in Toyotaism − even more than in Taylorism and Fordism − is stripped of all its discontinuities. The formal and the real duration of working hours are brought as close together as possible. It is not fortuitous that, in Toyotaism, management deliberately employs fewer workers in the production process than the number considered indispensable, in order to guarantee the highest possible level of tension in the workforce at all times.

There is a second, and not less important, aspect typical of the 'Toyotaist model', which, however, Ohno does not tell us about; namely, the particular length of working hours. Although there has been a slight reduction of hours in recent years due to the joint efforts of the federal government and Rengo, the major labour federation, coupled with a slump in production, in the early 1990s a Toyota worker was working about 2,300 hours a year (500 hours more than a European worker, which means almost 2 hours more per day), with a rate of absenteeism of around 5 per cent, which is about half the European rate. If we add to that a commuting time that has been continually on the rise since the 1960s, now amounting to a round-trip of between 1½ and 2 hours per day,[9] it would be no exaggeration to speak of the 'Toyota system' workers as men or women who, in the epoch of the greatest labour productivity in history, totally exhaust their vital energy in the production of goods. The former Toyota seasonal worker Satoshi Kamata summed the situation up very bluntly: 'Looking around me, I realize that the workers in this automobile factory literally work like slaves. What crimes have we committed to be punished with such hard labor?'[10]

Such a high and prolonged productive tension can be maintained only in an extremely disciplined factory environment, in an atmosphere described by Ronald Dore himself as like 'an army camp'. And such discipline, as in any army camp worthy of the name, combines different and complementary techniques of domination, based on generalized coercion, paternalistic relation-ships, and a strong, and carefully cultivated, *esprit de corps*. The result, as Michael Burawoy put it, with reference to another factory situation, is 'hege-monic despotism', a mixture of coercion and 'spontaneous consent'.[11]

Those experts, on the other hand, who underscore the 'anti-Tayloristic' character of the 'Japanese model' see in the company organized according to Ohnoistic principles one that encourages worker participation more than the 'old' autocratic company did. If by this one means the greater participation of workers in company decisions in defence of their own interests, the life of Japanese factories since World War II resoundingly gives it the lie. Indeed, the Japanese factory is characterized by the methodical action of capitalist entre-preneurs designed to uproot any form of independent organization of workers, and by that which Takagi calls 'discriminating control' – a type of control based on a company ideology that admits no possibility of an organized opposition within the 'company-community'. 'People who oppose their em-ployers must be punished'[12] – this is the fundamental principle of company democracy in Japan (and not only in Japan for that matter), which is not contradicted by the existence of eighty thousand company unions, since such unions have constituted, in Japan, a substructure of the company itself, whose aims they have entirely made their own. Neither is it contradicted by forms of egalitarian participation such as 'quality circles', since the theme and even the manner of these moments of collective life are rigorously dictated from above. And, of course, they are in line with the fundamental aim of reducing the cost and time of production. This, I repeat, is the one and only form of operative participation and autonomy that is encouraged: participation in the effort to increase company profitability, to beat its competitors, and to reduce the value of labour power – one's own, and that of the entire working class.[13]

What can we expect to happen with the diffusion throughout the West of the Toyotaist model of the organization of company work and life? Since it is taking place in a period of growing economic uncertainty (indeed, as the response to a relative loss of competitiveness of US and European firms) and one in which the welfare state is under attack, it is more than likely that material returns for the First World working class will be increasingly reduced. This makes the wholesale transfer of the extreme characteristics of the model more complicated, but even its partial exportation has already led to a clear worsening of working conditions in factories everywhere, especially as far as the intensity and length of working time is concerned. Workers have had just one thing in return: those among them who have been able to cope with the new criteria, pace and hours of production have managed to hold on to their jobs.

There are many examples of the consequences on working time of the diffusion of Toyotaism in the West, starting with the US and British auto industries, which were the first segments of production to be reorganized in compliance with Ohno's obsession with reducing non-value-adding work to zero.

In the Mazda plant at Flat Rock, a suburb of Detroit, the application of just-in-time introduced production times never seen before in the United States. In the early 1980s the usual work pace at the Ford, General Motors and Chrysler plants covered between 40 and 50 seconds per minute, while the remaining 10 to 20 seconds were waiting or idle time ('dead' time, in terms of increasing the value of capital). Mazda, however, which at its Hofu plant in Japan manages to attain a saturation of working time close to 60 seconds a minute, at Flat Rock set – and achieved – the goal of keeping its workers working for 57 seconds of every minute. It thus gained a considerable advantage over its competitors, since working 12 seconds more per minute is equivalent to 12 minutes more every hour, 96 minutes per 8-hour working day, 8 hours per 5-day working week, which amounts to about 400 hours more per year *for every single worker*. If we multiply this figure by, say, just two or three thousand workers, we understand just how much working time and labour power is saved with this intensification 'Japanese-style' of the pace of production. But if we look at things from the standpoint of the workers, of wage labour, we can understand just how much Toyotaist rationalization lengthens real working hours even when it leaves nominal hours unchanged (in the case in question the increase is 20 per cent). And then – as was the case at Flat Rock – if average daily working time is itself extended from 8 to 9 hours, the increase soars to over 30 per cent; which means that Mazda's relatively high wages,[14] if compared with the value produced, turn out to be lower than average.

The miracles performed by Toyota at the NUMMI plant in Fremont, California, a joint venture with General Motors, are even more astounding. Here, Toyota took an auto factory with low productivity and an even lower-quality product and turned it into a super-productive factory, modelled on the Takaoka plant in Japan. The average number of seconds worked per minute jumped from 45 to about 57, and the rate of absenteeism was slashed from the 20 to 25 per cent of the old plant to between 3 and 4 per cent – which means that real hours rose overall by 40 per cent, without taking into account the further lengthening of hours intrinsic to Toyotaism (workers going in early to work, working overtime, taking part in quality circles and other after-hours company activities).[15]

That the spread of the Japanese model has not been limited to ventures with Japanese capital may be clearly seen in Great Britain, the European country in which it has had the greatest impact. One now speaks of three forms of Japanization: direct, mediated and full. And in all three cases, not only in the Japanese-owned facilities (such as Nissan's Sunderland plant), we are presented with a vast transformation both of work organization and of industrial relations. Be it in auto components (at Bosch, Valeo, Lucas) or in electronics, 'learning from Japanese management' has meant the introduction of just-in-time, autonomation, *kanban* (the tag that accompanies each and every component, giving operating instructions), quality-control, worker 'participation' in resolving problems in the production process, and wages proportionate to performance. As a result, in a number of English factories, such as Austin Rover and Lucas Electrical, the tremendous increase in hours and in the intensity of the workload has led to the first anti-Toyotaist strikes in Europe.[16]

The reception of Toyotaism in France and German has produced similar effects, even if, especially in Germany, it has been filtered through organizational models that are already well established, and by no means antagonistic to Ohno's principles.[17] But the prime European example of the 'Toyota effect' is, I think, the Fiat–Sata plant at Melfi, crowned by *Motor Business Europe* in August 1996 as the most efficient full-cycle auto plant (and with the lowest production costs) in Europe, with a production of 64.3 vehicles a year per employee.

The example is particularly significant because, as we shall see, Fiat designed this plant to be a model of fully humanized, 'anthropocentric' Toyotaism, a place of continual dialogue and 'soft' integration between company and workers, of total horizontal cooperation and low-echelon decision-making, of generalized professionalization and multivalence. A place where the common worker would never feel estranged, but on the contrary would be motivated to give his/her all for the cause of 'total quality', for the company (mother and father rolled into one), and for the full satisfaction of that dearly beloved *deus ex machina*, the mythical 'customer'. We shall limit ourselves here to a look at the results of the first real study (1996) of working conditions at Melfi, which attempts to discover what the workers themselves think about this 'integrated factory' organized 'Japanese style'.[18]

Well, every worker interviewed judges the work pace to be 'excessive, stress-inducing, exhausting.' The lines run at breakneck speed and stop only for technical reasons; to make up for lost time the already high pace is pushed even higher – often higher than the 10 per cent increase agreed upon with the unions, and higher than is needed to make up the lost time. Vice versa, the possibility of a worker 'stopping the line' is purely theoretical. Even the management of collective breaks is fundamentally unilateral. (Management decides: One break at the beginning of the shift.) The overall picture that emerges is one of an 'extremely strong time-pressure' exerted by management on the workers. For that matter, in order to increase productivity the time system at Melfi was organized from the very beginning on the basis of a work pace 18 per cent faster than the average pace in other Fiat plants. (From the very beginning, in fact, everyone knew the system had been rigged.)

At Melfi there are three shifts per day, including Saturdays, with nightwork compulsory also for women. The shift system is 'unanimously judged to be extremely heavy, not only for the alternating of the three shifts, but for the particular internal structure of this work schedule ..., which makes even a partial physiological and "social" adjustment practically impossible'. Since the shift schedule itself quite often is not respected, workers may find themselves forced to put in as many as 18 consecutive nights. Maintenance workers even work on Sundays, and rest every 20 days. White-collar workers and supervisors only have one day off a week, and not always the same day either.

Apart from the overtime often demanded by the company, the suffocating pace also gives rise to forms of 'voluntary and unpaid overtime', since many workers 'prefer' to take their places on the line some ten minutes early to prepare the components and implements before the shift begins. And with a great many workers commuting from far, and even very far, away, overall working hours easily amount to 10 hours a day – at least 8 of them, if not more, of great intensity and with shifts that change from week to week. 'Lean production' thus translates into a genuine slimming cure for the possibilities of socialization (and organization) of workers, both inside and outside the factory.

But apart from the harmful effects of desocialization, at the Toyotaized Fiat–Sata also the harmfulness of work in the narrower sense of the term has proved greater than the company forecast. In addition to the 'traditional risks' connected with the use of harmful substances (as in some nonmechanized painting procedures), now there are risks due to the work pace for workers who have to 'leap' from one post to another, as well as those due to a lack of injury-prevention measures. To say nothing of the stress associated with the intensity of the work itself, which a union study sees as the cause – among other things – of a rate of automobile accidents above the norm.[19]

And to all this must be added: a general dissatisfaction with the low level of wages and with the gap between a worker's wages and his qualifications; discontent about the recrudescence of the 'old' logic of hierarchy and discrimination (there have been a number of politically motivated firings), which had been considered dead and buried; the practically nonexistent 'active role' of labour, except on the upper–middle levels of the company hierarchy; and the poorness of the 'bonus system' itself. So it is not surprising that in just four years over 700 young trainees (10 per cent of the entire workforce) have quit their jobs, and the study shows how 'almost nobody wants to stay at Sata'.

In sum, the Italian and European factory best equipped with the latest devices of the science of work organization for the necessities of globalization, the factory with the record levels of labour productivity,

> looks to a great many workers like a place 'to escape from as fast as possible.' But [the author of the study observes] the 'conditions for the escape' are not easy to create; whether this will contribute to translating the 'urge to escape' into a struggle for change is for the moment an open question.

This, in fact, is true; still, it should be noted how, from the opening of the factory till now, worker participation in union strikes has been on the rise.

The Diffusion of Variable Hours

Besides, where is one to escape to? Melfi is, unquestionably, a pioneering venture, on the 'new frontier'. Nonetheless, its work organization and its system of working hours are not the exception; they are fast becoming the rule, in Italy, in Europe, in the United States, in Japan – in what I have been calling the 'West', by which I mean the advanced capitalist world, the 'centre', what is often called the 'North', in opposition to the Third World, the 'periphery', the 'South'.

For the past twenty years the West has been one big building site of 'flexibility'.

> The need for greater flexibility in industrial relations became clear soon after the oil shock of the mid 1970s, which signaled the end of the post-war period of high economic growth ... and inaugurated a period of growing uncertainty and rapid economic and social changes.[20]

These changes range from the technological innovations 'that have led to an increasingly greater emphasis on flexible specialization' to the fickleness and turbulence of 'consumer markets', after the certainty and standardization of the previous thirty years; from the heightening of international competition to the rise in the percentage of women in the workforce. 'All these factors have contributed to a growing awareness of the need for flexible industrial relations in order to adapt to these changing conditions.'[21]

Making industrial relations (and thus working hours) 'flexible' means de-regulating – breaking – the old rules of the conflictual social compromise between capital and labour that had been in place since World War II, to replace them with new rules – far from, and contrary to, the 'old' practice of concertation or codetermination – dictated by companies, markets and global capital; which, in turn, are opening fire from all sides on the standard, union-regulated work schedules of the so-called Fordist factory – and all the more so on the demands of workers for a reduction of working hours.

This crusade in the name of 'flexibility' spares no dimension of working time. Shiftwork, nightwork, Saturday work, Sunday work, overtime – they are all spreading everywhere; only the proportions and the modes of the increase vary. Now that companies have broken the rule of the 8-hour day with the introduction of 'special' schedules (9, 10 and 12 hours a day), they intend to break the rule of weekly hours too, taking as their reference annual, if not pluri-annual, hours. This permits them to have their employees work from zero to 48 hours a week and even more, according to their own needs or those of the market, and breaks down any 'conceptual' distinction between ordinary hours and extra hours. (In France in May of 1996 an agreement was reached for the metalworking sector to precisely this effect.)

Moreover, to get an idea of what music is being marched to – in that Europe which presents working hours that are more measured and regulated, on the whole, than in the USA and Japan – we may take a look at the Delors Commission EEC directive of 23 November 1993, 'concerning some aspects of the organization of working hours'. The directive presents itself as a list of 'prescriptions' – 'minimum' prescriptions, to avoid hurting the delicate feelings of entrepreneurial organizations; but, in point of fact, it legitimates the abolition of the 'maximum prescriptions' in force up to that time, giving free rein to a fuller liberalization – and lengthening – of working hours. Implicitly, the directive makes some pretty important 'concessions': the working day may be stretched to 13 hours; nightwork hours are to be considered substantially 'normal'; weekly day(s) off may be regularly reduced to 1 day; a 48-hour working week is acceptable, even for long periods; and, last but not least, companies may invoke the 'particular characteristics' of their production ac-tivities to justify exemptions – collectively or individually 'contracted' – from these 'minimum prescriptions', including exemption from the principle of not

Table 3.1   'Atypical' work schedules in Europe, 1995
(% of workforce)

	Shift-work	Night-work	Saturday work	Sunday work
France	8.0	14.0	36.3	18.1
Great Britain	17.0	22.0	56.9	37.4
Germany	12.0	12.0	30.6	16.3
Italy	22.0	13.0	56.1	17.5
Denmark	10.0	15.0	44.9	33.5
Spain	7.0	9.0	34.3	14.2
Belgium	19.0	13.0	30.9	18.8

Source: Eurostat, *Labour Force Survey: Results 1995*, Brussels: Eurostat, 1996.

working on Sundays.[22] One year earlier, demonstrating a somewhat suspicious concern with gender equality, the same European Commission, falling in with an analogous decision made in 1990 by the Bureau International du Travail (which abolished a previous regulation of 1948), had abrogated the prohibition of nightwork for women. This, indeed, was a case of equalization not in the acquisition of 'rights' that had been 'denied' but in the suppression of rights that had been acquired.

But let us proceed in an orderly manner, beginning with a statistical picture (for Europe) of 'atypical' ('contingent', 'casual') schedules, then going on to an analytical examination of the various aspects of the increasing variability of working hours, and concluding with some remarks on the comprehensive effect of this process.

Even at a glance, these figures – which apply to all sectors of production – startle us by the magnitude of the phenomenon. In Europe, on average, one worker out of six or seven (around 15 per cent) habitually does shiftwork, a similar percentage habitually works at night,[23] nearly 50 per cent of all workers go to work on Saturdays (over 56 per cent in Italy and Great Britain), one worker out of five regularly works on Sundays; and, as we have seen, if these figures are not exact, rest assured that they are too low, not too high.

The diffusion of 'atypical' work schedules is a consequence of the company's drive for a greater utilization of its facilities, which has manifested itself on a large scale over the past twenty years; this, in turn, is linked to the massive introduction of new and costly machinery and plants to be productively amortized and 'worn out' as quickly as possible. But the shift system is by no means a product of recent years. Its origins go back two centuries; it is rooted, as Marx has shown, in the very nature of the capitalist mode of production:

> Constant capital, the means of production, considered from the standpoint of the creation of surplus-value [or, subjectively, from the standpoint of the obsession of Taiichi Ohno and his opposite numbers of every nationality, race and religious creed], only exist to absorb labour, and with every drop of labour a proportional quantity of surplus-labour. While they fail to do this, their mere existence causes a relative loss to the capitalist, for they represent during the time they lie fallow, a useless advance of capital. And this loss becomes positive and absolute as soon as the intermission of their employment necessitates additional outlay at the recommencement of work. The prolongation of the working-day beyond the limits of the natural day, into the night, only acts as a palliative. It quenches only in a slight degree the vampire thirst for the living blood of labour. To appropriate labour during all the 24 hours of the day is, therefore, the inherent tendency of capitalist production. But as it is physically impossible to exploit the same individual labour-power constantly during the night as well as the day, to overcome this physical hindrance, an alternation becomes necessary between the workpeople whose powers are exhausted by day, and those who are used up by night.[24]

This primordial instinct of capital has grown stronger with time, in relation to the more than proportional increase in the value of the means of production compared to the value of labour power. It has had to reckon, however, with the resistance of the working class to the lengthening of hours and the introduction and multiplication of shifts, and on some occasions with the struggle to reduce working hours. As soon as this struggle, or this resistance, weakened, as it has for some time now, the capitalist offensive to prolong the working day without limits until it covered 'all the 24 hours of the day' was not long in coming. In recent years, driven by the goads of diminishing corporate profitability[25] and harsher market competition, the offensive has become relentless.

The Diffusion of Shiftwork

We have already seen some of the damage caused by shiftwork, which conflicts with our natural circadian rhythm on the one hand, and with the 'normal' rhythm of social life on the other; there can be no doubt that the schedule it imposes is both unnatural and asocial. Neither can it be doubted that the three-shift schedule (morning, afternoon, night) is becoming increasingly harmful to both rhythms, and that damage to the health and the social and psychic life of workers increases with the passing of time, especially after a certain threshold of continuance, and in relation to the frequency of changing shifts.

Since the dawn of time (between one and two million years ago) the human being has been a diurnal animal; daily rhythms have been essential to human life. Activity and rest, body temperature, heartbeat, arterial pressure, the volume of circulating blood, the production of hormones, the replacement of many cells, the process of transforming food into proteins and lipids, the nervous system itself – all vary according to a temporal cycle that has a periodicity (approximately, and with a certain difference between individuals) of 24 hours.[26] Disturbing these natural biological rhythms, while not in and of itself unbearable, always involves a particular psychophysical effort with inevitable pathological consequences, especially in the long run. The first physiological function to suffer is sleep, followed by the others. The shiftworker – the nightshift worker in particular – is pressured by the systems of hours in which he or she is imprisoned on a 'merry-go-round' that is increasingly dangerous and uncontrollable:

> The fundamental problem of irregular shiftwork consists in the fact that if temperature rhythm, adrenal gland, heart and kidney rhythms, sleep/wake rhythm, and all the other biorhythms are not synchronized with working hours, workers will suffer from fatigue, various disturbances and psychosomatic illnesses (ulcers, colitis, decreasing libido, insomnia). Furthermore, work accidents due to distraction and fatigue become more frequent; the very quality of work suffers.
>
> The fatigue does not appear immediately in a clear form. The first symptoms are vague disturbances of the nervous system and of behavior: listlessness, dizzy spells, anxiety, digestive problems, etc. These are followed by depression and sleep disorders: difficulty in falling asleep, waking frequently during the night, insufficient periods of deep sleep. It is at this point that, very often, a dangerous *vicious circle* begins. The individual, no longer able to regain energy through sleep,

is assailed by psychosomatic disorders (colitis, hypertension, impotence, etc.) that make his/her suffering worse. These disorders can, in turn, modify the individual's relationships, both inside and outside the family, causing psychological problems.

When they find themselves at this stage, many people decide to turn to sleeping pills, to induce sleep, and to stimulants, to regain lucidity. At this point the circle is closed. Fatigue leads to insomnia and psychosomatic disturbances, which lead to the use of drugs to sleep, which leads to fatigue upon waking, which leads to the use of stimulants to increase wakefulness, which leads to the use of sedatives that not only alter the composition of sleep even further, increasingly impairing its restorative capacity, but also accentuate the fatigue syndrome, which threatens to become permanent.[27]

And the vicious circle goes on from there, spiralling, wounding, leaving its mark on the body and on the psyche, which are connected by a thousand threads and, in the end, are a single whole.

That this is the destiny of the shiftworker was confirmed, for the umpteenth time, by the Twelfth International Symposium on Night and Shiftwork, held in June 1995 in Connecticut. The studies presented at the symposium, however, have three evident limits: most of them are laboratory simulations, not studies of flesh-and-blood workers; they reflect the lack of real interaction between the researchers and the shiftworkers themselves; and, swayed by the supreme demands of the market, they are marred by the overriding influence of a 'compatibilist' approach to the problem, exclusively concerned with avoiding the issue of some of the most devastating effects of the chronic fatigue, psychical disturbances and grave safety risks connected with shiftwork, on the certainly not 'value-neutral' assumption that shiftwork is necessary and inviolable, and cannot but continue to expand.[28]

In this symposium, which also dealt with special shifts of 12 and even of 24 hours (the latter, obviously, were experiments done on 'second class' Vietnamese and Bulgarian workers),[29] the social consequences of shiftwork remained in the background. They too, however, are not unknown. However little and poorly they are studied, such consequences emerge – constantly, almost monotonously – from all the surveys. Shiftworkers, especially if they also have to work at night, meet particular difficulties in relationships with family and friends, in making use of social services, in participating in social life. 'Living time' outside the workplace is as atypical as 'working time' – out of sync with the dominant, or at least prevalent, time system of society. Even our 'expert' who, riding the crest of the spirit of the times, sets off with misguided enthusiasm in search of the 'comforts' and 'privileges' (his very words) that shiftworkers, 'in spite of everything', might enjoy, was duty-bound to write:

> we have demonstrated that a certain degree of congruence between conditions of inconvenience and the consequent behavior does exist. When these two factors, joining together, affect the social life of the shiftworker [which, by our author's own testimony, is true in the vast majority of cases, eight workers out of nine], the result is a *maimed social figure*, for whom the hands of the clock follow another logic, a shiftwork logic, significantly different from the one that moves the clock-hands of the rest of society.
>
> The feeling of getting out of time, or even going against it; running after social events and activities; finding oneself in the wrong place at the wrong time; feeling that society 'owes you something' [which is quite true]; having to neglect family, friends, relatives; living in the scraps of time left over from work; spending many hours of the day or week in total isolation – these are just a part of the consequences of living by a shiftwork logic.
>
> In comprehensive terms, the many indicators recalled above induce us to associate shiftworkers with a state of relative deprivation, which for some may be attenuated by more or less incidental circumstances, forming a niche, but which generally rests on the notion of 'social inaccessibility'.[30]

Since in human affairs – the only ones accessible to us mortals – everything is relative, we may as well speak of social deprivation and marginalization *tout court*, which joins up with the special psychophysical fatigue caused by shiftwork, making it worse. Who can envy the shiftworkers' fate? Who can deny that their working hours are particularly heavy, that their 40 (or, perhaps, 'just' 36) 'variable' hours, worked at the same intensity as normal hours, cannot be equated with normal hours? The shiftworker is a woman or a man who ages, who withers before their time. And if the day of the life of wage-earners is short, and not exactly overflowing with satisfactions, it is even shorter and sadder for the workers who are subject to the inflexible laws of capitalist flexibility. 'About 1 in 5 workers in Western industrialized countries work some kind of shiftwork, *more than at any time in the past*, as international competition becomes more intense.'[31] And the general forecast is for an even greater expansion both of shiftwork and of nightwork.

The social force that imposes these 'deprivative' and marginalizing work schedules, aseptically denominated 'flexible', 'variable', 'atypical' (why not 'eccentric' or 'lunatic'?) is the competition between companies – between capitals – for domination of the market. It would seem 'out of date', in fact, to call them by their proper names – namely, unnatural and asocial.

Such a judgement may seem too categorical. What about processes, from iron smelting to oil refining, that require a continuous production cycle? And essential services, from hospitals to railroads, from electric power to running water, that have to be guaranteed at night? These demand shiftwork, even if it is also true that automation applied on an even broader and more rational scale could greatly reduce the need for living labour in these areas. But the fact is that it is not in these areas that shiftwork is increasing, but in the production of T-shirts and diapers, soft cheese and cookies, cars and bicycles, medicine and computers, teddy bears and ballpoint pens, sneakers and soccer balls – and any mind that does not pulsate in unison with the need for increasing the value of capital finds it hard to fathom why these goods cannot be produced in broad daylight, without upsetting the biological and social rhythms of masses of human beings.

But – you may ask – what would become, then, of that one shiftworker out of nine who really wants to 'live against time', who relishes a hectic life? Will he have to submit to the dictatorship of diurnal work, just because social medicine and research say that nightwork is harmful? Of course not! A society no longer regulated by the law of value, and so a little less monotonous than the one we have today, could afford to be generous with this extraordinary 'nocturnal' individual, granting her a voluntary surplus of shifts, in the certainty that sooner or later she may, possibly, understand that 'atypical' hours are not the only option for 'atypical' individuals.

But the shift system is not only unnatural and asocial, it is also not very well informed. And thus, since nobody told it that the category of 'class' is now 'scientifically' out of date, it still lives in the old days. The shift system still believes in class! Indeed, who actually does shiftwork today? Certainly not shareholders or industrialists, managers or professional people, legislators, mayors or judges. The very experts who take such pains to make shiftwork acceptable (to others) give it a wide berth, as do high-level technicians and foremen. Very few white-collar workers ever fall into its clutches. But the shift system still has a strong partiality, a brute passion – and don't ask it for flexibility, passion is passion – for workers and low-level technicians, for nurses (more than for doctors), for immigrants and people of colour (more than for natives and whites), for the proletariat in general, and for its most oppressed elements in particular.[32] And when shiftwork's mechanical arm reaches out with its class-conscious hand and snatches up women who are already busy wrestling with their household work, the turmoil and distress are so acute that the woman shiftworker is often forced to quit her job. For the woman who manages – who *has* – to endure it, a work- and life-experience is in store that is rife with anxiety and with physical, psychical, sexual and family contradictions, and that leaves her practically no 'time for herself'. An experience, as Laura Corradi put it, of slow 'hemorrhaging of being'.[33]

The further diffusion of regular shiftwork (for the most part with 8-hour shifts, but the variety is truly remarkable) is only the most conspicuous aspect of the company pressure to make working hours 'flexible'. Other means have been employed. In France, for example, there is the recourse to overtime (for 1990 the official figure was 65.9 hours annually per worker, more than 1 hour per week); there are weekend teams with regular shifts on Saturdays and Sundays, in most cases of 12 hours; there are modular hours – that is, variable upwards or downwards (which raise the limit of weekly hours to 44 and even 48 hours); there are individual schedules – but they are 'class-conscious' in quite a different way (applying to 57 per cent of managers, 39 per cent of office workers, 19 per cent of manual workers, and 16 per cent of factory workers); there are a hundred different types of part-time job; there are work schedules dependent upon the educational trimesters; there is the annualization of hours.[34] *Et voilà!* A thousand different schedules! exclaims the ingenuous, or disingenuous, empiricist – meaning that there is no common thread. But in the eyes of the workers there is, indeed, the common thread – or common chain – of a comprehensive worsening of the quality of working hours. The more objective observers cannot but confirm this, even recognizing the fact that 'the new policies of time have been conditioned up to now by the necessities of companies, but very little by the necessities and the demands for change expressed by workers', and that the variability or 'flexibility' of hours 'is experienced differently by each social category – it represents a sign of greater freedom for the middle managers, but becomes a *bond* for the workers (bound to alternating shift schedules, for example)'.[35]

The transition from 'standard' to 'variable' hours is so far from being neutral and advantageous for all the 'social partners' that it can be depicted as a 'pressure to extend working hours to temporal spaces that once were sheltered from work', as a 'global colonization of time' on the part of working time[36] – or, to be more precise, on the part, and to the advantage, of the owners of working time (the colonizers), to the detriment of the sellers of working time (the colonized). This situation was denounced, with distinctly German vigour, by one of the leaders of IG Metall, who also identifies its fundamental cause:

> Together with the neoconservative policy of *deregulation* [of working time] also the imperialism of the time of capital has been raised to a new and graver level.
>   The increase of fixed capital with respect to living labour, in the production process, means that this new capital investment has to be amortized more quickly.
>   The intention to increase the velocity of capital means that machinery works longer and factories are open longer. The dictatorship of the working time of machinery – of dead labour over living labour, so to speak – has got worse.[37]

Listening to the metalworker speak of the 'working time of machinery', do not think of the large factory exclusively, or of industry alone. 'Machinery time' has insinuated itself into agriculture, and on an even larger scale into 'services'; it has broken down the doors (quite some time ago) of the small, and very small, craftworking shops. These shops, which resemble external departments of the big factories more every day (think of Japan, where a big firm may have as many as five to six thousand supplier plants, or of the company network model organized in Italy by Benetton), have working weeks of close to 60 hours, in an almost inextricable nexus of exploitation – in good measure by others, but also of self-exploitation. Such schedules are now so far from being 'abnormal' that they have been partially legalized by collective agreements admitting major exceptions from the 'norm' for craft enterprises. Furthermore, the 'bearable' length of such hours encourages big companies to continue their experiments with 'abnormal' shifts of 10 hours, 12 hours, and even more.[38]

This insatiable hunger of companies for working time and 'flexibility' of hours has meant, for shiftworkers, the progressive expansion of working time within living time as a whole, even when they work (slightly) fewer hours than dayworkers do, as is often the case. If the lengthening of working time leaves less and less time for 'living', and if its intensification leaves the workers too exhausted really to live the 'free' time they have, in its turn the diffusion of 'atypical' schedules further limits and hinders the occasions for sociality of common working humanity, even within the family itself. In the year of grace 1996 of the 'postmodern' era, a Swiss typographer for a large news-paper, after ten years on the job, talks about the life of a nightshift worker:

> When you work nights, it takes an enormous effort to maintain a family life and social ties. And it's even harder, now that most of the time the husband and wife both work. These days, to talk with your own wife you practically have to make an appointment. Younger people also want more time to look after their chil-dren's education. But if you are working shifts, you have to ask your daughter: when can we find some time to play together a little? These situations create enormous tensions and frustrations, which can lead to alcoholism, for example, or look at the number of people working nights who get divorced.
>
> The people who work in delivery are even worse off. Some of them have been doing this job for twenty or thirty years; they only have one day off a week; six days out of seven, they finish work at five in the morning. On their day off, it's impossible for them to change their rhythm; what can they do but sleep? A life like this often plunges people into real misery; what sort of relation-ships and affections can they have? The situation is hardly different from a form of modern serfdom [servage].[39]

In the so-called 'era of mass free time' – the era in which nonworking time lords it over working time, if one believes a sociologist like Sue – for a growing number of wage labourers life is forcefully invaded and turned topsy-turvy by working time. Indeed, Japan and the United States were the first to be invaded by a brand-new 'postmodern' disease, 'workaholism', which affects those workers for whom going to work has become a drug no less necessary than alcohol is for alcoholics. The paroxysm of the pathology has reached such a pitch that companies are now confronted with a paradoxical dysfunc-tion known as 'presenteeism', with workers so disciplined that they show up early or go home late, all on their own, but who are so stressed out that their contribution to company life is minimal, if not downright negative, however hard they try.[40] And there is no point in our smiling condescendingly about this here in Europe, because pathologies of the same nature, caused by the extension of the same iron laws of capitalist productivity to every sphere of social activity, are spreading right before our eyes. Spreading even to work-places – hospitals, for example – where it is not a question of tightening bolts

or packaging newspapers, but rather – and it ought to make *some* difference
– of caring for human beings.[41]

The Diffusion of Neoliberal Policies

That is not all. The flood – torrential here, creeping there – of neoliberal
policies aimed at demolishing the entire system of welfare guarantees in the
labour market and in pension mechanisms has also had a great many consequences on working hours.

The chaotic multiplication of increasingly precarious jobs, both in factories
and in services, has thrown the 'old' schedules into confusion. Just look at
how many *types* of contract we have today: apprentice, trainee, outside con-
sultant, part-time of *every* stripe (in France there are cases of up to six different types of part-time in a single store!),[42] temporary, daily (more frequent all
the time), seasonal, weekend – to say nothing of totally undocumented jobs
without contracts (for the immigrants of your choice, but certainly not just
for them). The casualization of labour is now *dominant*. In Spain 96 per cent
of the jobs created in 1996 were temporary, as are 75 per cent of those created
in France between 1996 and 1999. In the United States, the world leader of
flexible globalization, no more than 15 to 20 per cent of the employees of big
companies presently have open-ended contracts.[43]

The more this jungle of unsteady jobs thickens, creating fierce competition
between workers, bridling and dissipating the power (also bargaining power)
of the proletariat, the more the companies have free rein in managing their
employees' working conditions and working time according to their own
needs – which include the need for long hours. The already lenient rules laid
down by the Delors Commission are often not worth the paper they are
written on. Here too, then, the European industrialists and their governments
have learned the lesson of Toyotaism, and with a vengeance, in some ways
even pushing it to the extreme. In the classical 'Toyota system' the workforce
was carefully divided between lifetime (*honkò*) and temporary (*shagaikò*) employees, between men (mainly employed in the larger firms) and women
(mainly employed in the smaller factories, paid less and maltreated more). In
the Toyotaized and Thatcherized Europe of our day the dividing lines are even
more jagged and 'Bosnian', if only because here – unlike the case of Japanese

capitalism, whose workforce was ethnically compact until just a few years ago – companies can draw on an inexhaustible reserve of immigrants from inside and outside Europe, to be subjected to the latest forms of working conditions and hours.

The industrial zone in Marghera, on the Venetian lagoon, is a fine illustration of what this liberalization of industrial relations really means. We are not talking here about little factories or craftwork shops, but about a huge state-owned enterprise, Fincantieri, which way back in the 1960s put into practice a policy of cooperative industrial relations that was boasted of for some decades as an 'advanced model'. This 'model' enterprise, which in fact is booming (its cruise ships are very much in demand), was denounced by the metalworkers' union in 1997 in the following terms:

> In the dockyard around 150 subcontracting firms have been operating for months, at present providing jobs for over 1,600 workers [many of them from Yugoslavia, Romania, Africa, or southern Italy; the regular Fincantieri workers amount to about one thousand]; no one respects the contractual hours (the production workers work 12 hours a day on average); nearly all the firms avoid paying contributions through the system of 'all-inclusive wages' [wages that include a small part of the contributions that should have been paid to the state]; almost all of them operate as subcontractors; there is a risk [risk?] that a system of widespread illegality may take hold, in contrast with the history and tradition of Fincantieri.[44]

But such a system is perfectly in keeping with the prevailing trend towards the deregulation of industrial relations.

There has also been an extremely favourable external context for the generalization of situations of this type; namely, the jobless growth (without *steady* jobs in particular) of the 1980s and 1990s, resulting not only from the increasingly suffocating pace of world-scale accumulation but also from the sharpening of the contradiction inherent in the capitalistic use of machinery. Capital, from its very beginning, has made use of the latest machinery to reduce the working time needed for producing a given commodity and the number of workers needed for that production, on the one hand, while prolonging the working day, employing the greatest possible number of workers (in the new conditions), and intensifying their work, on the other. The (relative) novelty in recent years consists in the fact that the rise in production has not entailed an increase in employment, and in the fact that the process of replacing living human labour with new technological instruments has become an absolute precondition for growth.

Speaking of an 'end of work', as Rifkin and others before him have done,[45] is an exaggeration as gross as it is unilateral, because it fails to see the other side of the question, or pushes it into the background − namely, the intensification of the 'residual' work and the trend towards the lengthening of working hours. But the rise in the unemployment rate and in the mass of the unemployed is considerable, even in periods of economic recovery. In the 1960s the unemployment rate in OECD countries was between 3 and 5 per cent, in the mid 1990s it was over 10 per cent; in the meantime the mass of the unemployed grew enormously, from between 5 and 10 million to between 35 and 45 million, and its size had become increasing independent of the economic cycle. Indeed, the financial organism that presides over this curious 'development', the IMF, acknowledges the existence of strong structural or chronic unemployment, 'which is destroying the social fabric in many countries, regions and communities', and speaks with a certain alarm of 'marginalization of a large slice of the work force' in the West.[46] And the phenomenon is without exceptions.[47] A high unemployment rate leads almost automatically to a fall in the price of labour power, which is one of the fundamental causes of the lengthening of working hours, in the form of overtime hours and multiple jobholding, both of which were on the rise in the 1990s.

Calculating overtime hours is particularly difficult, as anyone with experience in the matter knows, because more often than one may think we are talking about hours worked and not paid, or paid in an arbitrarily determined lump sum, or paid and not declared or, for fiscal reasons, declared only in part. In any case, all the surveys are concordant in recording a conspicuous total of overtime hours all over Europe, from France to Germany, from Great Britain to Italy.[48] As for multiple jobholding, Eurostat estimates that there are more than five million people in Europe holding second jobs, where they work 12.2 hours a week on average, that two-thirds of them have a permanent second job and only the remaining one-third take a second job occasionally or in certain seasons.[49]

As for the decline in the purchasing power of wages, which is the other factor, along with the rise in unemployment, that fuels the increase in working hours, it is not worth dwelling upon, since the fact has been generally taken for granted in the United States for years, and is becoming common knowledge in Europe as well.[50] Less common knowledge, however, is the fact that the increased threat of unemployment and the increasingly authoritarian policies of control of the workforce and discouragement of union activity have cut down – in the true sense of the word – the rate of absenteeism in industrial firms (and not only there) in both its components: 'absences' due to strikes, and those for 'nonoccupational disease'. In Italy in 1975 the rate of absenteeism was around 14 per cent, with much higher percentages in the large firms; by the mid 1990s the absentee rate had fallen to less than 8 per cent. So, even if we consider just this single aspect, supposing that working hours remained formally unchanged over this twenty-year period, *real hours* would still have increased, both on average and for the individual workers. This is another one of those elementary considerations that are almost always left out of account – perhaps because they are considered just too elementary.

In sum, the diffusion of neoliberalism has produced a growth and intensification of working hours through deregulation, the rise in unemployment, the policies of containment and reduction of the purchasing power of wages, the attack on the feasibility of political and union activity in the workplace and in society (we have just been through twenty years of anti-union legislation), the measures to discourage absenteeism and labour conflicts. There are, however, three new fronts where this capitalist offensive for the re-lengthening of working time is now heating up.

The first is that of the counter-reform of the pension system. For the past ten years not a day has gone by without the IMF, the World Bank, the Stock Exchanges, the OECD, the EC (now EU), the national governments, employers' associations, and political economy pundits with their sumptuous salaries, perquisites (and pensions), all thundering against the present pension systems of workers – invoking, and introducing, measures against early retirement, measures for reducing the degree of coverage of the pension (in relation to wage or salary) and, more frequently all the time, measures to raise the minimum retirement age. And combined with these generalized trends there is another trend too, which is already making headway in the United States; namely, the trend towards a reduction of the percentage of wage-earning workers covered by the pension system, which fell in just ten years (1985–95) from 70 to 60 per cent. And the fall is not over, not by a long shot, if it is true that by now even the liberal economists, and not only the Chicago boys, are accusing the elderly (note well: the elderly *workers*) of being the ruin of the state budget, a cause of inflation, and intolerable dead weight for the entire USA, and especially for the new generations,[51] while promising them a new round of hidings.

In Europe the first step in this direction was taken in 1992 by Sweden, which raised the retirement age from 65 to 66 while, simultaneously, reducing vacation time from 27 to 25 days per year – measures which, together, mean 2,600 to 2,800 additional hours worked in a lifetime. But practically all the countries of Europe are now treading this path, raising the retirement age even more. At the moment, if on average European workers are required to put in 40 years of work and be 65 years of age before they can retire, there are already 'authoritative proposals' going around to raise the retirement age to 67, 70 (Iceland has already done so, though only for a few sectors), 75; while on the US front the *Monthly Labor Review* reports that the number of retired people who are coming back to the labour market (of their own free will?) is on the rise, and at the same time an Advisory Council on Social Security nominated by Clinton suggested raising the 'normal' retirement age to 69.[52]

Is it right or wrong – for society and for themselves – that people should work throughout the course of their existence? I, personally, see nothing wrong, provided this does not mean prolonging the long agony of a wage slavery already endured for decades – and in even more humiliating conditions, given the lesser 'productivity' of the elderly. But here let me just remark that also the trend towards a reduction of the years of work has been blocked and reversed, which means that also on this front working hours, rather than contracting, are getting longer. On the second front, the reduction of paid vacations (a practice that, for the moment, has become law only in Sweden) fuels the trend even more. In the US manufacturing industry in the course of the 1980s the already minimal two weeks a year were reduced by 2.3 days,[53] and the phenomenon is gaining ground even in Italy, where in August the once-deserted factories are now not so thinly populated.

On the third front we have a process that, while still embryonic, cannot fail to develop, if the relentless advance of neoliberal policies continues –

namely, the 'early' entrance of young people into the workforce, spurred on by legislation (highly advantageous for the purchasers of working time) that puts fresh wage labourers at the disposal of companies, who have the legal right to pay them 'entrance' wages well below the norm. The process may already be observed in some areas of northeast Italy, where, in the Veneto in particular, a fall in secondary-school attendance is matched by a rise in the number of young people entering factories before their sixteenth and even fifteenth birthdays. And in France the pre-apprenticeship age has been lowered to fourteen and a full-fledged governmental campaign to promote apprentice-ship is under way, with teenagers working 48 hours a week.[54]

In sum, the globalization of Toyotaism, of 'flexible' hours and of neoliberal policies come together to make working hours in Western industry and serv-ices more intense, longer (even when nominally or contractually somewhat shorter), freer from legal obligations, and more desynchronized with respect to other 'social times'. This trend, which is part and parcel of the leap forward of the globalization of finance and production in the 1990s, is increasingly homogenizing the partially diversified situations of the various countries of the West. And it is clear that the entwined sum of these processes is stamped with a single, unequivocal sign of class; namely, that of the concentrated (which does not mean unified) superpower of the market, of world capital. The president of the AFL–CIO summed up this very recent course taken by capitalism pretty well, and not just for the United States: 'In the last ten years American workers have been working like mules, and been treated like dogs.'

(Official) Hours and Labour Productivity

The United States is, in any case, the country where the fundamental dynam-ics of the process are most sharply delineated. In fact even the official studies now acknowledge without reservation that since the mid 1970s: the length of the working week in industry has increased (the official estimate gives 39.5 hours in 1975, about 42 hours in 1995); the percentage of individuals with 'very long' weekly hours has increased; average annual working hours have increased by 100 hours for men and 233 hours for women, just as the number of women working year-round has increased; and – surprise – a large slice of the atypical, flexible and variable hours, including working weekends, have fallen onto the shoulders of low-educated women.[55] At the same time the casualization of labour, which is the other side of this coin, has been generalized to such an extent[56] that at the United Parcel Service in the summer of 1997 we witnessed the first mass (185,000 strikers) labour struggle against the precariousness of labour, on a national and international scale.

If the United States, overtaking Japan, has become world leader in the lengthening of working time, in Europe the primacy of Britain, their traditional pupil, is now being threatened by Spain. Great Britain in 1996 vaunted some 4 million workers working more than 48 hours a week (up from the 2.7 million of 1984), and in November of that year was reprimanded by the European Court of Justice for the 60- and 70-hour weeks in its textile sector.[57] In Spain up to the mid 1970s, under Franco, working hours were considerably more than 40 hours per week and 2,000 hours per year. In the period from 1978 to 1991, thanks to the resumption of labour militancy, hours were reduced by about 10 per cent, approaching the European average. But since then there has been an about-face – a counter-reform – featuring every possible form of casualization imaginable (so far, they have come up with more than eighteen types of temporary job), with, of course, a rise in hours, overtime, work accidents (rising in the first half of 1997 to a record level of 3.2 per thousand employees) – in short, with all the necessary ingredients for making Spain into 'a model both for entrepreneurs and for conservative governments'.[58]

The rest of Europe is not moving in a different direction. Even in Germany, the only European country to have had some reduction of working hours (thanks to the struggle of the metalworkers), 'the tendency to shorten average working time towards 35 hours per week, which has occurred since the mid 1980s, seems to have stopped.'[59] That is not all. While the German Manufacturers' Association beats its breast over the *Lebercompromise* of 1984, there has been a succession of initiatives increasing hours without increasing pay, ranging from the government of Bavaria, which lengthened the working week of its employees to 40 hours, to a growing number of factories, beginning with those of the Siemens group, which, under the threat of dislodgement to Eastern Europe, are accepting a return from the 35- to the 38-hour week, with no rise in pay. But the most significant indicator of the changed social and political climate is the approval by the Christian Democratic Union, one

Table 3.2 Official weekly working hours of full-time workers in Europe, 1995

	Agriculture	Industry	Services
Germany	41.3	39.1	40.0
France	41.3	40.1	39.7
Great Britain	48.7	44.4	43.5
Italy	40.7	40.4	37.3

Source: Eurostat, *Labour Force Survey: Results 1995*, Brussels: Eurostat, 1996, Table 73, pp. 168–9.

of Germany's two main political parties, of a general policy statement that baldly asserts: 'Germans have to be ready to work more for the same wages.'[60]

After all, if we take a good look at the official European statistics the German 'difference' is pretty well cut down to size.[61] As Table 3.2 makes clear, *official* European working hours in the 1990s not only do not present us with a continent of milk and honey, but the decrease, since the mid 1980s, in Germany (from 40.2 to 39.1 hours per week), is offset by an increase in France (from 39.7 to 40.1), in Great Britain (from 43 to 44.4), and in Italy (from 40.3 to 40.4). And as we know perfectly well by now, *real* hours are quite another matter; for Italy, for example, as we shall see, the weekly figure for real hours is 3 to 6 hours higher than the official hours.

For the European countries as a whole we have the following annual series of weekly working hours in industry: in 1987, 40.6 hours; in 1988, 40.7; in 1989, 40.6; in 1990, 40.4; in 1991, 40.3; in 1992, 40.3; and finally in 1995, 40.5[62] – a clear picture of complete stagnation. In merely quantitative terms, of course, since these figures, which even quantitatively are inadequate, tell us absolutely nothing about the intensity, density, weight and quality of a working time that has meanwhile been Toyotaized, has become more variable and asocial (through the rise in shift- and weekend work), and more continuous (with the fall both in absenteeism and in vacations). And since from time to time in our daily information–disinformation the unlikeliest of figures (and they are *official* figures!) for average annual hours – 1,300 hours, no less! – fly like carnival confetti, permit me to report *these* official figures for European industry, sector by sector, for 1992: 1,799 hours in the sectors of energy and water; 1,826 in the mining and chemical industries; 1,814 in the metal-working industries; 1,821 in the other manufacturing industries; 1,840 in the construction industry.

If we go on to services, hours are even higher, both in the sector of transportation and communications with 1,861 annual hours (keep in mind the sharp rise in shiftwork), and in wholesaling and retailing, public commercial concerns, hotels, and so on (with a maximum of 1,875), and are over 1,800 hours in the sector of finance and insurance as well. Only in civil service jobs do they dip to 1,718 hours.[63] While it is true that these figures are still below the official hours of the United States and Japan (and even further below the proto-capitalist hours of the Third World), the difference is not as great as we have been led to believe. The big difference here is from Kahn and Wiener's 1,000 hours and Fourastié's 1,200 – prophesies that have not proved self-fulfilling.

Aside from the Franco-Italian smoke signals on the 35-hour week (we shall deal with that later), in the 1990s the only country in the West that saw a real reduction of working hours was Japan. There, in about ten years, hours were reduced by 7 per cent, in annual terms from the 2,050 hours of 1987 to the 1,919 of 1995, and in monthly terms from the 175.9 of 1987 (these are official figures, which do not include businesses with fewer than thirty employees – the ones, that is, with longer hours) to the 165.8 of 1996.[64] But it would be rash to call this the first step in a spontaneous reversal of the trend. While a host of factors have been responsible for this reduction, the conversion of Japanese firms to a non-Ohnoist conception of working time is not one of them. In the first place, Japan has been through a period of declining production, with a number of negative years. Second, Japan's competitors have been repeatedly asking it to open up its internal market with measures to increase mass consumption and dampen competitiveness (this explains the highly unusual pressure in Europe and the United States to reduce hours… in Japan). Third, there has been some sign of initiative on the part of Rengo, the 'general' Japanese union that is nonexistent in industry but present in some sectors of public services. Finally, there are the expectations of the younger generation of workers, who hope for a little more room for their own lives outside the workplace. Nevertheless, if we analyse this reduction, we observe how about one half of it, 59 annual hours out of 131, is concentrated in the two-year period 1992–93, and thus depends almost entirely on the halving of overtime during a period of recession, and not on any sort of agreement for the reduction of working hours; we also observe how the 165.8 monthly hours of 1996 is just a sliver less than the 167.8 of 1975, the other moment of serious difficulty for the Japanese economy.[65]

Once again, recent government measures to 'persuade' both companies and workers that it would be socially useful 'for everyone' to reduce working time – at least by taking a few more Saturdays off! – have indeed been rather bland. It is since 1980, if not earlier, that there has been talk in Japan – on the political level – of 'coming into line' with Europe, yet Hippo's 'seven enigmas' of Japanese working time, though weakened, still persist.[66] The re-structuring underway in 'the Japanese employment system'[67] presages no re-duction of hours. On the contrary, it can be interpreted as an attempt to renew a production mechanism that was showing signs of fatigue, giving it even greater dynamism than it had before. The main lines of the reform proposed by the Bank of Japan are modelled on the 'American system' of Reaganomics, and urge Japanese companies – especially the big ones – to make employment and wages more flexible. The means it suggests are: abol-ishing the 'lifetime job' system; shifting a part of the employees of the major companies to their minor, supplier firms; cutting seniority 'privileges'; in-creasing the use of immigrant labour; casualizing the workforce, in particular through temporary and part-time jobs; and, finally, raising the retirement age from sixty to sixty-five. These are all measures that, albeit 'gradually' (as recommended by the Bank of Japan), will slowly but very surely produce *an increase in working hours*, from daily and weekly hours to the working time of a worker's lifetime.

As a matter of fact, it is since the early 1990s that big Japanese companies have been dealing with the problem of the *madogiwazoku*, 'the tribe of those who sit at the windows' (often in offices), with mass firings, beginning in the iron and steel industry and in naval shipyards. And, together with this 'new' practice, it is to be expected that a firing or an unemployment 'psychosis' is

spreading among workers and that, if on the one hand this feeling of insecurity may undermine company loyalty and (to some extent) labour productivity, on the other the fear of downward mobility induces workers to
accept the 'inevitable' changes for the worse in their working conditions.[68] In
any case the 'slimming' of big companies that are already 'lean', but never lean
(and mean) enough in times of sluggish growth, has begun; and the new jobs
on the Japanese market are increasingly precarious and concentrated in smaller
firms. The impact of this situation on work time stares us in the face, if we
compare the hours in firms of different sizes. In 1990, in firms with more
than 1,000 employees only 3.2 per cent (say the official statistics) were working 6 days a week; the percentage rose to 17.5 for firms with between 100
and 999 employees, and shot up to 38.6 per cent for firms with 30 to 99
workers. The Japanese Ministry of Labour gives no figures for firms with
fewer than 30 employees, but if we want to get some idea of the enormous
mass of Japanese workers still working Saturdays (and thus, indirectly, of the
insubstantiality of the official statistics), consider the fact that over 44 per cent
of Japanese workers are employed in firms with fewer than 100 employees,
while the remaining 56 per cent are divided between large and middle-sized
firms.[69] And that, if the overall rate of unionization in Japan (and we are
talking about ultra-company unions, in industry) has fallen sharply since the
1980s, in small firms even the company union is effectively banned.

As we have seen, there is an increasingly evident convergence between the
three main poles of the West, and between the companies that operate in
them. This convergence is founded on a combination of Toyotaism and
neoliberalism, and on what has been called 'time-based competition' – in
particular, on the quantity of labour time companies manage to expropriate
from 'their' workers.[70] At this point, I do not think it would be rash to
conclude that the trend (broached in the previous chapter) towards the
nonreduction, indeed towards the lengthening, and in any event towards the
worsening of the 'quality' of working hours, is entirely confirmed by our
multilateral analysis of the processes 'in progress', and not yet fully completed,
in the 1990s. With the warning that we are talking about a *general* trend –
general not because it is realized contemporaneously in every single country
and every single company in the same way, with an automatism extraneous to
social relationships, but because it leaves its mark on the evolution of the

Table 3.3 Labour productivity, production and employment in industry, 1979–95 (% change)

	Productivity (per hour)	Production	Employment
United States			
1979–95	2.6	2.1	−0.8
1979–85	3.3	2.0	−1.4
1985–90	2.2	2.2	−0.1
1990–95	2.3	2.1	−0.6
Japan			
1979–95	3.4	3.4	+0.5
1979–85	3.5	4.7	+1.2
1985–90	4.3	4.8	+0.8
1990–95	2.3	0.4	−0.5
Germany			
1979–95	2.2	0.4	−0.9
1979–85	2.1	0.2	−1.1
1985–90	2.1	2.3	+1.1
1990–95	2.4	−1.2	−3.5
Italy			
1979–95	3.8	2.3	−1.9
1979–85	4.9	1.7	−2.9
1985–90	2.6	4.0	+0.3
1990–95	3.7	1.3	−2.8
Great Britain			
1979–95	4.2	0.7	−3.2
1979–85	4.4	−1.2	−4.9
1985–90	4.6	3.4	−1.2
1990–95	3.7	0.3	−3.1

Source: *Monthly Labor Review*, February 1997, pp. 29–30.

entire system of hours. Let me conclude this chapter with a look at the question of labour productivity, which will provide further confirmation of this state of affairs.

Even in the most recent period, despite the production indices and rate of capital investment that are rather low, labour productivity in Western industry has continued to grow (in 'services' the situation is more complex) precisely by virtue of an intensification of the exploitation of the employed workforce, which meanwhile has been reduced almost everywhere, as Table 3.3 shows.

Comparing Table 3.3 with Table 2.2 (p. 32 above) we note several things that are new. The biggest change is that the British tortoise, dead last in long-term labour productivity (1870–1981), has been transformed into a hare, attaining indices even higher than those of its period of greatest production growth (1950–73). This spectacular recovery of productivity in British manufacturing industry cannot be explained by the rate of increase of GDP, which over the period 1979–95 was semi-stagnant (+0.7 per cent on average). Neither can it be explained, as Husson suggests, by an accelerated replacement of labour with capital, since the growth rate of capital per employee is the same on average as in the 1960s. Furthermore, the increase of fixed capital per employee has proceeded in extremely strict (even 'mechanical') correlation with the drastic reduction of industrial workers (-24.9 per cent in the period 1979–84 and substantial also in the period 1990–95). This, then, was the basic cause of the 'big bang' of labour productivity, which continued to grow at a fast pace even after the 'institutional rupture' (*rupture institutionnelle*) provoked in 1979 by the Thatcher government – growth that was a direct consequence of the combined policy of 'new' flexibility of the labour market at the social level[71] and the adoption of the principles of Toyotaist 'rationalization' at the company level.

Great Britain is the European country where the diffusion of Toyotaism, variable hours and neoliberal policies has been most thoroughgoing, and we can see the resuls. We can see, by the same token, how maintaining working hours above the European average – indeed, lengthening them even more – by no means conflicts with the growth of productivity, so long as there are mechanisms, in and out of the workplace, that 'advise' workers to discipline themselves – 'advice' that serves to weaken the workers' union and political organization.[72]

The fact that a greater diffusion of 'Ohnoism', 'flexible' hours and neoliberal policies (combined with longer hours, not as an alternative to them) pays off in terms of labour productivity can also be seen in the results obtained by the United States and Italy, the only countries that in the period 1979–95 *reversed* the long-term trend (albeit just barely) towards a slowdown of labour productivity; and, once again, we are talking about two countries where an increase in working hours is taken for granted.

In the performance of Japan and of Germany we see no such reversal of the trend. In the case of Japan it was the sharp rise in production that, until 1990, supported the productivity index, while the slump in employment had the opposite effect. In the case of Germany, there was a small rise in productivity only when the workforce was cut back (what Ohno calls the 'elimination of waste in time and labour'). There was, however, no reduction of working hours in either case.

But the most significant fact of all – and one more confirmation of my thesis – is that, while labour productivity has continued to grow in the West, together with production, and with the replacement of living labour by fixed capital, working hours have not moved in the direction prophesied by Keynes, and publicized by a certain sociology of labour. A sociology so far removed from the reality of wage labour that it fails to see the sarcasm implicit in its talk of *révolution du temps choisi* when in fact we are faced with a 'counter-revolution' (or, at least, a counter-reform) of a time that is increasingly coerced. A time beaten by the commands of the market, and by competition for the snapping up of profit.

4

A Reply to Some Objections

The Numbers, Today and Yesterday

This analysis of the course of working hours in the past half-century has met with a series of objections that need to be addressed.

The first objection – to a certain extent the most radical – is that the estimates, the numbers, regarding the length of working time to which we have lent credence are not true. Or at least, if one looks at them from a different, and more comprehensive, point of view, relating working time to the other times that condition us, or the working times of today to those of the past, they end up losing all their weight.

It has been remarked, for example, that the first Italian study based on 'time budgets' turns the picture we have drawn upside down.[1] Working time, in fact, proves to be just third on the list of everyday times. At the top of the list we find 'personal care' (sleeping, eating, toilet, dressing, etc.), accounting for 11½ hours a day. Next comes leisure time, which 'occupies 4 hours and 50 minutes in the 24-hour span of the average individual'. And then, in third place, we come to working time, which – the story goes – is on average 'only 2 hours and 43 minutes a day', a sort of residual time, after that 'of care' and of amusement, and hierarchically subordinate to them.

Quite frankly, this objection does not worry me; it is a classic example of the ideological use of statistics, based on glaring manipulations. The first manipulation is in this 'detail' – the estimates refer indiscriminately to all subjects between 14 and 75 years of age. This is nonsense, since in Italy one enters the labour market, on average, well beyond the age of 14, and leaves it – for the time being, at least – well before 75. The second manipulation is that these estimates refer to all subjects whether employed or not, presupposing for all people of working age an extra-domestic employment rate of 100 per cent, which is patently absurd. The third is that these estimates hide away within 'personal care' a hefty portion of domestic work, which is rarely taken by official statistical wisdom for what it is, namely work – material and psychical, socially necessary (in the framework of the market economy), and provided for free almost entirely by women.

But the very author who proffered these estimates in support of a 'different' perspective on present-day working hours then feels the need to cut them down to size. European studies based on time budgets[2] in fact show that if only employed subjects are taken into consideration (but isn't it obvious?), then average European working hours amount to 6 hours and 12 minutes a day for men, and 4 hours and 36 minutes for women. What is more, even these figures are averages that include Saturdays and Sundays, since the data is calculated on a *weekly basis*. Then, for women employed in extra-domestic work the overall time of daily work includes (at the least) another 4 hours of 'reproductive labour', for a total of 8½ hours of work per day.

So, we have come somewhat closer to reality, in which the great mass of male workers put in (at least) 8 hours per day on average, and the female workers even more. The weekend days of 'rest' do not reduce the real time of daily labour by a single nanosecond (as occurs in the not-unbiased fantasies of certain statistics we have seen); they simply allow the workers to reabsorb it, to recoup their energies in order to face a fresh week of work. This is the 'average' situation. In the West, of course. Because in the dominated countries, as we shall see, working hours are far longer. It is this real situation that, like it or not, has to be explained. Vice versa, the 'paradoxical situation whereby, if we take everyone between 14 and extreme old age, regardless of whether they are employed or not, we have a television viewing time that is relatively close to the official time of paid labour',[3] amounts, purely and simply, to a party game. And why leave children under 14 out of the game? Why leave out smaller children? Infants? If they, too, were included in the calculation of average working time, the 'scientific' estimates of working hours would no doubt be even more shocking.

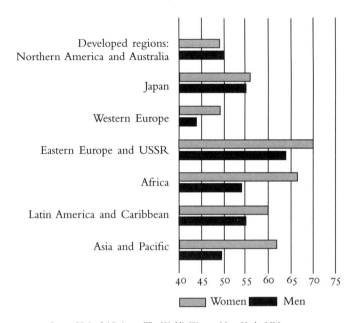

Developed regions:
Northern America and Australia

Japan

Western Europe

Eastern Europe and USSR

Africa

Latin America and Caribbean

Asia and Pacific

40 45 50 55 60 65 70 75

Women   Men

Source: United Nations, *The World's Women*, New York: UN, 1991
(based on studies conducted between 1976 and 1988).

Figure 4.1   Hours worked per week (official estimates) by women and
men, including unpaid housework

This does not mean, however, that time budgets can give us nothing other
than 'desperately poor' information;[4] but it is certain that, if they are formulated in this way, they are not only poor but also rigged, and a hindrance to
social knowledge.

From the world of badly manipulated figures let us return, at least, to the
certainly not impeccable world of official figures closer to... weekly experience (I was, mechanically, about to write 'daily' experience, which would, of
course, have been a better unit of measure).[5] If we look at the United Nations
numbers in Figure 4.1, while they vastly underestimate overall working time
in the West, the image of 'a society where leisure time greatly prevails over
working time, as the final result of the evolution of industrial capitalist society',[6]

bursts like a soap bubble. Certainly, in the wealthier societies comprehensive working time is, relatively, reduced, since 'wealth is disposable time, and nothing more'.[7] Today, however, even in the wealthiest industrial capitalist society, the United States, and in the entire West along with it, the working time of wage labour continues to prevail – *greatly* – over 'free' time, and to *determine it* externally and internally, on the surface and in the depths of the unconscious, as time coerced for the reconstitution of working energy to be alienated to the owners of social time. To say nothing of the fact that, given the ever closer integration of the world as a whole, the persistence of far longer working times in the dominated countries cannot but negatively feed back on the conditions of wage labour in the dominating countries themselves.

Another objection, however, which is analogous to the first but more substantial, regards the *historical trend* towards the reduction of working hours. It runs like this. Whatever the possible controversies regarding the present day, even if it be true that in such-and-such a country, in such-and-such a sector, in such-and-such a conjuncture, working hours are temporarily rising, not falling, it is indisputable that compared to a century ago annual working hours have been halved. Figures are figures, not opinions: 1,600–1,700 hours of work per year are half of 3,300–3,500. This affirmation is normally pre-ceded, or followed, by predictions of new, sure reductions of hours since, or so one says: 'The length of working time, in developed societies, decreases *regularly* from one decade to the next';[8] or, more prudently: 'The trend toward the reduction of working hours is a long-term *structural* phenomenon that regards most of the developed countries, with the partial exception of Japan.'[9]

In the liveliest moments of debate on further reductions of working hours, this affirmation has been able to avail itself of illustrations similar to Figure 4.2, which we find in the special issue of *Futuribles* on working times.[10] Let us examine it, momentarily putting in brackets the far from neutral choice of the 'working year' (instead of the working week or working day) as its unit of measurement, and the apparent eccentricity – even less neutral – of not calculating working hours in wartime, as if in such periods production had been suspended and not, in fact, ruthlessly militarized; or as if there were no data for those periods, which were precisely the periods of the century when the hours and the weight of work increased most sharply. But we shall come to this shortly.

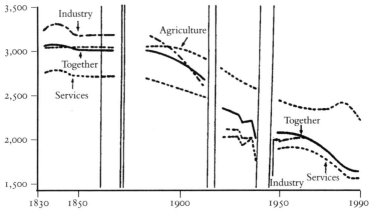

Source: Futuribles 165–166, May–June 1992, p. 34.

Figure 4.2   Annual working hours in France, 1830–1990
('objective' representation)

Let us begin by examining the bald quantitative estimate that, while *almost* true, is pressed into the service of two completely false theses. It is almost – not entirely – true, because, in 150 years, there has been no full-fledged halving of working time. First, because nineteenth-century working hours have been generally overestimated, since the widespread practice of 'Saint Mondays' and other forms of labour discontinuity have almost never been taken into account; while, vice versa, contemporary working hours have been underestimated, since they have often been calculated on the basis of contractual rather than real hours, and of larger rather than smaller firms. But, above all, two working times of very different density are being compared. The first is still marked, as Andrew Ure lamented, by the 'desultory habits' of workers who do not yet identify themselves with 'the unvarying regularity of the complex automaton';[11] the second is continually more compact and despotic, ruled, precisely, by that 'unvarying regularity'.

What we have, then, is a partial and by no means indisputable truth, at the service of two completely false theses. The first, and usually explicit, thesis is that, as was the case in the past century or century and a half, in the future, too, working hours will continue to diminish *regularly* because such is their 'natural', *structural* trend in the framework of capitalist development. The second, which is usually implicit, is that it is due to capitalism if, compared to a more distant past, working hours have been reduced. Let us examine the second thesis at once, postponing our analysis of the first until Chapter 6.

Since time is a 'social institution', any given form of organization of social life corresponds to a given conformation of social time and a given structure of working time. Since in the social existence of humanity everything is historical, having a birth, a process of development and an end, this is also true of work and working time. There is a history of work, and of working time. There is a history of their respective concepts, which, in the case of natural economies, is the history of their *absence*. In such societies, in fact, we often find no term that indicates 'work', to say nothing of 'working time', or even 'time' in general. It would be fascinating to make excursions in space and time among the Bushmen with Sahlins or among the American Indians with Clastres, to study their working times, so remote from our own, and so much shorter.[12] And such excursions would also be more relevant to our question than one might think, since in many parts of the world industrial capitalism has had to come to terms with practical and mental habits generated by natural economies in the millennia of their existence. Nevertheless, for reasons of... space and time, it is preferable to focus our attention on the transition from feudalism to capitalism and on the quantitative and qualitative transformations working time has undergone with the evolution of capitalism itself. And let us begin with a fact that, while self-evident, is generally ignored: compared to feudal society, capitalism *immeasurably lengthened* (not shortened) the working day, week and year. It did so for as long as it could exploit – with the complicity of the nobility and the clergy, the two estates 'dethroned' in 1789 – the laws against 'combination' (in England, the Combination Acts), which prohibited any association ('combination') of workers.[13]

In the Middle Ages the 'normal' working day was about 10 hours, but the discontinuity was far greater than today. Legislation and social practice ensured the workers, besides Sundays, several dozen days off a year – 'feast' days, when working was strictly prohibited. In fact, from the early Middle Ages until the middle of the seventeenth century the number of feast days, apart from

Sundays, continued to increase; in addition to the holidays of the liturgical year they included Carnival, celebrations of military victories, happy occasions of the ruling or aristocratic families, and so forth.

> Hatred of feast days did not begin to develop until the fifteenth and sixteenth centuries, in the constitutive phase of the modern industrial and commercial bourgeoisie. The French Revolution eliminated most of the religious holidays and replaced the seven-day working week with one of ten days.[14]

The studies by Le Goff and Thompson, and the more technical works by Landes and Cipolla,[15] have described the epochal transition from 'Church's time' to 'merchant's time' to the time of capitalist industry. They have shown how, in this transition rife with social conflict on two fronts (the first labour struggles against the lengthening of working time date from the late fourteenth century; the first papal bull on the reduction of feast days was issued by Urban VIII in 1642), the bourgeoisie – capital – progressively detached time, and working time in particular, both from nature (as far as possible) and from any bond of sacrality, transforming it into an increasingly social and secular product. Time became an object that can be measured with new criteria, and at the same time an instrument of measurement. It became something that has a price, and that gives a price to 'things', first of all to work and to money; something that belongs to man, no longer 'to God', and can therefore legitimately be a source of lucre, to be used and abused. This was new time, measurable, oriented and predictable, in keeping with a new socio-economic space, the space of the expansion of mercantile social relations, of the flowering of urban life, of trans-oceanic traffic, of manufacturing that opens the way to heavy industry, of the second – eternal – youth of science and technology.

This grandiose process of transformation also gives rise to a new working time. Until that 'moment', says Le Goff,

> On the whole, labor time was still the time of an economy dominated by agrarian rhythms, free of haste, careless of exactitude, unconcerned by productivity – and of a society created in the image of that economy, *sober and modest*, without enormous appetites, undemanding, and incapable of quantitative efforts.[16]

From that 'moment' on, the old working time is flanked by a new one, in keeping with the new urban economy and its daily rhythms of man-to-man commerce. This new time is measured with increasing care and precision, now in terms of *hours*. Always denser, always more avid, because on this time the 'givers of work', who are the takers of time, measure 'their earnings'.[17] Clock time. An abstract time, which has already become money. A time no longer *passed* but 'spent', because it has become the object, on an ever greater scale, of the crucial mercantile exchange between wages and working time of people who are without any reserve. A new working time, regular and continuous, which a 'nonindustrial institution', the school, is already drumming into children.[18] A time that is disciplined, disciplinary, military; upon which 'new habits of work' and the 'new discipline of time' are shaped – the social discipline, and labour discipline, demanded by the relentless, endless, accumulation of profit.

The qualitative transformation of working time is nothing other than its quantitative transformation (and vice versa). The bourgeoisie has fought for hundreds of years and in hundreds of places to shatter any limit to the length of the working day. Since the dawn of capitalism, this is how the working day of 12, 14, 16 hours was born. Marx, in his matchless analysis of this unitary, quantitative and qualitative, social and technological, material and spiritual, economic and politico-juridical process, in Volume I of *Capital*, tells us how, why, and at what price this breach came about:

> *What is a working day?* What is the length of time during which capital may consume the labour-power whose daily value it buys? How far may the working-day be *extended* beyond the working-time necessary for the reproduction of labour-power itself? It has been seen that to these questions *capital* replies: the working-day contains the full *twenty-four hours*, with the deduction of the few hours of repose without which labour-power absolutely refuses its services again. Hence it is self-evident that the labourer *is nothing else*, his whole life through, *than labor-power*, that therefore *all his disposable time* is by nature and law *labor-time*, to be devoted to the *self-expansion of capital*. Time for education, for intellectual development, for the fulfilling of social functions and for social intercourse, for the free-play of his bodily and mental activity, even the rest time of Sunday (and that in a country of Sabbatarians!) – *moonshine!* But in its blind unrestrainable passion, its were-wolf hunger for surplus-labour, capital oversteps not only *the moral, but even the merely physical maximum bounds of the working-day*. It usurps the time for growth, development, and healthy maintenance of the body. It steals the time required for the consumption of fresh air and sunlight. It higgles over a meal-time, incorporating it where possible with the process of production itself, so that food is given to the labourer as to a mere means of production, as coal is

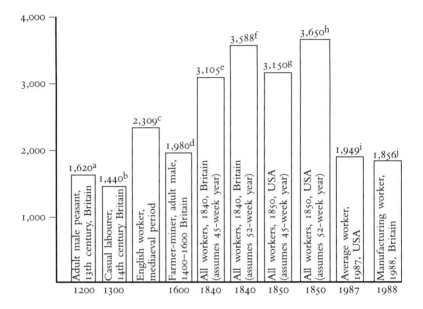

a   Calculated from Gregory Clark's estimate of 150 days per family, assumes 12 hours per day, 135 days per year for adult male ('Impatience, Poverty, and Open Field Agriculture', mimeo, 1986).

b   Calculated from Nora Ritchie's estimate of 120 days per year. Assumes 12-hour day. ('Labour Conditions in Essex in the Reign of Richard II', in E.M. Carus-Wilson, ed., *Essays in Economic History*, vol. II, London: Edward Arnold, 1962.)

c   Juliet Schor's estimate of average mediaeval labourer working two-thirds of the year at 9.5 hours per day.

d   Calculated from Ian Blanchard's estimate of 180 days per year. Assumes 11-hour day. ('Labour Productivity and Work Psychology in the English Mining Industry, 1400–1600', *Economic History Review*, vol. 31, no. 1, 1978, p. 23.)

e   Average worker in the United Kingdom, assumes 45-week year, 69 hours per week (weekly hours from W.S. Woytinsky, 'Hours of Labor', in *Encyclopedia of the Social Sciences*, vol. III, New York: Macmillan, 1935).

f   Average worker in the United Kingdom, assumes 52-week year, 69 hours per week (weekly hours from Woytinsky, 'Hours of Labor').

g   Average worker in the United States, assumes 45-week year, 70 hours per week (weekly hours from Joseph Zeisel, 'The Workweek in American Industry, 1850–1956', *Monthly Labor Review*, 81, January 1958, pp. 23–9).

h   Average worker in the United States, assumes 52-week year, 70 hours per week (weekly hours from Zeisel, 'The Workweek in American Industry').

i   From Juliet Schor, *The Overworked American*, Table 2.4.

j   Manufacturing worker in the United Kingdom, calculated from Bureau of Labor Statistics data, Office of Productivity and Technology.

Source: J.B. Schor, *The Overworked American*, p. 45.

Figure 4.3   Eight centuries of annual hours

supplied to the boiler, grease and oil to the machinery. It reduces the sound sleep needed for the restoration, reparation, refreshment of the bodily powers to just so many hours of torpor as the revival of an organism, absolutely exhausted, renders essential. It is not the normal maintenance of the labour-power which is to determine the limits of the working-day; it is the greatest possible daily expenditure of labour-power, no matter how diseased, compulsory, and painful it may be, which is to determine the limits of the labourer's period of repose. Capital cares nothing for the *length of life of labour-power*. All that concerns it is simply and solely the maximum of labour-power, that can be rendered fluent in a working-day. It attains this end by *shortening the extent of the labourer's life*, as a greedy farmer snatches increased produce from the soil by *robbing* it of its fertility.[19]

This process, Marx adds, was followed by 'a violent encroachment like that of an avalanche in its intensity and extent', after 'the birth of machinism and modern industry.'

In this light, let us go back to Figure 4.2 for a moment and note, on the upper left, that the peak of 3,300 annual working hours, which today seems like the monstrous legacy of forms of precapitalist society, in truth has just one name: *capitalism*. Instead, this 'value-neutral' Figure of ours, and the equally 'value-neutral' comments that accompany it, invite us to put, 'spontaneously', the (virtuous) term 'capitalism', or 'market', or something to that effect, on the lower right, where we find the (inexact, according to Eurostat surveys) figure of 1,700 annual hours. But let us look at a different Figure – this one drawn by Juliet Schor – that presents us with a very different picture: a picture of the historical process of the enormous lengthening of the working day produced by capital. And despite the fact that Schor, too, adopted annual hours as her unit of measurement, in the desert of (also figurative) conformity that assails us, we are glad to stop at this little oasis. After all, Figure 4.3 puts the numbers in their proper places, and gives us an idea of how even dry numbers can be used to make historical and social processes clear, rather than obscure.[20]

The Driving Force of the Reduction of Hours

Setting aside for the time being the issue of numbers (the *right* numbers) of today and of yesterday, and granting the argument that (annual) working time in the West has indeed been substantially reduced compared to the orgies of the first half of the nineteenth century, we are still left with the fundamental question: what has been the driving force of the reduction?

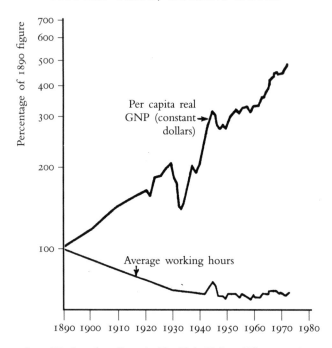

Source: P.A. Samuelson, *Economics*, New York: McGraw-Hill, 1973, p. 81.

Figure 4.4   Gross national product and working hours in the
United States (mystified representation)

We already know the answer given by Keynes and by the prevailing socio-
economics: It has been the combined power of technical–scientific progress
and of 'compound interest.' In short, it has been capital, capitalism. Samuelson,
in his introduction to economics, translates this answer into a figure regarding
the United States, which visualizes it very well. We reproduce it in Figure 4.4;
the caption reads as follows:

> *Higher productivity gives us more output and chance for more leisure.* Technological
> improvements, better capital goods, and more highly trained labor have raised
> production faster than the growth of population.[21]

The terminology and the logical construction are more halting in Samuelson than in Keynes, but the substance is the same. Higher productivity (of labour, I might add) *automatically* brings with it both an increase in production and a reduction of working time – for workers. This is the point at issue, not some generic increase in social free time. But Samuelson's own Figure belies his assertion. If we draw a vertical line corresponding to the years 1948–50 and then, from there, two horizontal lines for the per capita GNP and for the hours worked, we shall see at a glance that in the period 1950–73 per capita GNP almost doubled while average hours remained the same. Note, furthermore, how there was a sharp (albeit inadequately represented) rise in hours during World War II (1941–45). According to the automatic connection cited above, we ought to expect this rise in hours to be coupled with a fall in productivity and production. Just the opposite was the case. How shall one explain these two 'minor' anomalies, which moreover have continued to this day? How shall one explain the fact that in the past half-century (since nothing changed from 1973 until now) labour productivity has more than doubled in the United States while working hours have grown somewhat longer, not shorter?

There is a third reason for rejecting the validity of Figure 4.4; namely, that the course of working hours from 1890 to 1941 was not, in fact, that gradual and regular descent that Samuelson depicts. Things did not go so smoothly. After the strong labour movement of the early 1880s, culminating on 1 May 1886 (with the events in Haymarket Square), which nonetheless produced no immediate tangible results, the issue of the reduction of hours and conquest of the 8-hour day remained in the background until after the turn of the century. The working day in 1872 was (on average) 10.5 hours, and was still set at 10 hours thirty years later. The 6-day working week was still in place. There was no real change until the years between 1908 and 1919, 'the decisive period in the battle for the 8-hour day' in the United States, in the judgement of Roediger and Foner. In 1919, 8 hours (6 days a week) became a reality for the majority of industrial workers. A definitive conquest? By no means. In the late 1920s, just before the Great Depression, the overwhelming economic development led to a new rise in working hours. Only 45 per cent of the workers were at or below the 48-hour level; the other 55 per cent found themselves above the 1919 level, with 20 per cent working more than

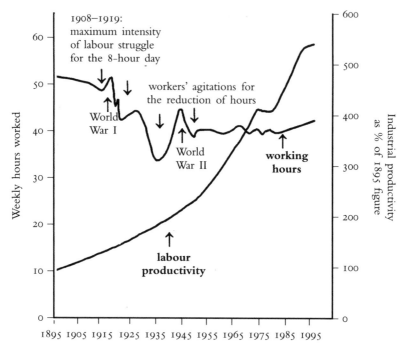

1908–1919: maximum intensity of labour struggle for the 8-hour day

workers' agitations for the reduction of hours

World War I

World War II

working hours

labour productivity

Weekly hours worked

Industrial productivity as % of 1895 figure

1895 1905 1915 1925 1935 1945 1955 1965 1975 1985 1995

Sources: For hours: D.R. Roediger and P.S. Foner, *Our Own Time: A History of American Labor and the Working Day*, New York: Verso, 1989, *passim*; T. Liesner, ed., *One Hundred Years of Economic Statistics*, London: Economist Publications, 1989, pp. 98–9; *Monthly Labor Review*, various issues. For productivity: A. Maddison, 'Comparative Analysis of the Productivity Situation in the Advanced Capitalist Countries', in J.W. Kendrick, ed., *International Comparisons of Productivity and Causes of the Slowdown*, Cambridge MA: Ballinger, 1984, p. 73; C. Sparks and M. Greiner, 'U.S. and foreign productivity and unit labour costs', *Monthly Labor Review*, February 1997, pp. 26 ff.

Figure 4.5 Labor productivity and weekly hours in the United States, 1895–1995

55 hours per week. The battle for the reduction of the working day and working week flamed up anew in the midst of the great crisis, with proposals within the AFL calling for a 30-hour week (5 days of 6 hours) and with a mass mobilization of both unemployed and employed workers for shorter hours. In the 1930s working time in the United States did fall, on average, to

less than 40 hours, due to three interacting factors: the labour movement, the crisis, and state intervention to regulate social conflict. It was not before the end of World War II – which, once again, greatly intensified and lengthened working hours – that the battle of US workers produced 'stable' results, with the transition to the 5-day week, but of 8-hour days (the same daily hours as in 1919).[22] Figure 4.5 gives us an idea of how things really went.

Thus both Figure 4.4 itself and the logic with which it was constructed are belied by the facts. Above all because the principal driving force of the reduction of working hours is not taken into consideration; namely, the *organized struggle* of the industrial proletariat. In Samuelson's schema wage labour is taken into consideration for its specialization and its productivity merely as labour power, as an object, as a subordinate part of capital, never as a subject, as a class capable of acting in defence of its own interests in conflict with the capitalist class. But if truth be told, the history of the length of the modern working day has always been a history of conflict between social classes, since, apart from the relations that these two collective social actors have had with the other classes of society,

> the capitalist and the worker represent, on the commodity market, two starkly opposing viewpoints and the actual length of the working day can only be decided through the struggle between the capitalist class and the working class as a *question of power* [*Machtfrage*].[23]

Although there has not yet been a proper work of synthesis on the history of this centuries-old and international struggle, there is certainly no lack of documentation,[24] for anyone who wishes to look into the question. It should be noted that on this point, too, Schor stands out from the crowd, when she formulates a judgement in deliberate contrast with the prevailing opinion of the economists (and others):

> Once we realize that capitalism entailed an expansion of working time [compared to natural, ancient or medieval societies], the mid-nineteenth-century turn towards leisure no longer appears as a structural imperative of the market system, as proponents of the conventional wisdom believe. It occurred because workers struggled mightily *against* the normal processes that determined the length of working hours. In this sense, leisure exists *in spite of* rather than as a result of capitalism.[25]

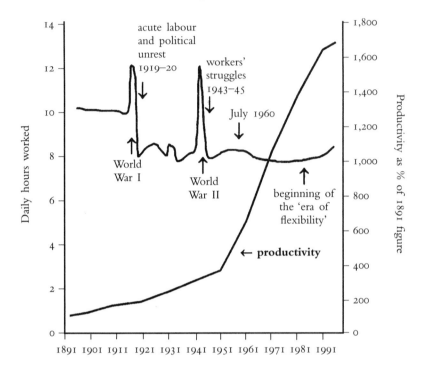

Figure 4.6 Labour productivity and daily working hours
in Italy, 1895–1995

Sources: For working hours: G. Procacci, *La lotta di classe in Italia agli inizi del secolo XX*, Rome: Ed. Riuniti, 1978; A. Marchetti, 'Per chi suona la campana. Ricerca esplorativa di storia del tempo del lavoro (1880–1919)', and G. Garbarini, 'La disciplina del tempo. Gli orari di lavoro durante il fascismo', in M. Bergamaschi, ed., *Questione di ore. Orario e tempo di lavoro dall'800 ad oggi*, Pisa: Biblioteca F. Serantini, 1996, pp. 17 ff., 73 ff.; M. Isnenghi, ed., *Operai e contadini nella grande guerra*, Bologna: Cappelli, 1982, pp. 262 ff.; A. Camarda and S. Peli, *L'altro esercito. La classe operaia durante la prima guerra mondiale*, Milan, Feltrinelli, 1980, ch. 6; D. Bigazzi, 'Gli operai alla catena di montaggio: la Fiat 1922–1943', in *Annali Fondazione Feltrinelli*, anno XX, 1979–1980, pp. 895 ff. (p. 946); P. Spriano, *Storia del Partito comunista italiano*, vol. 6, Turin: Einaudi–L'Unità, 1990, Chap. 10; Liesner, ed., *One Hundred Years of Economic Statistics*, pp. 242–3; G. Olini, 'Anni ottanta, lavorando meno solo sulla carta', in *Politica ed economia*, no. 1, 1994, p. 49 ff.; author's estimates for the years 1993–95. For productivity: N. Cacace, *107 anni di lavoro italiano (1891–1997)*, Table provided by the author, whom I thank (the data on productivity refer to all sectors); C. Sparks and M. Greiner, 'U.S. and foreign productivity'.

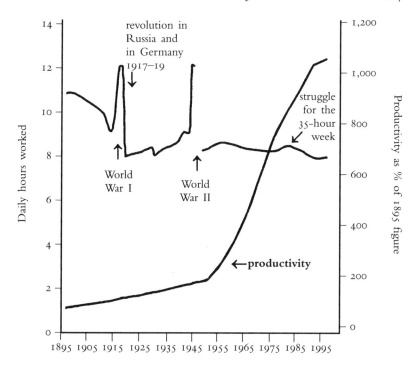

Sources: For working hours: G. Scharf, *Geschichte der Arbeitszeitverkürzung. Der Kamp der deutschen Gewerkschaften um die Verkürzung der täglichen und wochentlichen Arbeitszeit*, Cologne: Bund Verlag, 1987; S. Bologna, *Nazismo e classe operaia*, Rome: Manifesto Libri, 1996, pp. 145 ff.; E. Collotti, *La Germania nazista*, Turin: Einaudi, 1962, ch. X; for the last ten years, Eurostat. For productivity, as Figure 4.5.

Figure 4.7   Labour productivity and daily working hours
in Germany, 1895–1995

The post-World War II period has confirmed this fact. With the collapse of the labour struggles for a further reduction of hours, 'the inevitable [capitalist] pressures towards long hours reasserted themselves', to the point of creating a full-fledged 'crisis of leisure time' for US workers.[26]

The driving force of the reduction of working hours has operated within organizational, political, technological and production contexts in continual evolution, and in one way or another has been conditioned by them. While a full reconstruction of this entire system of variables is not possible here, before going on to the next question I would like to present two Figures (4.6 and 4.7) that finally give us a true picture of the two social forces that have been fighting for centuries over the issue of working time. The Figures are, intentionally, incomplete, because they abstract from most of the contextual factors, with the exception of labour productivity, and because they under-score the action of the two forces in conflict at their moments of maximum tension; which for the working class are the highest points of its organized struggle, and for the capitalist class the two world wars, maximum expression of the competitive struggle between companies and between states for supremacy on the world market. Let us particularly note the two points I consider to be essential: (1) the substantially uninterrupted growth of labour productivity *has not generated* an uninterrupted, even if nonproportional, de-crease in the length of the working day; (2) the real length of the average social working day has been *decisively influenced* by the struggle of the working class for the reduction of working time, and by the counterthrust of capital aimed at keeping it intact, or even making it longer.

Contradictions in the Calculation of Working Time

The reader will have noted that in the studies and Figures examined here, apart from the imaginary day of the 14-to-75-year-olds of the time budgets, we have found three different units of measurement of real individual work-ing time: the day, the week, the year, and sometimes even a fourth unit, referring to the individual's entire lifetime. These units are not equivalent – either as regards quantitative results (how much one works) or for qualitative aspects (the place work has in one's life). The choice of one unit of measure-ment rather than another gives us very different pictures of things. It is thus not fortuitous that defenders of the market economy are so partial to annual or, at most, weekly working hours, while critics of the market economy have always focused their attention on the working *day*.

The partiality for annual hours does not simply depend on the fact that the work *year* makes it easier to highlight the reductions of hours that have taken place since World War II – one reduction on the weekly level with the conquest of Saturdays off (not for everyone), and the other on the annual level with the 4 to 5 weeks of vacation (in Europe). It depends, fundamentally, on the fact that the reference to annual hours is more consistent with the accounting needs of company budgets and the planning needs of company production – and, indeed, is more consistent with the conception of the worker as a simple provider of labour power.

Companies formulate their budgets on an annual basis, calculating the quantities of the production factors to be employed (raw materials, machinery, labour force) and their respective costs. The utilization time of the labour force comes into this calculation in the same way that the utilization time of machinery does – indeed, as a variable *dependent* on machinery time, and more generally on the times of capital and of the market. There is no room here for the human needs of the workers, no room for taking their *day* into consideration. Indeed, if the need arises to amortize the increased costs of machinery quickly or to increase production because a booming market demands it, then new work shifts, including night shifts, can be introduced without further ado. And if such shifts upset the everyday life of workers, and their family life in particular – well, that's too bad, but competitiveness demands it. The increasingly frequent agreements between management and labour subordinating the variation of hours to the more or less pressing demands of the market (on a one-year, two-year, three-year basis, or longer) are an optimal expression of this way of seeing the function of living labour – that is, this way of treating it *materially*. Not only are company necessities occupying the workers' Saturdays, Sundays, nights, and imposing endless forms of job instability; in certain cases they even provoke the reduction, or arbitrary shifting, of summer vacations – and this is not the end of the road. After all, such a *commodity* is not something to be treated with kid gloves. Even the setting of an annual limit to its use (which, however, may not be respected) is, indeed, a substantial 'concession'!

But, to the contrary, if wage labour is seen as the bearer of human needs to be satisfied that go beyond the pure and simple securing of survival, and, even more so, if it is seen, collectively, as the bearer of the need to emancipate itself from its condition of wage slavery, then the central, and not interchangeable, criterion of measurement both of working time and of 'disposable' time can only be the working *day*, since the satisfaction of these needs demands daily, incessant, activity (or attention).

And care for our 'higher' human needs requires time and application of even higher quality. Caring for loved ones and friends, for education and health, reviving an exchange with nature that has been impoverished by urban living, taking active part in social and political life – just on weekends or during summer vacation, in the time *left over* from alienated labour? No! These must be *everyday* activities. But it is just this 'everyday' care that is impossible for working men and women, for wage labour in general, if most of the days of the year (from 220, minimum, in Europe, to 320–330, and perhaps more, in Asia) they *have to* spend most of their time and energy, directly or indirectly (commuter time), on the job and resting up and recuperating from their accumulated fatigue, to be fresh again for the next morning, afternoon or night.

Here, we shall not get involved in the debate on the question of 'everyday life', on the birth of this 'dimension' and its concept, content and function.[27] But we do wish to note how, while this 'level' of human experience was greatly emphasized in general sociology after 1950, there has been no trace of that emphasis in the more recent sociology of labour. In the 1970s the Bergers wrote:

> Our experience of society is, first of all, an experience of other people in *every-day life*. By the latter is meant, quite simply, the fabric of familiar routines within which we act and about which we think most of our waking hours. This sector of our experience is the most real to us, it is our habitual and ordinary habitat....
>
> For better or worse, our experience of society is very largely an experience of *routines*.... The insight into the routine, and necessarily routine, character of society has a very important implication: because most of our experience with other people consists of routines, this experience becomes discernible as a fabric that endures over a period of time.[28]

One may agree or disagree with this conception of social life. My point, however, is that in the sphere of institutional social sciences you will not find anyone asking these days, 'What is the everyday life, the routine, of a worker? What is his experience of time in everyday life and, above all, in the most "familiar" of his habits – his place of work?' The question is considered unimportant, apparently. Yet on those rare occasions when the question is posed directly to the workers, the answers are important ones indeed.[29] 'We don't have enough time.' 'We have *no time*.' Working time, which is the first and most central of all times, is a time full of fatigue and empty of satisfaction; or, in the vivid expression of a French working woman, '*On court, on court toujours après le temps.*'[30] We do nothing but run run run, always running after time – which means running after *life*; after the genuine, deep, emancipative needs that flee, that escape people who have to spend most of their day, of their 'routine', and thus of their lives, working for wages.

Hence quantity and quality of actual working time appear in a profoundly different light if looked at from the side of management through the distorting lens of the working year, or from the side of labour, 'live', through that unit of measurement better suited to a proper understanding of the real condition of workers, which is the working day. From the workers' point of view, the last great conquest of the proletarian class dates back to 1917–19, with the advent of the 8-hour day. Since then, reductions of hours have been on the weekly or yearly level and, indeed, over the worker's entire lifetime[31] – but without ever touching the heart of life. Of course, there are more 'free' Saturdays, or more vacation days, than fifty years ago (principally in Europe, since, as we have seen, the 'exception' represented by Japan has been joined by another 'exception' – the United States). But what does this mean? Apart from the fact that such an increase in 'free' time was no 'gift' to the workers; apart from the fact that the capitalist class has demonstrated that the current situation is by no means inviolable; apart from the other side of the coin, namely the '19th century' working hours of the dominated countries – apart from all this, there is a precise material connection between the increase in weekly and annual breaks granted workers and the almost total suppression of breaks in daily working time. Precisely to the extent that the squeezing of labour is carried out today with highly 'rationalized' presses, producing great physical but also psychical and general fatigue, the time needed for the full recuperation of the workers' (physical and nervous) capabilities – for their 'breathing-space' – has to be somewhat extended, at least on the weekly and yearly scale. 'Long' summer vacations are useful for a necessary retuning of the mind–body labour machine, to avoid having to scrap it before its time. As in the past, the proletariat was the first to feel such a need, which the entrepreneurial class – although it put up a fight and carefully dosed out its concessions – was unable to ignore. Also for a reason that is not directly related to the production process, but rather to the comprehensive development of social life.

In a society where overall social wealth has increased enormously, even if appropriated privately by only one part of society; in a society where labour productivity is eight (for the United States), fourteen (for Germany), sixteen (for France and Italy), seventy (for Japan) times greater than it was 130 years ago; in a society where the number of well-off do-nothings, and the level of their returns on capital, is so great that the parasitism of the feudal courts and of Late Empire patrician Rome was slim pickings by comparison; in a society where not only the increase in wealth but also the increase in disposable social time is immediately perceptible – in such a society it is unthinkable that the 'breathing-space' of a worker be no more than it was a century and more ago. But the social promotion of Western workers to the rank of consumers – programmed and controlled consumers of 'free' time in particular – has not changed their *structural* condition, which is that of being expropriated of the product of their labour or, which is the same thing, of being expropriated of their *time*. Indeed, this social promotion – socializing them to the (bourgeois) conviction that the highest act a human being can perform is the act of purchasing for cash – has represented a way of forcing them 'voluntarily' to work longer hours.

A Return to the Nineteenth Century?

Closing the parentheses round the true driving force of the reduction in hours, and the most appropriate unit of measurement of that reduction, let us return to the objections.

My insistence on the expansion of the trend towards the lengthening of working time and on the prevalence of the negative aspects of the restructuring of hours has earned me the following reproach: 'Are you perhaps claiming that, going forward, we are going backward, to the nineteenth-century English worker?' To evaluate the pertinence of this reproach we first have to reach an understanding about the frame of reference. Is it Italy? Europe? the West? the world? It is obvious that the answer to the question varies according to the socio-economic situation that is being considered. The object of this study is, principally, the West. But, as we mentioned in Chapter 1, if it is true that we are in an age of maximum (uneven) integration of the market and of world capitalism, then any examination of the question of working time – say, in a single Western country – that fails to consider the *world* context would be no more than a feeble and impoverished abstraction, since, as company management never fails to remind us (and this reminder is no pretext), globalized competition must be taken into account. The globalization of the competition between capitals goes hand in glove with a globalization of the problem of working hours, and of its possible solutions.

If, then, we keep to this objective level,[32] my answer can only be this: At the end of the twentieth century, the 'nineteenth-century English worker', far from having vanished, is by far the most common 'social figure' of the world industrial proletariat. He has been *internationalized*. And this internationalization is fraught with (potentially antithetical) consequences for the condition, and strength, of European, US-American and Japanese workers. Immanuel Wallerstein wrote on the subject:

> The overwhelming proportion of the world's work-forces, who live in rural zones or move between them and urban slums, are worse off than their ancestors five hundred years ago. They eat less well, and certainly have a less balanced diet. Although they are more likely to survive the first year of life (because of the effect of social hygiene undertaken to protect the privileged), I doubt that the life prospects of the majority of the world's population as of age one are greater than previously; I suspect the opposite is true. *They unquestionably work harder – more hours per day, per year, per lifetime.* And since they do this for less total reward, the rate of exploitation has escalated very sharply.[33]

On the relation between globalized Western capital and world labour power, Ronaldo Munck tells us: 'As Manuel Castells puts it, the dream of monopoly capital to overcome its crisis is "*a twenty-first-century capital; and a nineteenth-century proletariat*".'[34] One may disagree, as I do, with the theoretical viewpoints of these authors; there is no question, however, that if their judgement on the state of affairs and ongoing trends may be ignored – as is habitually the case – it cannot easily be refuted. In 1995 the cost of labour was 0.46 dollars per hour in Thailand, 0.30 in Indonesia, 0.25 in China and India, against the 31.8 dollars per hour in Germany, 23.66 in Japan, 19.34 in France, 17.20 in the United States, 16.48 in Italy.[35] This, I believe, does tell us something. In the Third World, where large families struggle just to reach the threshold of 'survival wages', it is *inevitable* that we find what we have called 'ancient hours'. Let us examine two examples from two industrial sectors – textiles and metalworking – with heightening competition between countries of the 'periphery' and those of the 'centre'.

In 1988 the annual working days of employees in textile plants (the plants with the greatest number of working Saturdays and Sundays) were between 212 and 239 in the EC countries, 248 in Japan, 260 in the United States, while totalling 287 in Morocco, Hong Kong and Malaysia, 288 in Mexico, 290 in Indonesia and Thailand, 301 in South Korea, and 318 in Taiwan. The number of days the plants themselves functioned annually were between 222 and 292 in the EC (291 in Italy), 274 in Japan, 301 in the United States, but 325 in Tunisia, 330 in Hong Kong, 339 in Mexico, 346 in India, 348 in Indonesia, 353 in Thailand, and – last but not least! – 354 in Taiwan.[36] One wonders whether European plants of the 'dead and buried' nineteenth century ever went that far.

In the metalworking sector, according to a recent International Metal-workers' Federation study, there is a legal working week of 48 hours almost everywhere, which can reach 56 hours, as it does in South Korea. But there is above all a forced prolongation of hours, whose figures speak for themselves. Average weekly overtime amounts to between 7 and 9 hours in South Korea, 10 hours in Hong Kong, 12 in India and the Philippines, 15 in Taiwan, and 25 in Malaysia. And we are speaking of 1995, not 1895. For overtime, the maximum legal limits range from 500 to 1,920 (in Malaysia) annual hours. Overall official hours often exceed 2,100 hours a year, with Mexico, which hosts plants of the major multinationals of the sector (General Motors, Toyota, Volkswagen), vaunting between 2,200 and 2,300 hours.[37]

How long is the working day in the Third World? The official information provided by the governments of the dominated (or 'newly industrialized') countries have a degree of reliability that is below zero.[38] Organic research, to my knowledge, does not exist. The most significant and best documented comprehensive studies on Third World working conditions and organized labour movements[39] do not provide sufficient details and comparisons, while taking it for granted that there are, ordinarily, long daily hours with no international or local regulation. Thus we have to base ourselves on a variety of still rather fragmentary sources, which – however – agree in indicating a working day, on average, of from 9 or 10 up to 12 hours; except in the 'islands' – almost all of them now being dismantled or restructured – of state

Table 4.1   Third World annual working hours in the metalworking
industry

Asia			
Taiwan	2,496	Hong Kong	2,023
India	2,496	South Korea	2,685
Malaysia	2,160	Philippines	2,304
Singapore	2,288	Thailand	2,833
Latin America			
Brazil	2,112	Argentina	1,900/2,133
Colombia	2,368	Ecuador	2,080
El Salvador	2,328	Mexico	2,250
Guatemala	2,160	Curaçao	2,080
Africa			
Benin	2,080	Kenya	2,340
Ghana	1,920	South Africa	2,051
Ivory Coast	2,080		

Source: International Metalworkers' Federation (IMF), *I metalmeccanici e l'orario di lavoro nel mondo*, Geneva: IMF, 1997.

industries or of the largest national private industries, in which at least some union organization exists.[40]

A report on Indonesian workers 'discovered' factories in the main urban areas with people working 12 to 14 hours a day, or with only two nonworking days per month (at Nike), compulsory overtime, to say nothing of such things as verbal, physical and sexual abuse and the denial of any possibility of organization. A fire in a doll factory in Bangkok led to the 'discovery' of people – most of them young girls – working 12 hours for $3 to $4 a day, and of the fact that the foreign-owned factories with this type of work organization and working hours are legion. From Singapore Giovanni Bonazzi, in his report on that 'state-managed market economy', describes workers getting home after their generous helping of daily labour as a 'heap of bodies going limp', a 'silent surrender of organisms exhausted by their 12-hour shifts'. *Newsweek* – a source not exactly on the workers' side – takes for granted a working day of 12 hours in industry throughout Asia. And *Time* makes it clear that this is precisely the attraction for US-American capital: 'In most of Asia, factory workers have traditionally put in long hours for low wages and that, in fact, is why American enterprises have moved in.'[41]

Until just a few years ago, Asia, industrially, meant the explosive development of the Four Tigers. But more recently a new world frontier of accumulation has been activated, and auto-activated, capable of imposing rhythms, working times and wages unknown even in such universal models of the 'new industrialism' as South Korea, Taiwan, Hong Kong, Singapore, Malaysia, and so on. From the country that is the emblem of this brand new (but not last!) frontier of the superexploitation of labour, the 'People's' Republic of China, star pupil of the World Bank, we are now receiving travellers' reports and (legal and illegal) reports from the interior that, to say the least, should give us pause. Here is a quick survey, going from south to north, centred on the question of working hours.

Despite the fact that a (legal) working week of 44 hours had been in force until May 1995, when it was (officially) supplanted by a 40-hour week,

> these reforms have been generally ignored and workers of the coastal areas are often forced to work 60 or even 70 hours a week with no extra wages for their overtime hours. Furthermore, the new law on the right to work does not recognize the right to strike.[42]

Working conditions are particularly harsh in the special economic zones (with a high concentration of Western capital) and in the smaller firms. In Shenzhen,

> workers often put in between 12 and 16 hours a day. And if it's necessary, if the delivery dates demand it, they work even more. In these 'marvelous' factories there are certain rules. For example, the *toilette* rule: Workers have the right to two or three breaks a day, five minutes each. If you take more than five minutes once, you get fined; if it happens again, the fine is doubled; and the third time, you're fired.[43]

There are factories, like the Gaofu ('Great Fortune') clothing factory in Canton, in Guangdong province, where – to increase productivity – management imposes hours like this: from 8 to 12 in the morning, then 2 to 4 in the afternoon, then 7 to 11 in the evening – and this is a single 'shift'! – for 25 days a month if one respects the law, otherwise, as at 'Great Fortune', for

29 or 30 days a month. In Guangdong province, the most developed industrially, although the Labour Code calls for a maximum of 36 hours of overtime per month, the monthly overtime of the workers at foreign firms (the
ones that export all over the world not only their capital but also the 'immor-
tal principles of 1789') is 70 to 80 hours on average, and in extreme cases as
many as 130 hours; that is, from 2½ to 4 hours more than the legal limit of
8 hours per day. In the same report we read that in 85 per cent of the foreign-
owned textile and garment firms the laws on female labour are not respected.[44]
With the rise, for years now, of a disorganized – but vigorous – movement of
strikes and protests,[45] the situation has come to present such great social risks
that a certain disquiet has seeped in all the way to the lacquered halls of the
People's National Assembly. There, in October 1996, a member of the Assembly and former president of the official state union presented a report on the
(lack of) application of the Labour Code, stating:

> Exceeding the legal limit of overtime hours is common practice in the private
> foreign-owned firms or in the rural municipal cooperatives. In the firms in
> Guangdong, average overtime varies between 70 and 80 hours a month.... The
> legal rights of working women and children are not well protected. Some firms
> have a discriminatory attitude towards women, demanding that they work harder
> than the men. They are treated as cheap labour to be sent packing after a three-
> month trial period on any pretext at all.[46]

The fate of commuter workers or of those with temporary permits is even
harsher; even though many of them, who end up sleeping inside the factories, may actually consider themselves lucky, since they do avoid the extra
fatigue of the long commute. But here we are in the north, where we find
the 'spectacle' of inhuman 'cities without children', almost entirely inhabited
by workers imported – or 'deported' – from the interior to the coast. Cities
where – according to a travel report by European union representatives –
there is just one thing going on: 'Production, more production, nothing but
production.' Cities where 'the overwhelming majority of workers live inside
the factories.' (Were there cities like this in the nineteenth century?) Factories
with extremely harmful working conditions where, given the lack of any
system of social welfare, a serious injury means the loss of one's job. Factories
with long hours, 'from a minimum of 10 hours a day up to, at times, as many

as 14 hours, for six days a week, and sometimes even seven.' And we are not just talking about textiles or garment or other mature sectors, but also about electronics – in one such factory the employees were obliged 'to work un-interruptedly for three days and three nights'.[47]

Kenichi Ohmae, the 'business theory' advocate, speaks excitedly of this El Dorado of 'compound interest'. He is like a gold-seeker who suddenly happens upon a boundless valley of nuggets as big as boulders and, after a moment of disbelief, realizes that it really exists, it's not just a dream. At the sight of this 'extremely talented and hardworking northern Chinese labour force', which has 'already reached a steeper learning curve than Japan – with higher produc-tivity and only 2–3 per cent of comparable wage levels – in the manufacture both of printed circuit boards for laptop computers and of cylinder heads for videocassette recorders'[48] – at such a sight, how can one *not* go into ecstasy? But let the superproductive northern Chinese beware of resting on their laurels – the 'businessman' (never mind the 'theory', which has nothing to do with it) who has just been fawning on them can afford no sentimentalism. Indeed, two pages later he hisses the following warning, in perfect 'white-collar criminality' style:

> At present, the coastal regions of China, which have really just gotten on the development map, are already beginning to price themselves out of the running [the 'price', of course, being that of labour], compared with inland areas and with countries like Vietnam and, before too long, Myanmar.[49]

No, I really do not think the 'nineteenth-century English worker' has disappeared or is about to disappear. He has simply reproduced himself, and continues to reproduce himself at dizzying speed and on an enlarged scale in the countries, and continents, that only now are fully entering capitalism. This is no return to the past. It is not a 'return to Dickens' and 'to the worst forms of 19th century capitalist exploitation'.[50] The fact is that none of this ever left us – never left history and capitalist social relations – but afflicts the living and working conditions of areas that are today home to four-fifths of humanity. If it is true that we are still in the midst of 'nineteenth-century England', we may at least console ourselves with the fact that 'twenty-first-century' Europe and America make no bones about entering 'nineteenth-century' China, Asia and the entire Third World with their calculating rationality. In this way, the cogent, impersonal need of Max Weber's *Zweck-rationalität* finds its interpreters in China – on our very question, the question of time. One of these interpreters, an expert on 'time allocation', after lamenting that 'the total time structure of city and town residents' is 'lax' and 'the rhythmic coordination of time' is not that of 'modern industrial society', offers us this little gem:

> The phenomena that the time structure is lax and the rhythm is slow can be observed at any time in the real life of city residents. According to our observations, the average Heilongjiang city and town resident needs 50 seconds to walk 30 meters, while the Japanese need only 20.07 seconds. In recent years quite a few cities have introduced fastfood services. However, according to our observations in the Hahale Restaurant, Harbin, regular customers more often than not sip drinks slowly and smoke cigarettes leisurely and carefreely. Some even spend two to three hours over a meal. Thus, 'snack culture' has been assimilated into 'slow meal culture'.[51]

The length of hours, then, or their intensification, are not 'alternatives' as they were, to a certain extent, in 'nineteenth-century England'. We are in fact *still* in nineteenth-century England but beyond the limits it reached. In Asia, the capitalist need for longer and more intensive working time calls for an intensification of eating, drinking, socializing, smoking and physiological times, as well as – and the spread of prostitution is a symptom – the very 'time of love' (prostitution is the time, without the love). And do not say that such a world is far away, because the world is progressively becoming *one* world, even in its lacerating conflicts and inequalities. Indeed, it could not be *one* in communication – the so-called 'global village' – if it were not *one* in production. And being one in communication progressively locks its production unity into a closed spiral. The fact is well known, not only by big-time entrepreneurs whose natural dimension of action and analysis is the entire world and in whose 'thoughts' Asia has a special place, but also by the leaders of the Western trade unions, who have been concerned for years about the negative repercussions of financial and production globalization[52] – repercussions that, unfortunately, they think they can combat not by working to unite the workers of the world, but rather by keeping them divided and in competition with one another.

The Presumed Disneyland of 'Services'

Let us get back to our objections. Three more present themselves hand in hand, as if one objection could not stay on its feet without the others, like a little chorus chanting with a somewhat mechanical air. The first: 'Industrial workers, industrial workers! But there are lots of other workers these days! What about the new 'service' professions? We have many different types of workers, and their working times are very different from the ones you have described.' The second: 'The Third World! Japan and the United States, OK! But Europe has been different. There are different types of market society. For sure, some are based on long hours. But there is also the "European model", which is moving towards the 35-hour week. Have you no eyes to see!' The third: 'Long hours, long hours! Maybe so. But you still haven't said anything about one of the greatest novelties of recent years, namely, part-time work! Working part-time doesn't just solve the problem of women who want to combine extra-domestic and domestic work. As in the Netherlands, it may constitute a new model of work organization, with reduced times for everyone.' Let us examine these objections one at a time.

Premiss: The 'services' category is a category totally devoid of scientific value, 'invented' by social scientists in difficulty, and propagandized in the interest of mass befuddlement by the ideologues of 'postindustrial' or 'post-material' society. Those who have been perplexed for years about how to measure the productivity of labour in this irreducibly heterogeneous, multifarious heap of activities have discovered that such a 'category' is of no use for any serious study of the structure and functioning of society. It is not fortuitous that the better-advised among them have drawn some distinctions between the many types of 'services' on the basis of criteria linking them, somewhat, to production, to distribution, or to persons (to reproduction), in an attempt to put *some* order into this chaos of things with just *one* thing in common: they are other than industry and agriculture.[53]

The term 'services' itself ought to cause us to pause. In the service of what? There has never been a society whose central and dominant social activity is an activity in the service of something else. If, then, the 'service society' is not a new social formation that upsets all the paradigms used for interpreting capitalist industrial society, then it can only be interpreted as a form that has evolved from that very society. At bottom, 'services' – from transportation, which is in the first place transportation of commodities, including the commodity called 'labour power' (from schoolchildren to mature workers) to communications (likewise), to wholesaling and retailing (of commodities, what else?), to services for the maintenance and repair of commodity-machines, to mass schooling (instruction, training and discipline of the prospective labour force), to hospitals (repair and recuperation of deteriorated labour power) – are all in the service of the accumulation of capital and of the reproduction of social (capitalist) relations. If these quite obvious facts are kept in mind, one should not be surprised to see models of work organization, technology and working time systematically transferred from industry to the thousand branches called 'services', not the other way around.

Let us reverse our usual procedure and begin this time with the quality of working time in 'services', coming later on to the length of the hours. And let us begin at the furthest possible point from industry, with the sociologist as far as possible from our own point of view, Niklas Luhmann. If his systemic sociology needs, generally speaking, to be carefully deciphered, his reflection on the theme of 'administration time' is illuminating in itself. As he puts it:

> In all sectors of public and private administration the working day is determined for the most part by deadlines.... The beginning of work and, in a less coercive form, the end of work are established temporally. Within working time there is a certain quantity of interconnected deadlines that have been agreed upon with others, be it the case that we have to go to others or that they have to come to us.... With growing specialization and the growing need for coordination such deadlines can no longer be isolated but are increasingly interdependent. They have to be coordinated not only temporally but also thematically.[54]

In this general picture of temporal coercion – setting the times of individual operations, seeking synchronism and combination between operations for a better quality of finished product, division and specialization of functions – what do we see if not the basic characteristics of industrial work organization, a mix (albeit mediated by the specific needs of each activity) of Taylorism and Toyotaism? For Luhmann administrative activity, too, is dominated by the 'pressure of time' and by the 'shortage of time', which afflict what he calls 'the epoch of big organizations', and which is nothing if not the epoch of the highest development of capitalism – distinguished, indeed, by the predominance of big businesses, big banks, big stock exchanges, big states, big wars, big 'private' criminal organizations, big communications networks (with their big, big lies).

Luhmann, the realist, notes how this relentless drive to 'increase the pace of behavior' in administration has made the principle of 'working conscientiously' obsolete and forced administrators to make 'objectively less than optimum decisions'. Willy-nilly, the 'growing demands of rationality of organized behavior' impose the single criterion – certainly not 'of value' but purely quantitative – of 'saving time'. Whatever saves time is good – this is the supreme criterion that has to dictate the actions of an administration, even at the cost of nonrational behaviour. This obsessive temporal pressure shrinks the space and shortens the time 'for unconstrained action'. In short, the working time of public and private administrations is also becoming – Luhmann tells us – increasingly more coerced, abstract, constrained, synchronized, rational, fast, compact, intense. There really is not much to add, except the fact that the time of public and private administration is unlikely to take on these qualities to the degree to which we find them in the working time of the contemporary Taylor–Toyotaist factory, the key time of the production of profits, which shapes all other times of social living. It will, however, attempt to do so. But why? Why is everyone always in such a hurry in administration too (with due exceptions, of course)? And why has this haste come to be an ideological taboo?

Curiously enough, along with the predictably tautological answer ('because we are in a complex world'), we also find an 'open' suggestion:

> Summing up, we can say that the selective effect of time can have different *causes*. It can emerge from a politically recognized ideology of accelerated economic development. It can also be the consequence of certain structural particularities of the social system. This selective effect will produce, then, certain secondary ideologies of work – those, for example, of teamwork, of tolerance, of comprehension – that are capable of justifying the constraining character of deadlines...[55]

The administrative ideology and practice of doing things in haste is, indeed, *caused* by necessities rooted – through 'politics' or directly – in the processes of the economy, in the 'structural particularities' (if properly understood) of mature capitalist societies. The course of, and rush to, the privatization of a broad range of public services do not just concern a change of juridical ownership of the companies that provide them; it is a change in the organizational and operational criteria and is a change, in the sense Luhmann describes, of the temporal criteria. And the process is not fortuitous.

Thus the working time of industry is entering deeper and deeper into the, by definition, slow and dusty world of the bureaucratic apparatus; and it is doing so also by means of an incessant technological revolution that has entirely redesigned offices and office work with the automatic and informatic means of the factory.[56] And the last-born of all production times is making its entrance along with it; namely, *real time*. This is extremely fast time, time that 'is speed itself', 'punctual' time (reduced to a point),[57] which presents itself as time inscribed in the new machines (immateriality indeed!) but which progressively expands, and imposes itself, as the *new time of office work*, time that cadences office time, making it faster, more intense, more 'productive' – be it the offices of private firms or professionals, municipal services or banks, laboratory analysis or post offices.

Think, for example, of a university copying (once simply photocopying) office. The employees – say, two or three – have to manoeuvre in the midst of a formidable throng of machines: photocopiers, personal computers, scanners, plotters, printers, binders, paper cutters, faxes, and phones that always ring at a bad time. I have counted as many as nine such (immaterial!) production machines in a single office, packed like sardines into a cramped, humid room, without natural light or air, polluted by the humours of the machines. With the employees working like *Modern Times* Charlie Chaplins on a variety of production lines simultaneously, relentlessly, for at least 43 to 45 hours a week (Saturday mornings included).

And there is certainly no lack of such examples. From the prohibitive working times of truck drivers (in France they report 60-hour weeks, which they are fighting to cut down to 50 hours!) to the holidays that have become 'normal' working days in catering; from the cleaning workers with their long and irregular hours to the strict time calculation at office counters; from the continuous loading and unloading hours reinstated in the ports (where for a certain number of years nightwork had been eliminated) to the new work rules dictated by the 'for profit' principle in hospitals. The list is endless: of times that are binding and never short, cadenced by night shifts, tighter all the time (since the customers, too, are in a hurry), and harmful in a thousand ways.

Times, principles and modes of work organization ('services', too, have learned about 'just-in-time'!), the use of technology and, most radically, functional links are progressively assimilating many 'services' to the production of value. Saskia Sassen acutely examines the situation from the perspective of 'service' cities – that is, service-based urban economies. Sassen portrays them as *two* cities, *two* economies, *in one*. On the one hand, 'an urban economy dominated by finance and specialized services' and, on the other, a vast informal economy and 'downgraded manufacturing sector'. At first blush, these two economies may appear separate and alternative (where the first develops, the second regresses). But the opposite is true. If one way of seeing the financial world exalts, unilaterally, its immaterial character and capacity for creating highly paid jobs, Sassen rejoins:

> There is a whole infrastructure of low-wage, nonprofessional jobs and activities that constitutes a crucial part of the so-called corporate economy. A focus on the *work* behind command functions, on *production* in the finance and services complex, and on market*places* has the effect of incorporating the material facilities underlying globalization and the whole infrastructure of jobs and workers typically not seen as belonging to the corporate sector of the economy: secretaries and cleaners, the truckers who deliver the software, the variety of technicians and repair workers, and all the jobs having to do with the maintenance, painting, and renovation of the buildings where it is all housed.[58]

Furthermore, if it is true that the (unproductive and antisocial) 'production' of financial services is capable of augmenting the high-income echelon of the social stratification, it is also true that this increase entails a transformation both in the production and in the supplying of consumer goods and services. The demand for luxury goods and services on the part of the high-income social sectors demands a network of production circuits with high intensity of labour. Indeed, a critical analysis of the 'global cities' of finance shows us the true – if 'invisible' – social face of the majority of their inhabitants. It shows us the faces of workers, many of them immigrants, women, and poor, with low wages and long and inconvenient hours working in sweatshops, or in 'industrial work done at home', in subcontracting, in the expanding territories of informal production – which is coming to mean, more and more, the 'production of services'. This analysis reappraises the equation between the growth of financial centres and of 'advanced services' and a general rise in the quality of employment, and reverses it: the 'postindustrial' cities are places where we find vast areas of casual work, great social polarization, and an extreme income differentiation that reshapes the 'consumer structure' itself, polarizing it; which, in turn, has repercussions on work organization. And so we find luxury taxis and collective taxis, super-homes and sub-homes, boutiques with sky-high prices (often supplied by low-paid work done at home) and supermarkets for second-rate products. In these 'service' realms there is no more social cohesion or 'organic solidarity' than there was (or wasn't) in the 'old' traditional industrial society. Indeed, in Sassen's opinion (and not only hers), there are signs of 'a segmenting of the middle class'.[59] Yes, there are new social figures, but with basically the same – if not wider – social gap as before between the class of the accumulators of capital (and their functionaries) and the working class, due to a general worsening of working conditions evidenced by 'the decline of unions in manufacturing', a weakening of unions in the 'service' sector, and 'the loss of various contractual protections'.[60]

It is very hard to understand how the 'service' economy can be depicted as the realm of, if not quite liberated work and time, at least work that is less constrained, lighter, softer, shorter, and, in any case, more varied and creative – a veritable Disneyland for the adults lucky enough to work there. Who, indeed, would exchange an office job for a factory job? Things go the other way around! And yet the combined power of technical–scientific progress and compound interest is doing its utmost to bring offices and 'services' *closer* to the factory – even as it takes pains to demonstrate that it is turning factories into quasi-offices.

But let us press forward to the ultima Thule of 'unconstrained' work, foretold by Toffler; namely, *teleworking*, which the 'services' world assures of vast possibilities of expansion. Well, a recent report by the European Foundation in Dublin expressed great concern – and even criticism – about the 'social implications' of teleworking. The report would appear to dwell more on the risks than on the potentialities: the risks of 'a fusion and overlap of work and private life, of working time and leisure time, of work place and home', so much so that 'the right to respect for private and family life is at stake'; the risk of teleworkers being left 'in a more difficult position to negotiate with their employers'; the risk (or certainty?) of a low wage and a lack of social protection; the risk of having to do 'repetitive work, especially work involving keyboard use'; the risk of stress, as someone put it, from 'the never-shut-down terminal syndrome'; the vitally important and primary risk of 'marginalization from the work collectivity', such that work would be a means of isolating the teleworker instead of strengthening social ties through work; the risk of women not being able to have their say, of not being informed and not being consulted about decisions that concern their work; and, finally, the duration of the work? '*It is difficult to control*. Long working hours might have adverse health consequences especially in a badly designed workplace and when performing repetitive tasks.'[61] Two circumstances in particular show us that these risks of teleworking are by no means imaginary: first, the almost total lack of labour negotiation (even though teleworking has been going on for a good fifteen years); and, second, the exceptionally high proportion of women, who represent the weakest part of social labour power.

Therefore the fact that the thousand-and-one different 'services' are in expansion and that they create 'new figures' in the world of work does not mean that such 'services' give rise to social relations, work relations, forms of work organization, working techniques and working times that are 'different' from and 'alternative' to those that exist in industry and agriculture. It is the relation between capital and wage labour that determines and structures also the entire world of 'services' in its production and reproduction. And the times that emerge here, as we saw earlier with regard to administration, al-most blindly follow the general trends towards a freeze in the reduction of working time, the intensification of work, the introduction of 'atypical' sched-ules and, in many cases, the lengthening of hours.

Certainly, in 'services', besides the enormous mass of more or less skilled manual workers, of clerks, of proletarians and workers on the way to proletar-ization, there are also higher-echelon 'new professional figures' who have margins of autonomy and self-management of their working time that are far greater than those of a barman or a cashier, a warehouse keeper, a bus-, subway- or truck-driver, or a maintenance worker. That is self-evident. But the question we are asking is this: is the social figure that represents the vast majority of the 'service world' – namely the *common worker* supplying abstract labour – so very different, so much more protected and more satisfied, than the industrial worker, as certain mythical portrayals of that world seem to suggest? And, as regards working hours, does this worker have different and better opportunities than the very heavy 'opportunities' weighing upon the industrial proletariat? On both counts the answer is no.

The fact is unequivocally demonstrated by EC surveys on working hours. On a European scale, the sectors with the longest annual hours are wholesale and retail trade, hotels, public commercial concerns and repairs (on average 1,875 annual hours per employee), followed by transportation and communications (1,861 hours on average). These figures are just a few dozen hours higher than the ones for construction and for manufacturing – which also exceed 1,800 hours, lightyears away from the 1,300–1,500 hours of certain tables for mass consumption! In another major sector of the service economy, finance and insurance, we find average annual working time per employee amounting to 1,811 hours, in 1992. The level is substantially the same as five years earlier. There is just one 'service' sector where total hours are sharply less than in industry – namely, public administration (with 1,718 hours). The situation in Italy is analogous.[62]

Even more revealing, because measurement based on the working week better reflects the real life of workers, are the figures on (official) weekly hours in the *Labour Force Survey 1997* compiled by Eurostat. It shows that the average hours of male workers in the various sections of 'services' is between 42 and 45 hours per week while those of women are between two and three hours less; as usual, we are at the level of average hours in industry, if not slightly higher.

The Presumed Difference of Europe

These figures can also help us dispel certain illusions regarding the 'difference' between Europe and the United States and Japan; although, as I said before, we do not know whether or to what extent the survey took small businesses and the 'underground economy' into account. In this regard, the results of the *Second European Survey on Working Conditions* are even more useful. This is an official survey carried out, at last, with a certain degree of accuracy, which, I am sure, will not be well received, because it gives the lie to the rose-coloured view of contemporary working conditions. The reader will find an adequate synthesis in Appendix A to this chapter. For the moment, let me quote from the presentation prepared by the European Foundation itself:

> The working population of the European Union (15 Member States) is 147 million, of whom 83 per cent are employees and 17 per cent self-employed.
>   In 1996 the European Foundation interviewed a representative sample of 1000 workers in each Member State, or 15,800 persons in total.
>   The survey reveals that:
>
> - the most common work-related health problems are:
>   back pain (30 per cent of workers)
>   stress (28 per cent of workers)
>   muscular pains in arms or legs (17 per cent of workers);
> - health problems are most often connected with poor working conditions;
> - absenteeism due to work-related health problems affects 23 per cent of workers each year (averaging out at 4 working days lost per worker);
> - exposure to physical hazards (noise, vibration, dangerous or polluting products or substances) and to poor workplace design remains very common (28 per cent of workers are exposed to intense noise, 45 per cent to painful or tiring working positions);
> - the pace of work is increasing all the time;
> - repetitive and monotonous work is still very common (37 per cent of workers perform short repetitive tasks and 45 per cent perform monotonous tasks);
> - workers are gradually being given more autonomy over their work, although in general this is still rare;
> - work is largely dominated by external constraints (the client has replaced the machine as the main factor dictating the pace of work);
> - computers have now become an important feature of work (38 per cent of workers use computers);
> - only 32 per cent of employees have had training provided by their company in the last 12 months;
> - violence at work is not a marginal phenomenon (9 per cent of employees claim to have been subjected to intimidation);
> - the main feature of the organization of working time is its dispersion (irregular hours, weekend work, night work);
> - working conditions differ widely between occupational categories, sectors of activity, countries, types of employment status. Casual and temporary work is on the increase, and is characterized by poor working conditions.[63]

These data, of course, are then broken down in various ways: by employees and self-employed; by sectors and branches of activity; by gender, employment status, etc. In all cases, this breakdown reveals heavier than average

working conditions for industrial workers, and for casual workers (who represent the vast majority of the workers hired in the past five to six years). It
also shows that 'the pace of work has increased sharply' since the previous
survey in 1991. And it shows that '"blue-collar" workers (especially in manufacturing) and workers in the transport and hotel and catering sectors have
very little autonomy in their work'. And finally, as regards working hours,
here we have the most up-to-date picture to come from an official source
(up-to-date but static, since it gives no historical comparison capable of grasp-
ing their dynamics). We find 'a high proportion of part-time workers (14 per
cent of all workers work fewer than 30 hours per week)', there is 'a high
proportion of workers with long hours (49 per cent work more than 40 hours
per week, 23 per cent more than 45 hours)', and atypical hours are on the
rise – '52 per cent of workers work at least one Saturday per month, 29 per
cent at least one Sunday; and 21 per cent at night, at least occasionally'.[64]

This is common knowledge, it might be said. But if it were really so
common, it would be impossible to understand the insistence on a sort of
(presumed) *genetic* difference of the social relations between capital and labour
in Europe, which would then be reflected in the field of working hours. A
'social market economy' opposed to the 'ultrafree market model' in the United
States as something more in keeping with the 'European spirit' – historically,
it's hard to come up with a taller story than that! In a hypothetical, and futile,
contest to see which 'model of capitalism' is more 'social' than the other, a
democratic American might remind us that Keynesianism had to emigrate
from the 'social' Europe to emerge from the books and journals and become
state policy. And he might also remind us that the cradle of liberalism and
neoliberalism (of Hayek, Mises, Popper, Robbins and their ilk) was, once
again, Europe. And he might add that it was Europe, with the Nazi fascism
of which Europe (I would say 'European capitalism') was the cradle, that
perpetrated the most complete eradication of any 'social' guarantee for workers
anywhere in the Western market economy. And as a last 'unkindest cut' he
might mention unemployment: can a continent and a 'model' that tolerates
higher and higher percentages of unemployment be termed 'social'? Shall we
declare the contest 'no contest'?

In just one respect European capitalism is actually different from capitalism
in the USA and Japan: it has had to deal with a more substantial and organized

proletarian movement. As regards our theme, since World War II the only struggles of some substance for the reduction of working hours in the West have been in Europe: in France and in Italy in the late 1960s; in Germany in the 1980s; and once again, on a lesser scale, in France (the truck drivers) in the 1990s. Even without obtaining results comparable to those of the struggle for the 8-hour day in 1917–19, these mass workers' agitations did succeed in lowering, slightly, the average level of weekly hours – at least until management launched its full-scale counteroffensive, solidly supported by state policies and by the liberalizing measures of Brussels. For years now, this offensive has been dismantling the legal, union and de facto mechanisms of guarantee that were opposed to the lengthening, intensification and maximum flexibility of working time – mechanisms that are by no means in the DNA of Europe, homeland of 'wild capitalism' (or perhaps Great Britain is Asia?). Still, they do arise and stay alive, as long as the proletarian movement manages to hold its position in that creeping civil war over working time, and over everything else, which is going on even when it is undeclared, or is waged unilaterally by management under whatever label is most convenient (flexibility, full utilization of plants, increase in productivity, competitiveness, entering Europe, combating unemployment, and so forth).

The most clamorous *battage* about a presumed 'European model' comes from France. Here it is the state, first with Mitterrand (who soon gave it up), then with Jospin, that presented itself as the driving force for a reduction of hours, in the direction of the 35-hour week. For at least fifteen years the French talked, incessantly, about the *réduction–réorganisation*, *réduction–aménagement* of working time. And the result? Much ado about nothing, in quantitative terms. But quite dangerous in terms of the capacity of workers to put forward collectively their demand for the reduction of working hours. The balance sheet drawn up by J.Y. Boulin is meagre indeed. Management's short-term production logic (but what other logic does it know?) has imposed itself, he admits, on every other demand. The reorganization of working time has complied, fundamentally, with this logic. The workers have been given, at most, some individuals sops, and one certainly cannot speak of a 'positive-sum solution' for companies and workers together. On the contrary, 'the trio individualization/heterogeneity/irregularity' of working hours leads to 'disintegration and segmentation on the social level'[65] – and for workers in particular, with the corrosion of their bargaining power. Boulin's final plea to the state, entreating it to become the engine of social change, is a reflection of the fact that concertation between management and labour has not weakened the 'collective actors' but only one of them, the proletariat, since management has emerged fortified and more entrenched than ever *against* a reduction of hours.

State initiatives for the reduction of hours are, in any case, not new. There was a first example in France itself, when the Popular Front government introduced the two-week vacation.[66] Sixty years have passed since then, and it shows. Compared to the 'summertime' of 1936, state initiatives today are far more timid, far more favourable to management (which is assured of all kinds of support and financial facilities), far more gradualist, far more sparing of promises to the workers, far more detached from any form of appeal to the masses to press directly for the reduction of hours. Summer has turned to autumn. More than an action truly promoting a generalized reduction of hours, the action of the French government is designed to bolster social cohesion; it is more of a 'spectacle' to lend credibility to the state's role *super-partes* than a real, even moderate, reform of working time.

If, then, we consider the fact that in Great Britain, in Sweden, in Italy, working hours have been rising for years, the whole presumed 'European difference' boils down to this: in Germany hours are slightly shorter than in the other Western countries. Quite true. This is because in Germany several categories of industrial workers, especially the metalworkers, have struggled mightily to reduce working time. Even this acquisition, however, is now called into question. Not by a central decision, like the one made by the Bavarian government to increase the working week of its employees from 36 to 40 hours with no rise in pay;[67] but rather with the use, by management, of the ruse of local agreements, plant by plant, and the method of eroding workers' resistance by the threat, and practice, of decentralizing plants to the East and to the South. Meanwhile, not even the most reckless of gamblers would bet a red cent on the generalization of what was called, wrongly, the 'Volkswagen model', which was in fact no more than a provisional compromise, and one which proved to be short-lived.[68]

This 'different' Europe has been pursuing the reacquired dynamism of the United States for years, while attempting to counter the Japanese challenge.

How? Bosch and Lehndorff's answer, which in terms of observation of brute fact coincides with mine, is: by prolonging the utilization time of plants, and the consequent diffusion of atypical hours. Today there are at least six automobile plants in Europe that beat their Japanese counterparts when it comes to total utilization time: the General Motors plant in Zaragoza, Volkswagen in Brussels, Opel in Bochum, Fiat in Cassino, General Motors in Antwerp, Ford in Genk. The second aspect of this European competition over time has to do with 'long hours with massive overtime' – as at the Nissan plant in Sunderland, which, together with the Fiat plant in Melfi, is the 'model factory' of the European response to Toyotaism on its own ground – including the company philosophy of 'combining constriction and consent'. Bosch and Lehndorff suggest that Europe follow another way to defeat US–Japanese competition: namely, the way of investment in 'human capital' and in 'cooperation'. They are forced to recognize, however, that the company policy prevailing today, also in terms of working time, is quite different: 'The Germans (or the Europeans) have to have longer working hours.'[69] To stop and reverse this trend something very different will be needed from what Bosch and Lehndorff are hoping for.

The Presumed Cure-all of Part-time Work

Now for our last objection: is the diffusion of part-time work a form of reduction of working hours? Does it run counter to the trend of freezing or lengthening hours? Is it a possible anticipation of the comprehensive solution of the problem of hours, even over the long term? The answer is no.

It is not a form of reduction of working hours, first of all because in the vast majority of cases one moves up (in terms of hours) to a part-time job from unemployment, not down from a full-time job. Second, because part-time female workers (who make up three-quarters of all part-time employees) have no significant reduction of their domestic working time, which means that their extra-domestic is added to their domestic work. And third, because part-time work presents a series of negative characteristics that portray it, as a rule, as a depreciated and ghettoizing form of employment. Let us begin with this third point.

The great diffusion of part-time work took place after the crisis of 1974–75, and is connected with a need to reduce costs and to increase the flexibility of the labour force, particularly in the 'service' sector. As can be seen from the reports of the European Foundation in Dublin, we are not exactly talking about an ideal form of work:

> Part-time work often has characteristics of marginality, insecurity and depreciation of the work activity. Generally, the kind of jobs assigned to part-time female workers involve less skill and, consequently, less possibility of improving the work quality and conditions. In many cases, part-time work means increase of work paces and transfer to more monotonous and heavier jobs. Part-time workers are often required to have high 'mobility' in order to meet sickleaves, extra-time activities and unforeseen demands....
>
> In practice, part-time work often tends to overlap with occasional or seasonal work without guarantees and continuity of employment.
>
> For these reasons part-time work is still considered as *'second class' work*, which favours discrimination and social outcasting among workers, and therefore it is still not popular with most employees.[70]

This rule, of course, has its exceptions. It is possible that 'some individuals in very high-powered jobs', such as consultants, prestigious journalists, university professors or highly skilled technicians, use part-time work as an advantageous opportunity not only to reduce the stress from overwork, but also and above all to 'mix and match' a series of interesting jobs.[71] The exception, however, does not invalidate the rule. And the rule is that part-time work is, in general, work that is relatively unskilled, badly paid, marginalizing.[72] It is not fortuitous that most of it is done by women, whose subordinate condition in the labour market and in society is well known.

But, it is said, women *choose* part-time jobs. This platitude of a socio-economic literature committed to exalting part-time work as a genuine social cure-all is called completely into question by a critical reading of the official figures.[73] Let us suppose nevertheless that many women do actually 'choose' part-time work. It is not hard to understand that such a 'preference' for 'second class' work depends on a lack of alternative 'choices' open to them, and on the fact that the reproduction of labour power, a basic social necessity, is assigned to the female gender as a 'private' task (and more so all the time, given the deepening crisis of the welfare state). When all is said and done these women 'choose' what they cannot not choose, and end up having to cope with a double job that certainly does not represent a reduction of *comprehensive* working time, of women in particular and of wage labour in general.

The heightened feminization of the labour force in late capitalist societies stems, on the side of capital, from the same need that fuelled the widespread use of female labour in proto-capitalism, or during the two world wars – the need to compress the comprehensive value of labour power. Of course, behind this need there is also a woman's need, which is entirely different: namely, to break out of the stifling isolation of the home to enter social life fully. But the ways in which ever greater numbers of women are entering the labour market have not been chosen by these women; such ways do not, as a rule, depend on their 'strategies'. Instead, they are dictated by the extremely tight objective constraints of the capitalist compatibilities of this new phase of 'globalization'. A 'social' state stripped barer and barer and a labour force more flexible and casualized all the time: these are the 'social' (*antisocial*) demands to which the extension of part-time work responds – and that of women in particular. These demands have as much to do with the reduction of extra-domestic working time as they do with the attainment of equality between men and women: nothing at all.[74] Not too 'friendly' conflicts will be needed if such *truly social* (and anti-capitalist) counter-demands are one day to assert themselves.

There are, however, solid grounds for affirming that the diffusion of part-time work is part of the trend towards the lengthening of the working time of wage labour. What Schor and others have demonstrated for US-American women with full-time jobs – namely the sharp rise in their extra-domestic working time compared to the limited contraction of domestic working time – holds, *mutatis mutandis*, for the women of the other developed countries.[75] And what holds for women with full-time jobs also holds for women who work part-time. For that matter, the condition of (female and male) part-time workers is so unenviable and uncertain that, according to the first reports in Europe, more than a third of them declare their desire to obtain a full-time position as soon as possible, while an even higher percentage see part-time work as just the first step towards a full-time job.[76]

A recent study by IRES in Paris confirms these observations to the letter, at least for the French situation. Some 47 per cent of part-time workers have come to see their condition as a risk, and wish they could work more. Their fear stems from a precise material contradiction: the low level of wages paid to part-time workers. The percentage of workers with a low level of pay has risen, in France, from 11.4 per cent in 1983 to 15.3 per cent in 1995, while the percentage of workers getting poverty wages has actually doubled; so that in France too – the phenomenon has been ingrained for years in the United States – a *pauvreté labourieuse* is beginning to emerge. And this not-so-small stratum of poor workers (one out of six) is mainly composed – fully 72 per cent – of people working part-time. The French study remarks, bitterly, that with the diffusion of part-time work the phenomenon of the working poor is no longer exclusively an Anglo-Saxon concern.[77]

It is thus quite unlikely that the 'Dutch model' with its recourse to part-time work can really be taken as a prototype to be imitated, particularly as regards its effectiveness in combating unemployment. Apart from the doubts that have been raised about the accuracy of the Dutch statistics,[78] it remains to be seen whether the so-called 'Dutch miracle' is, in fact, an effect of the diffusion of part-time work. There are two different interpretations of this 'miracle'. One links the relatively low unemployment index to the role played by active policies favouring employment (including incentives to part-time work); the other, to a rate of development somewhat higher than in the rest of Europe.[79] But one fact is indisputable: with part-time work on the rise, the number-one company in the Netherlands, Philips, together with the industrialists of the metalworking sector, spearheaded a sharp offensive against the reduction of working hours, which forced the unions to abandon all their demands.[80] This demonstrates that, for full-time workers, the freeze of working hours along with the drive to make them heavier and longer is not an alternative to the diffusion of part-time work. The two phenomena take place in different fields of social activity, and if it is true that part-time work is seeping into industry as well, it is doing so, for the most part, in the form of weekend work, with 12-hour days on Saturdays and Sundays. So part-time work in industry appears, for the moment, to be no more than a collateral instrument, but one that is useful for broaching and stabilizing the atypical hours to which the entire labour force is to be habituated.

At the same time, Sylos-Labini's prediction that 'over the very long term the reduction of hours and the diffusion of part-time work tend to converge',[81] on the basis of the hard facts at our disposal, proves to be no more than a baldly ideological claim. The period of greatest recourse to part-time work (the past twenty-five years) has been one in which average hours in industry have ceased to fall. And there is a real correlation here, since both long and part-time hours, in combination, are called on to produce the 'flexible rationalization' in the use of labour power that has to ensure a lasting pick-up of profits. And if it is true that the rise in part-time work is a drag on wages in general, it cannot possibly have a beneficial effect on hours. In a capitalist market economy, low wages have always brought long hours with them. This is another mechanism through which part-time work contributes to the expansion of the hours of full-time workers, not to their contraction.

Quantity and Quality

One last observation before closing the chapter of objections, once again on the subject of the quantity–quality relation. In many cases, unfortunately, the qualitative dimension of time has been not simply distinguished but *separated* from its quantitative dimension. As a result, the two dimensions have proceeded, both in reality and in theoretical research, parallel to and independent of one another, 'noncommunicating, when not in direct conflict'.[82] The first dimension, on the one hand, has been assigned to an evanescent psycho-sociology that takes as its object an individual free from the determinations of the material structure of society – an individual who in fact does not exist. The second dimension, on the other, has been delivered into the hands of a socio-economics that thought it could limit its sphere of competence just to measurable, nonqualitative factors – which, accordingly, were not of decisive importance for 'human experience', for the 'meaning' of our actions. Once again, in the 'heaven' of consciousness, of intimacy, of spirit, we find values, symbols, foundations, 'visions of the world' and 'qualitative' time, self-generated and self-generating in and from the void. And on the earth, in the concreteness of socio-economic relations, we find vulgar quantitative time, with its measurements, its mechanical rhythms, its rules, and its statistics, which would appear to be less and less related to 'inner' time, to the 'intimate feeling of time', and to the representations of time.

But the real world has nothing to do with such dualism. 'Consciousness', the 'inner world', the *psyche*, is a plant – in flower or withered, as the case may be – that is entirely rooted in the relations of material production proper to the market economy, from which it draws its – more or less polluted – lymph. The psychical life, the state of psychical health (or sickness) of workers is therefore decisively conditioned by their working and social relations and life. If it is true that working time is at the centre of the system of social and individual times (this is our thesis), then also on the psychical level we cannot but see the effects of the trend towards its lengthening and intensification. And this is indeed the case.

Today, many voices are crying out in alarm about the increasing nervous 'costs' of labour. Rifkin notes that the problem of stress from work and overwork has become an extremely serious international problem, telling us that of the 200,000 Toyota workers who are members of the company union, 124,000 have reported periods of nervous exhaustion.[83] The situation in the United States is certainly no less alarming: 55 per cent of sick days are due to stress. The first major US study on the psychical disorders of people between the ages of fifteen and fifty-four revealed the enormous extent of nervous pathologies (about 50 per cent of the respondents reported at least one permanent disorder), and the existence of a substantial stratum of the population (14 per cent) suffering from multiple complaints. Depression, anxiety, drug addiction, alcoholism, simple phobias and 'social' phobias – all of them proved to be highly sensitive to the class division of society. In fact the rate of all nervous disorders rises with the decrease of income and falls as income increases.[84]

While this study tells us nothing specific about the causal link between working conditions and psychical pathologies, other studies have in fact dealt with the question. Cru and Volkoff, for example, after speaking of a marked deterioration in all aspects of work activity – exertion, harmfulness, work pace, hazards – go on to emphasize the internal, family and social repercussions of the overall destabilization of hours connected with the diffusion of 'atypical' work schedules. Unstable, variable and uncertain hours, besides being destructive for the natural rhythms of the body, are equally so for those of the mind and of the entire inner world.[85] And not only during working time. Christophe Dejours writes:

Common sense agrees that work materially occupies an important part of life – eight hours a day. But this crude evaluation falls short of the truth. The subjective relation to work stretches its tentacles far beyond the space of the workshop, office or company, and *colonizes in depth the space outside work*. The analyses of the psychodynamics of work are eloquent in this regard....

Psychical functioning is not divisible. The man who is engaged in defensive strategies to struggle against suffering at work does not leave his psychical functioning behind when he goes out of the door. On the contrary, he takes his mental constraints with him and needs the cooperation of his loved ones to bolster his defences for the moment of his return to work. It may thus be shown that the entire economy of the family is called upon to help its members cope with the constraints of the work situation.[86]

Thus the mental suffering caused by abstract and alienated work, on the computer no less than on the assembly line, passes from the place and time of work to the places and times of the workers' social and family lives, from the workers themselves to the people around and close to them. In short, the working of the mind is not divisible; by the same token, one cannot and must not divide the inner from the social, the spiritual from the material, the psychical from the physical, the symbolic from the 'normative', the individual from the (full) system of her social relations, the 'qualitative dimension' of experience from its 'quantitative dimension'.

We note the huge delay of the medical and social sciences in investigating the pathogenic effects of wage labour, the pathological inclination of these sciences to look at the problem merely in terms of adjustment–maladjustment to work,[87] the backtracking that has been going on for the past twenty years[88] and the hushing up today of any 'occasional difficulty' that might tarnish the shining image of the market economy. And as a result of all this, only a part – perhaps only a small part – of the deep, inner, even unconscious malaise that is accumulating in the spirit of the proletariat comes to the surface. One can continue to conceal it, even, as Dejours remarks, 'from the workers themselves, totally engaged as they are in the profuse efforts of production'.[89] But this malaise will explode in the end – like in 1968, and even more so – suddenly finding its voice and its lost time. It will become clear, all of a sudden, that it had not been nursing 'just' a mass estrangement from work, as in the years following the post-war reconstruction, but something even more radical.

Also, because if the new factors of psychical risk are on the rise, the 'old' factors of physical risk are still very much present, in industrial production and agriculture in particular. The World Health Organization reports that, worldwide, 220,000 people are killed in the workplace every year (with more than 90 per cent of the total represented by wage labour – a ceaseless holocaust, unchronicled and unsung); 120 million workers are injured; 160 million contract work-related diseases; and every day new pathologies emerge, linked to the use of new toxic substances, to new technologies, to the adoption of new methods of work organization – and to too many hours spent in stress-inducing environments.

We want to repeat that the health of a worker is not a commodity, and that health does not just mean absence of disease but entails a 'state of physical, mental and social well-being'.[90] But within the social relations in force today, the worker's health can be nothing other than the optimum condition of his capacity to produce; which means that it is indeed a commodity, and of rather low value to boot, given the increasingly abundant labour supply on a worldwide scale. The foundation of this commodification, so far from the 'state of physical, mental and social well-being' prescribed by the United Nations, is in the commodity condition of labour power itself. The pathology of industrial work and, within that pathology, the process of spiritual pauperization of workers, stems – more radically than from individual aspects of the capitalist organization of the process of production – from a determinate *social relation* of capital and labour. This relation *structurally* entails the 'loss of self' – an inseparable body–mind self – of men and women who, to make a living, have to sell their working time and their living time as well.[91]

That this may appear 'excessive' is an ugly sign of the times. We have no need to call on the sensibility of an Adam Ferguson to tell us about the effects of the division of labour on the personality, and humanity, of workers. Let me just remind the reader that even such a sworn and militant adversary of the working class as Alexis de Tocqueville could still write: 'In proportion as the principle of the division of labour is more extensively applied, the workman becomes more weak, more narrow-minded, and more dependent. The art advances, the artisan recedes'; he could still see how in capitalist industry 'as the workman improves the man is degraded'.[92] Today it has become a commonplace – without foundation, as we have seen – that such things went out with nineteenth-century capitalism. Meanwhile, when people talk about industry or the economy, they do nothing but ask – or reassure – themselves about the state of health of corporations, banks, state budgets, currency; and if they speak of 'restoring to health', the *health* (or 'well-being', as the WHO put it) is still always that of corporations, of *capital*. Small wonder, then, that problems of health, like the problems of hours and wages, of pensions and, above all, of decision-making power, in the factory and in society, are growing worse for the working class. And the diffusion of Toyotaism, of long, intense and variable hours, of neoliberal policies, all herald a further worsening of this unhealthy trend. Unless…

APPENDIX A
Second European Survey
on Working Conditions (1997)

The first survey by the European Community on working conditions dates from 1992 (*First European Survey on the Work Environment 1991–1992*); over thirty years had gone by since the creation of the EEC in 1958. Elaborated by the European Foundation for the Improvement of Living and Working Conditions in Dublin, the study, coordinated by Pascal Paoli, admits that information on working conditions in Europe 'often either does not exist, or is not accessible' (a curious admission, coming from a government institution), 'or, if available, is not comparable because of the differences between the monitoring of the various member states' (p. XI). The source cannot be suspected of a hypercritical spirit.

The survey concerned a sample of 12,500 workers, both 'independent' (self-employed) and 'employed', and was carried out through direct interviews in March/April 1991. From this 'not very large' sample (only 12,500 respondents out of 137 million workers), moreover, 'foreign workers were excluded' (p. 5).

Although the survey is a prototype, it does tell us a number of interesting things. First, it divides the mass of workers (137 million) into employed (111 million, or 81 per cent) and independent workers (26 million, or 19 per cent), and into male (61 per cent) and female workers (39 per cent). The highest percentages of employed workers are in the regions of the former East Germany (91.7 per cent), Denmark (90.8 per cent), the Netherlands (87.5 per cent), Great Britain (86.4 per cent), western Germany (85.4 per cent); the lowest percentages are in Greece (50.1 per cent), Italy (68.1 per cent), Portugal (70.7 per cent). Industry is the production sector with the highest percentage of employed workers (close to 90 per cent, with a peak of 95 per cent in the metalworking section). The total number of people employed in industry in the strict sense – factory workers, technicians, office workers, middle managers – amounts to 41.5 million, which becomes 50 million if we add the 8.5 million workers employed in transportation and communications. *This is nearly one half of the total number of employed workers* (50 out of 111 million). If we consider the fact that the overwhelming majority of them are wage-earning proletarians, we get some idea of the substance in Europe of what we jokingly referred to earlier as 'phantom activity' and a 'phantom class'.

Compared to the European average, Italy is one of the countries bringing up the rear both for the relation between employed and self-employed workers, and for the proportion of female workers (33.5 per cent of the Italian labour force is composed of women against the average of 39 per cent in Europe as a whole, with 46.4 per cent in the former East Germany, 42.3 per cent in France, 40 per cent in Germany).

As for working conditions, 52.7 per cent of the workers of all sectors and all conditions declare they have no particular problems; 30 per cent, however, consider their health and safety to be at risk on account of their work. The group most at risk are the unskilled manual workers.

Younger workers, on the whole, would appear to be subjected to the hardest working conditions, as regards exposure to toxic substances, submission to time pressure, and the 'Tayloristic profile of jobs and tasks (short cycles, lack of autonomy)' (pp. XIV–XV).

As for working hours (pp. 53 ff.), they are longer in smaller firms (46.4 hours a week on average for businesses with a single employee) than in larger ones (39.4 hours); longer in agriculture (48.3 hours), in transportation and distributive trades (43 hours), in construction (42.2 hours) and in the manufacturing industry (41.6 hours); and, predictably, shorter in services of the public administration (36.6 hours) and in banking (39.7); longer for the self-employed than for the employed.

The text of this first survey admits 'there is little data available on night-work and shiftwork' (p. 52), but it does give us a few figures: 'More than 20 million workers in the EC work at night at least a quarter of the time and 6 million' [five times the inhabitants of Naples or of Milan, a hundred times that of Venice] 'work permanent night shifts.' Here pride of place is held by a section of the 'service' Disneyland, transportation and communications, where some 40 per cent of the workers work at night at least a quarter of the time. But the energy and chemical industries are close behind.

The second survey (or study) on working conditions in Europe is, unquestionably, of greater interest; carried out at the end of 1995 and the beginning of 1996, the results were published in 1997 in the volume *Second European Survey on Working Conditions*, also coordinated by P. Paoli.

Methodologically, the survey has at least three major flaws. First, as customarily occurs, there is an over-representation of some sectors, such as services and public administration, while agriculture and industry are under-represented; and this is openly acknowledged (p. 8; but why is no attempt made to remedy the imbalance?). The second flaw derives from the first: there is an over-representation of the middle and upper-middle classes and social strata of society compared to the class of industrial and 'service' workers. For example, 7 per cent of the sample comprises 'legislators and managers' and 14 per cent are 'professionals', while 'plant and machines operators' make up only 9 per cent. This obviously leads to a 'sweetened' picture of the existing working conditions. The third flaw is that the sample is, once again, quite small (15,986 respondents), which is bound to affect the extrapolations and averages. It also means that little or no attention is paid to the 'underground' sector, where work is longer and heavier, paid less and less protected, and which here, again, is left in shadow.

It is impossible, then, to take the results of this survey as a faithful likeness of real working conditions in Europe. But, despite its flaws, the study does give us food for thought. And on the positive side: (1) the basic questionnaire was richer and more detailed than it was in 1991 (41 questions instead of 19); (2) the sample also included immigrant workers from non-EU countries (p. 11), even if we do not know to what extent and with what criteria; (3) the survey sought to ascertain workers' 'self-perception' of their working conditions. In this regard, we should note that the survey was conducted during a period in which working-class political and union activity was particularly slack, and this had an immediate impact on 'self-perception'; workers were inclined to accept a state of affairs they would have found intolerable if the labour movement had been stronger. Let us examine the principal aspects of the survey.

Composition of the 'labour force' (in quotation marks because the Foundation's conception of 'labour force' is very different from mine). Compared to 1991 the percentage of 'employed workers' rose to 83 per cent, while that of 'independent workers' fell to 17 per cent (only in Italy does one take, or pretend to take, the mini- or micro-business for the quintessence of modernity). The proportion of female workers rose from 39 to 41 per cent. 'Service' employees rose from 59 to 63 per cent, while employment in agriculture and in industry fell to 6 and to 31 per cent respectively. Nothing is said, however, about the 'outsourcing' operated by large industrial companies that artificially swells the ranks of 'service' workers.

Working environment 'The exposure to ambiental factors such as noise, vibrations, extreme temperatures, dangerous products or substances, was high in 1991 and remains high in 1996. *Approximately a quarter of the workforce* [of all sectors] *is exposed* at some stage to high level noise (28 per cent), to vibrations from hand tools or machinery (24 per cent), to intense heat (20 per cent) or intense cold (24 per cent), to inhaling vapours, fumes, dust or dangerous chemicals (24 per cent), to handling dangerous products or substances (15 per cent).' Those most exposed to these 'traditional' risks are the younger workers, workers in agriculture, construction and manufacturing, manual workers, workers with a precarious status, employees of middle-to-large sized companies (pp. 17–18). Those least exposed are 'legislators and managers', 'professionals', 'clerks'.

An even greater proportion of workers are forced to work in physically painful positions (45 per cent) or to carry or move heavy loads (33 per cent). The capitalist work organization reserves these privileges for the usual transportation, agriculture, manufacturing industry, construction and catering workers, for younger workers, manual workers, and – with 'striking' care – for temporary, or generally precarious workers (pp. 43–6). The least exposed? Those who have to 'lift' or 'carry' books, reports, law codes, microphones, faxes of congratulations, bank cheques, and so on.

Working hours 'Overall Europeans *work long hours*' (p. 72). So it is not just the invention of some hothead that '50 per cent of them work over 40 hours a week and 7 per cent of them over 60 hours. There are big differences between countries; the shortest average working hours are to be found in Denmark and the Netherlands, the longest in Greece and Italy.' By Jove! If one trusted the official figures, Italy would be in a completely different position. But this little sampling of 1,032 Italian workers, while not impeccable, is enough to give us some idea of the *real* figures.

The survey reports that 48 per cent of workers in the manufacturing industry, 64 per cent in construction, 55 per cent in wholesale and retail, 58 per cent in hotels and restaurants, and 58 per cent in transportation and communications work over 40 hours a week; and 21 per cent of Greeks, 13 per cent of Irish and Portuguese, 11 per cent of Belgians, and 9 per cent of Italians work over 60 hours a week. In an era – so they say – in which leisure time greatly prevails over working time!

In this same era, in our 'different' Europe, 55 per cent of all workers work at least one Saturday a month (83 per cent of the self-employed, 48 per cent of the employed), 25 per cent work every Saturday, while 29 per cent work at least one Sunday a month and 8 per cent every Sunday. Meanwhile, 33 per cent of the 'labour force' work shifts and 'irregular hours'.

And we still have to add the commuting time to and from work to the hours spent in the workplace. (Or are we talking about 'real hours', with breaks and meal time deducted? The survey does not say.) In general it is shorter for the 'independents' than for the 'dependents.' Of the latter, 23 per cent spend less than 20 minutes, 49 per cent between 20 minutes and an hour, and 28 per cent from 1 to even more than 2 hours commuting. With some elementary time-budget arithmetic, we have a working day that amounts to – on average, and supposing the (certainly reductive) estimates of the survey are exact – 8 hours and 10 to 20 minutes for a quarter of the workers, between 8½ and 9 hours for half the workers, and from 9 to 10 hours, or more, for the remaining quarter.

And **work rhythms**? A total of 54 per cent of the respondents (in all sectors, employed or self-employed) tell of working for more than a quarter of the time 'at very high speed', 56 per cent report 'working to tight deadlines', and 21 per cent say they do not have enough time to get the jobs done (p. 94). What is more, it is not just the automation speed of machines (22 per cent), production norms (35 per cent), or the 'direct control of the boss' (34 per cent) that hurry workers up; there are also the customers (in 67 per cent of the cases) or colleagues at work (37 per cent). While entire libraries are filling up with books showing how the centrality of the fast pace of industry has become a thing of the past, a little serious investigation shows us that, to the contrary, the haste of the machines has infected everyone and everything. What 'impersonal force' has made not only the workers on the assembly line into such a hurry, but also their colleagues and bosses, clients and customers, and society as a whole? And why? And is it not the case that this general *intensification* of work, of (almost) *all* work, which is declared by 70 per cent of construction workers, 64 per cent of industrial workers, 67 per cent of transportation and communications workers, is wearing out the men and women who are subject to it well beyond the 'long hours' (as the Foundation tells us) they are working? After hours, what *quality* time do they still have 'for themselves'? What is the quality of their 'free' time, leisure time – living time?

Job content   Some 45 per cent of the respondents 'consider their tasks as being *monotonous*, especially young workers, temporary workers, low-skilled workers, and blue-collar workers' (p. 140). Monotony, moreover, 'can be linked to the repetitiveness' of the tasks, reported by 37 per cent of respondents. The capitalist market does not have much imagination where the division of labour is concerned. The mechanism, from the very beginning, has been 'automatic'.

Temporary (or precarious) work   This eminently modern form of work catalyses everything the capitalist could possibly want: more working on Saturdays (p. 84), more working on Sundays (p. 87), more working at night (p. 90), more intense rhythms (p. 97), more piece work (p. 105), more direct control by the 'boss' (p. 119), less autonomy (p. 121), more monotonous tasks

(p. 148), more repetitive tasks (p. 160), less possibility of being 'consulted' on work-related decisions (p. 198), greater exposure to unwanted sexual attention (p. 246), greater possibility of being subjected to intimidation (p. 249). The elegant 'value-neutral' sheath enveloping all these marvels is called 'flexibility'.

Violence at work   A total of 9 per cent of the respondents report being subjected to intimidation, 4 per cent to actual physical violence, 2 per cent to unwanted sexual 'attention' (p. 240). Then there are the various forms of discrimination: sexual, nationality, racial, etc. Who knows whether the survey, which at least had the merit of posing the questions, was able to ascertain the real extent of these phenomena.

Results   Some '57 per cent of workers (56 per cent of employees) think that their work affects their health in a negative way', with the highest incidence of this fear also in such 'reduced hours' countries as Sweden, Finland and Denmark.

'The most important problems indicated are: backache (30 per cent), stress (28 per cent), overall fatigue (20 per cent), muscular pains (17 per cent), headaches (13 per cent)' (p. 263). We find stiff competition between 'old' and new complaints, as confirmed by one of the Foundation's recent publications, *Stress at Work* (Dublin, 1997), which states that stress is a growing problem in the working life of Europeans, in particular for the Finns, Greeks, Italians and Swedes (p. 6).

Despite these aches, pains and related fears, what is absolutely remarkable – and we are in Europe, not in Japan or the United States – is the rate of *presenteeism*. Some 77 per cent of all workers (84 per cent of 'independents' and 75 per cent of 'dependents') 'declare not having missed a day's work over the last 12 months' for health reasons, and another 6 per cent declare having missed 5 days or fewer. Presenteeism is particularly high among precarious workers and in small businesses. And it does not surprise us that, after everything they declared, 84 per cent of the workers say they are satisfied with the job they have. This is not acute schizophrenia; it is (apart from the real satisfaction expressed by a minority of workers) the normal, necessary realism of the wage labourer, selling his time to capital. Better a wage, and a hard, repetitive job with the same working hours as in 1919, than no job at all. Or not?

Comparison between 1991 and 1996 In the five-year period there was a slight increase in the exposure to noise (from 27 to 28 per cent), working in physically painful positions (from 43 to 45 per cent), carrying and moving heavy loads (from 31 to 33 per cent). But the most notable thing is *the sharp rise in the intensity of work.* The proportion of workers obliged to work at very high speed rose from 48 to 54 per cent, and those working to tight deadlines rose from 50 to 56 per cent. It is true, then, that we are rapidly 'progressing' beyond the times of Taylorism and Toyotaism and that 'Prometheus is leaving his place to Dionysus' (M. Maffesoli, 'La fine di un mondo', *Reset*, January 1994, p. 64). 'Our grandchildren' of the new millennium can dream of future delights.

APPENDIX B
Vietnam: 24-hour Continuous Shifts

Apropos of 'things that went out with the nineteenth century', there is an experiment going on today in Vietnam that deserves special attention for its futuristic and, one might say, 'humanitarian' character. Our source is the article by T.T. Khai, T. Kawakami, L.M. Toi and K. Kogi, 'Improving Safety and Health of Rural Sugar Cane Factories in the Mekong Delta Area in Vietnam', published in *The Journal of Science and Labour*, March 1997, pp. 14–22.

The article concerns field research conducted in two rural small-scale sugar-cane factories located in the Mekong Delta area in Vietnam (in the Hoa Luu village, Vi Thanh district in Can Tho province). The two purposes of the research are: (1) to identify the safety and health risks for the workers in these small sugar-cane factories; and (2) to establish the roles of the field researches for strengthening the local initiatives to improve working conditions. The research was conducted (in August 1994) by a joint Vietnamese–Japanese team.

First very minor detail 'Both of the factories [12 workers in one, 14 in the other] adopted a 24-hour long continuous shift system alternately worked by two teams.' No, this is not a misprint: they work for 24 hours *consecutively*, then rest for 24 hours, then come back to work another 24. That's 48 hours of work every four days, 72 every six. Well, with great zeal, our researchers set out to investigate (with their thirty-item 'fatigue questionnaire') the reactions of these workers to fatigue. The researchers, on their 'walk-through survey', scrupulously applied the 'action-oriented checklist developed by the ILO'; and with exemplary evenhandedness their investigation involved both workers and owners of the factories alike.

Careful records were made of the conditions of temperature and humidity of the working environment, and of the three 'fatigue categories', each consisting of ten items: (1) drowsiness and dullness; (2) difficulty in concentration; (3) projection of physical disorders. To supplement the fatigue evaluation, continuous heart-rate monitoring was applied to one worker engaged in extracting the sugar-cane juice and to one worker engaged in boiling the juice; the time study used 'an every 30-second snap-reading' applied to four extracting workers and four boiling workers during the whole shift. Ten breaks were inserted in the 24-hour shift; and, since the workers lived close to the factories, they were even allowed to go home during the breaks. Despite these breaks, our 'objective' researchers noted with some surprise that 'working a 24-hour shift increased fatigue symptoms markedly'. At the end of the shift, the workers' fatigue complaint rates were very high in the 'drowsiness and dullness' category, and high in the 'projection of physical disorders' category. A series of Figures illustrate the different reactions of the two types of worker, the different forms of fatigue, the effects of temperature variation, the difference in heart rate, and so forth. A number of improvements in the working environment were made, from increased ventilation to local lighting for nightwork, from cover for waste canals to cement floors, along with increased communication between owners and workers.

The last paragraph of the article reads:

> In conclusion, our experiences in [two] small-scale sugar cane factories in Vietnam demonstrated that widely applicable field research approaches were useful to identify multiple work-related risks in local workplaces and produce practical recommendation for improving working conditions. Given practical advice and sufficient discussion in the local context, the local small-scale factories could implement substantial improvement actions in their own initiatives.

Second very minor detail   Despite the fact that we are dealing here with 24-hour continuous shifts, and despite the fact that at the tail end of our researchers' list of problems in the workplace they do mention, somewhat distractedly, that 'reducing continuous working hours was identified as another priority for action' (some of the workers may well have come up with a similar idea on their own – with all due respect for the grandeur of 'science'!) – despite all this, our staff of researchers, in their conclusions, make not the slightest mention of reduction of hours as an absolute priority. They list all sorts of improvements, except the most elementary and basic improvement of them all – a drastic reduction of the inhuman length of working time. Lacking this, the whole research project boils down to applying all the latest scientific devices to habituate workers even to 24-hour continuous shifts.

'Promote *adjustment* to given social conditions and functions' is a symbolic *locus classicus* of nineteenth-century 'social science' that a certain industrial medicine has made its own. In short, promote the adjustment of the working class to the role that capitalist division of labour imposes on it – the adjustment to the supreme interests of the expansion of capital.

What international capitalism 'expects' of Vietnamese (and kindred) labour power can be easily deduced from *Rapporto Vietnam*, edited by G. Capannelli:

> One of the main sources of the comparative advantages of Vietnam consists in its abundant supply of low-cost, relatively well-trained, disciplined and growth-motivated workers.
>
> The legal minimum wage for industrial workers is 35 dollars a month. Foreign companies that intend to make direct investments [down payments on the 'comparative advantages of Vietnam'] can calculate the cost of labour on this basis. According, for example, to indications provided by an Italian–Vietnamese joint venture operating in a rural area in the South of the country, the overall final cost would add up to between 50 and 60 dollars a month, bonuses and production incentives included, which is an unquestionably low figure compared not so much with Europe, but with the other developing countries of Asia....
>
> We should also consider the fact that a part of the labour force can speak French or English and, more generally, that the Vietnamese are quite good at learning foreign languages. This is an important characteristic, generally not to be found in other countries of the region. (Turin, Edizioni della Fondazione Agnelli, 1995, pp. 52–3)

If only they could work 36-hour shifts every 24 hours!

5

Towards the 35- or
the 45-hour Week?

We still have to reply to the greatest of all the possible objections, which regards in particular the German and French (and Italian) situations. In Germany the 35-hour week has been a *fait accompli*, in some categories, for more than a decade. In France the 35-hour week has, indeed, been sanctioned by law. In Italy there had been talk, for several years, of a similar law. Doesn't this resoundingly give the lie to everything we have claimed?

The German Case

As regards Germany, quite frankly I see nothing that belies my thesis. The 35-hour week of the metalworkers and typographers was the outcome *only and exclusively* of a period of intense labour struggles. There was no spontaneous gift from companies or from the state. On the contrary, companies and the state have been working together for years to gut and reverse the 1984 agreement, even when, as in the case of Volkswagen, they seem to prefigure further permanent cuts in working hours.

Outside of Germany people find it very hard to accept the fact that the German proletariat is ahead of the other sections of the European proletariat. Anti-German chauvinism, whose targets include the German workers, holds such a thing to be impossible. But it is, quite simply, a fact, and has been for more than a century. In 1918 the workers of Berlin, Hamburg and Munich were the first in Europe to obtain the 8-hour day. And it was these same workers who paved the way for all the others, with a quasi-revolutionary social and political uprising that shook the European capitalist order to its foundations. Contrary to the racist historical 'reconstructions' à la Goldhagen, the German proletariat was in the forefront of the resistance against the rising tide of Nazi fascism – before and after Hitler's coming to power, up to the eve of the war and even (from a far weaker position) during the war itself.[1]

After World War II, the 'antifascist' democracies on the winning side did everything possible to prevent a resurgence of the German working class. The country was broken into two parts, and with the decisive complicity of Stalinism was kept in this condition of physical and moral disability for half a century. While these democracies effectively did nothing to denazify the German political and administrative institutions,[2] they did a great deal about radically decommunizing the German proletariat, tying its hands with an ultra-authoritarian system of restrictions. The German Communist Party (KPD) was outlawed, political strikes were strictly forbidden, political activity of the unions was prohibited, and legal limitations on the right to strike were imposed even for the unions themselves, which were under intense pressure to break themselves down into small company unions, organized not nationally but provincially. These coercive measures were patently designed to lobotomize the German proletariat through an operation of rank socio-genetic engineering.[3] The operation, moreover, was of international import, since it was aimed against the proletariat that since the mid nineteenth century has been in the theoretical and organizational vanguard of the European labour movement.

Sharing in the tragic defeat of the international proletariat in the 1920s, unjustly criminalized for the horrors of Nazism, defeated in its attempt to become 'spokesman for the renewal of the socio-economic structure' in Germany, disillusioned by the 'Soviet' suppression of the proletarian uprising in East Berlin in 1953, the German working class set out anew, in the West, from the depths of its abyss – through *economic* struggle waged at the *company* level. But it succeeded, gradually, in making up lost ground, progressively stamping *Mitbestimmung* – the German form of the post-war 'social compromise' between capital and labour – with its working-class mark.[4] For decades this slow reaccumulation of strength progressed uneventfully within the formal and substantial meshes of co-determination, confined to the issues of wages and employment. But in 1973 – the German workers' '1968' – a new social and political phenomenon emerged with the refusal by a part of the working class (spearheaded by the metalworkers) to submit to management dictates regarding working time and pace. And something else of great importance emerged from the confrontation: namely, the active role of immigrant workers, harshly discriminated against in society but key players in union organization.[5]

Since then *Mitbestimmung* has been a hotly contested issue between capital and labour.[6] The labour movement's trade-union and, in a broader sense, political activity continued to expand, culminating in June 1996, in Bonn, with the largest workers' demonstration since the end of World War II – 300,000 demonstrators 'against the demolition of the social services, against unemployment, and against the wage reduction imposed by the state'.[7] This was in fact a demonstration against the comprehensive policies of the Kohl administration and of the capitalist class, which reiterated the struggle of German workers against the 1993 budget, but on a larger scale. And all this took place – not by chance – after German reunification, after a series of workers' agitations in the eastern Länder, and after a timid beginning of reunification of the material conditions, the forms of work organization, and the feelings of the German proletariat. The dramatic forced break-up of the country after World War II was, slowly, becoming a thing of the past.

But let me say it once more: the conquest of the 35-hour week by the metalworkers and the typographers – a small conquest compared to that of the 8-hour day, but a conquest nonetheless – was due only and exclusively to the reawakening of the struggle of the German working class, which in the mid 1970s began to demand and to obtain greater respect for its expectations and needs – a reawakening, it must be said, that failed to call the politico-ideological foundations of co-determination into question. And this failure ultimately cost the workers dear, since it was co-determination itself that was becoming the real issue; the framework of national and company capitalist compatibilities within which workers had hoped to improve their material conditions proved, instead, increasingly binding and rigid. It was precisely in the name of the 'higher' claims of national competitiveness that German banks and businesses mounted their counterattack against the working class, gravely eroding its unitary structure. This, clearly, had negative repercussions on working hours, at the very height (in the 1990s) of the workers' struggle to respond cohesively to the capitalist class and the government. And this was due to the political delay – not only of the German workers, of course – in casting off a *Mitbestimmung* that was everywhere on the wane, together with the impetuous cycle of post-war development that had made it possible.

Not even in Germany, then, the heartland of European capitalism, do we find any trace of a spontaneous, mechanical, progressive reduction of working time corresponding to the increase of gross national product, labour productivity and company profitability. On the contrary, we find abundant evidence of the efforts of German capitalism to abrogate that 35-hour week, which, in any case, it has successfully kept from infecting other sectors of industry. The 1997 official statistics on weekly hours speak for themselves: 42.9 hours on average for agriculture (the production sector with the longest average hours, and which – strangely enough – almost never appears in the statistics publicized by the mass media); 40.5 hours for 'services' as a whole, with record figures for the hotel and restaurant sector (44 hours) and rather high averages also for transportation (41.3) and banking and financial services (41 hours); only for public administration is the figure just barely below 40 hours (39.7). In industry the official average is 39.3 hours per week, with a maximum of 40.2 hours for construction and a minimum of 39.0 for manufacturing.[8] This, on the whole, gives us a fairly faithful picture of the relative strength of capital and of wage labour in the different sectors of the economy. Where wage labour is more concentrated, organized and combative, average working time is shorter; where, on the contrary, it is more dispersed, disorganized and passive, average working time is longer.

So where is the German exception? Where is the realm of the generalized 35-hour week, obtained once and for all? Certainly not in Germany. A serious look at the true state of affairs – and the government's own figures could not be any clearer – shows that the 35-hour week actually exists only in a few industrial enclaves, the big factories of a couple of sectors, surrounded by an overall situation that is zigzagging towards the lengthening and intensification of working time. The attainment of the 35-hour week by metalworkers and typographers in 1984 (which did not come into force until 1995) was not even the beginning of that 'opening up of new perspectives of social development', of that 'qualitative turning point' in the organization of social life which had been hoped for (in some circles). This was due not only, and not so much, to the grave limitations of the labour movement, but principally to the range and power of the capitalist counterattack that was not long in coming.

Yes, there were lots of second thoughts about the *Lebercompromise* expressed by company managers; but the material attack on workers – starting with the workers of the 'privileged' companies – carries far greater weight than the verbal attacks that presaged it. For these workers, the introduction of the 35-hour week was accompanied by relentless management aggression against all elements of their working conditions. New shifts; maximum flexibility of hours, dictated unilaterally by company needs; growing pressure to transform Saturday (and, eventually, Sunday) into a normal working day; annualization and individualization of hours, with the diffusion of *Zeitkonten* (time accounts) and the related practice of unpaid overtime; methodical recourse, wherever possible, to outsourcing, both internal and external, national and international. Management fought relentlessly to appropriate every split second of working time, no longer calculating it on the basis of time spent in the factory but rather of time actually employed in production.

It would be opportune, at this point, to examine briefly three of the innovations that specifically concern working time.

The first innovation regards the enormous boom in the past ten years, especially in the larger companies, of 'à la carte' work schedules, different every day, dictated by management day by day.

> This form of management of working time is based on the will to broaden the base of legal or contractual working hours while reducing or abolishing fixed hours – which makes it possible to increase a company's real working time overall. Extremely flexible hours [*horaires de fonction*] are thus introduced in the place of fixed hours, in order to better synchronize the working time of each employee with the needs of production, in each sector.[9]

But 'à la carte' schedules, besides pursuing the goal of 'zero dead time' in factory work (companies are free to 'send their employees home' when work is slow), 'lead to an increase in the intensity of work and to a rise in invisible overtime'. The 'impossibility of precisely establishing the length of the working day' increasingly blurs the confines between variable hours and overtime. What is more, this impossibility effectively voids the real impact of the 35-hour week, since workers have to be permanently – and instantly – at their bosses' disposal to stop work and start it again, which leaves them even less possibility of planning their nonworking time than before.

The second innovation, which in fact preceded the 'à la carte' schedules and in a certain sense represents their 'institutional' frame of reference, is the so-called *réglementation des 13/18*. This permits companies to 'prolong weekly working time' while establishing an 'overtime limit' that has to be respected. Experience, however, shows that some 20 per cent of firms consistently fail to respect the limit, while the others too – the capitalist cannot change his spots – display a pathological interest in 'increasing the volume of working time'. In such a trend many union leaders see, realistically, the beginning of the end of the 35-hour week.[10]

The third innovation is that of *Zeitkonten*, time accounts or banks.[11] With this system, the workers of a company taken as a whole, and above all individual workers, are provided with 'time bankbooks' in which to record their credits (the hours worked in excess of contractual norms) – not, however, to be paid as overtime, but to be exchanged, over a given span of time, for as many hours of time off from work. Companies were wildly enthusiastic about this system because it allowed them to vary the quantity of production time according to the demands of the market, without having to hire more workers when the market was brisk – and without paying overtime either. As for the workers, they are supposed to profit from 'greater opportunities in managing their time'. These opportunities, however, are worth about as much as the paper they are written on. The chances of getting time off from work in periods of intense production are nil, since it is management – not the workers – that decides when the time accounts are to be settled. Furthermore, the timespan for making the 'exchange' is growing continually longer. At first it was limited to a couple of months, then it was extended to a full year, then to a number of years, then to the entire span of the working life, and finally, at Volkswagen, even to retirement years!

This limitless extension of the timespan multiplies workers' risks, since consistently, in all production sectors, their credits exceed their debits. In the North Rhine-Westphalian waterworks we find a spectacular asymmetry: +600/ -40 (which corresponds to an average working week of over 50 hours); even in the packaging sector in Hamburg (+224/-170) or in the advanced-technology machinery of Baden Württemberg (+150/-72), to cite just two cases, the balance is weighted against workers. *Zeitkonten*, then – and things could hardly be otherwise in a capitalist context – are nothing but the umpteenth form of that *uneven exchange* between capital and labour which is the cornerstone of the entire capitalist market economy. We can see why the workers – failing to obtain the hours, days, weeks or even months off from work that are due them, and expecting the worst – often ask for their accounts to be settled in cash. In this way they reveal the true nature of *Zeitkonten*, which are means not only for making working hours more flexible, but also for making them *longer*.

The social and individual consequences of this extreme flexibility and extreme variability of working hours from one company to another are also of great significance politically. Oskar Negt remarks:

> I think it is a grave danger for people if they lose their collective rest times. Brushing up the old biblical adage, the idea that after a number of days of work *everyone* has to rest seems to me a great conquest of civilization. The 'always available' man that the entrepreneurs see as ideal ... constitutes the prototype of the heterodirected individual – of the man who always has to be available for the orders that come to him from outside. When the company calls, he works for two days, and then just waits....
>
> I don't believe that flexibility leads to an increase in people's autonomy, but, on the contrary, to an increase in their dependence on what is outside, and to a loss of their social and family ties. This leads to the creation of a new type of politically manipulatable individual: when people are accustomed to responding when called, the risk of a rise of political authoritarianism becomes even higher....
>
> At this rate we shall end up with a man [or woman] who spends his [her] entire life inside his [her] company, the ultimate company [wo]man. With the enormous wealth that we produce, why do people have to become more dependent than before, reduced to being pure satellites of the sun of capitalism?[12]

Why? Because with all the 'enormous wealth' of commodities we produce, unfortunately we are still inside and under the mechanism of the 'exploitation of one class by another', of the oppression of one class by another. And this mechanism does not allow a fair and equitable distribution of the benefits of technological and organizational progress; as in the times of formalized slavery, it always proceeds antagonistically. With their struggles, the German metalworkers and typographers managed to wrest a 35-hour week from bosses who were by no means consenting or content. But these bosses immediately launched their counterattack, to conquer the totally *unilateral* management of the working time of wage labour. This action is making the workers' entire existence more dependent on the commands of the market than ever; it is wringing every drop of unworked time out of working time; it is making the pace of working time even faster; and it is succeeding, for now, in reducing in number and in *splintering* the most important section of the German and European working class, which had been consolidated and unified by its successful struggle for the 35-hour week. What is more, this action is laying the foundations for a *reversal* of the 35-hour week even in those limited areas of production where it has been broached.

The parallel offensive of the German Manufacturers' Association and the Bundesbank against the 'high cost of labour' has been no less implacable. The political philosophy here – embraced by Christian Democrats and Social Democrats alike – is as follows:

> Germany has to learn from America, where the percentage of workers is higher but wages are lower, there are practically no social services, working hours are longer and working conditions are worse. At least one of the advocates of an increase in returns on capital speaks of it openly: 'Before-tax wages have to be reduced by 20 per cent if we are to return to full employment.' This is the formula proposed by Norbert Walter, former director of the Institut für Welt-wirtschaft in Kiel and currently head of the economic research division at Deutsche Bank.[13]

This is a formula embraced by Schröder himself, who maintains that to absorb unemployment it is necessary to work more.

Diligently, capital and the state in Germany are learning the 'American' lesson. How they are going about it goes without saying: counter-reforming insurance regulations and sickness benefits;[14] using fiscal policy to shift wealth towards capital; raising interest rates to impose stable wage moderation;[15] pitilessly reducing company personnel; decentralizing production abroad; gutting national labour contracts; deregulating the labour market. In this regard Ulrich Beck went so far as to speak of a 'Brazilianization' of the German labour market, and with good reason. He estimates that in 1960 only 10 per cent of German employees were doing casual work, while in the 1990s the percentage rose vertiginously, with casualization reaching 33 per cent. In real numbers we are talking about 13,700,000 employees subdivided into various groups, many of them 'nomad' workers holding part-time jobs. Then, we

Figure 5.1 Wages and profits in the German metalworking industry, 1980–97 (% growth over period)

Wages and salaries		Profits	
gross	*net*	*gross*	*net*
94	74	147	251

Source: Statistisches Bundesamt, IG Metall.

have to add the 4,800,000 who are unemployed and the 3,100,000 in social welfare programmes, for a total of 21,640,000 people in precarious situations, over against the 38,500,000 workers with 'permanent' jobs. It is an enormous jungle getting bigger all the time and threatening to choke out the few and isolated Edens of the 35-hour week, which are themselves already infested from within by rampant flexibility.

This process of the *general casualization of labour* was given further impetus by the capitalist exploitation of German reunification. We saw earlier how the formal end of the two Germanys brought workers of the east and west closer together, also in contractual terms. But, indeed, the reaction of the German capitalists was not long in coming. After granting the inevitable wage hikes in the east in the first few years, they consistently exploited the high skills and low wages of workers in eastern Germany (and throughout eastern Europe) to blackmail the western German workers. And the blackmail proved highly effective also as regards working time. In the west even good-sized companies of the metalworking sector – Viessman in Kassel, Drager in Lübeck, Dasa in Hamburg, Sinitec–Siemens in Munich – imposed *additional hours without pay*, with a return to the 38- or 40-hour week.[16] Then, the other side of the coin, companies exploited the worsening of contractual and working conditions in the west to counter the demands for full equality in the east, where, especially in the last few years, there have been frequent reductions of the negotiable part of wages and frequent violations of contractual or legal obligations 'in the domains of working time, overtime, and flexibilization of annual working time.'[17] Little by little, playing off actions in the east against reactions in the

Figure 5.2   Labour productivity, wages and employment in the metalworking industry of the eastern Länder, 1991–97

	Change (1991 = 100)
Productivity	355
Hourly wage	204
Output per worker	160
Employment	31

Source: Statistisches Bundesamt, IG Metall.

west and vice versa, the German capitalist class has been calling into question the entire system of national collective bargaining, with the result that workers are increasingly at the mercy of individual companies – companies that, to escape any form of contractual obligation, be it regional, national or sectorial, often do not hesitate to cut all ties with their trade unions. Figures 5.1 and 5.2 show the ongoing results of this shift in power relations to the advantage of profits and thus of capital.

Upon closer inspection, the Volkswagen affair itself is part of this picture of increasingly hard, intense and casual work, albeit with the anomaly (provisional, in my opinion) of the under-35-hour week.

There has been a lot of confusion about what really happened at Volkswagen. Let us recall that the 1993 proposal was made by the company, and its decision was not free but forced. It was absolutely inconceivable that on the day after unification the biggest company in Germany should dismiss 30,000 employees without notice; it would have been a death blow – economically and politically – for the foreign and domestic prestige of the reunified Germany (Volkswagen is, after all, to a considerable extent state-controlled). A less traumatic way *had* to be found to achieve management's purpose of a sharp reduction in the workforce, a rise in work paces and productivity, a lowering of the costs of production, and a drastic curtailment of organized labour (in Wolfsburg nearly all the workers were unionized). The Volkswagen solution was not a reduction in working hours but the by no means equivalent one of reducing hours *and wages* together, which broached, in Germany, a possibility unknown until then – wage cuts, which fast became the rule in other sectors (chemicals, for example) as well.

That agreement is usually identified with the introduction of the '7 × 4 model'. Wrong. The number of employees who work 7 hours a day, 4 days a week, is rather small. It would be more correct to speak of 140 different work schedules, of which the 7 × 4 is just the most widespread. And 140 (or, according to another estimate, 164) types of schedule means, inside and outside the factory, the maximum fragmentation, desynchronization and individualization of working time and social time alike, since working and nonworking times are indissolubly linked. Then there is also the diversification of work schedules between the various plants of the group.

So at Volkswagen there was not a pure reduction of working hours but rather a comprehensive reorganization of the process of production and of working time, with the extension of shiftwork, nightwork and holiday work, of flexibility, of mobility (within the plant and between plants), and also of overtime – requested by management and often sought after by the workers themselves, even on weekends, as a form of at least partial compensation for their reduction in wages.[18] Another important aspect of the restructuring of the production organization at Volkswagen was the extremely sharp rise in work paces, as evidenced by all the research studies.[19]

But as for what this 'experiment' has really meant for the working class, note that between early retirement, transfers, and the freeze on turnovers, since 1993 there has been a forced or 'voluntary' exodus from the workforce of some 25 per cent of the employees – which shows that the agreement certainly did not safeguard jobs, as promised. No, indeed, Wolfsburg is not the joyous paradise on earth of reduced hours and free time that was promised. 'The dominant feeling [there] is *fear*, and you go to work even if you're sick or in precarious physical condition.'[20] And it is precisely the fear of losing one's job in a Germany where the unemployed are over 4 million that, in the surveys, makes the number of workers who declare themselves wholly or partially 'satisfied' prevail over the dissatisfied. After all, they have reason to be satisfied since they have avoided the greater evil – the loss of their jobs. It is not fortuitous that we find the highest percentage of positive judgements on the agreement among the workers who are less skilled and paid less – and more threatened with job loss and social exclusion; while we find the highest percentage of negative judgements among the most highly skilled and best paid – and least worried about losing their jobs.[21]

In fact, a close inspection of the workers' overall conditions of existence clearly reveals the painful effects of the 'Volkswagen experiment'. The socialization and solidarity among workers that formerly existed was shattered, since the occasions for workers to socialize inside and outside the factory (moments of collective recreation, for example) were sharply reduced. The centres of assistance for real or prospective alcoholics were populated by early retirees. There was a rise in divorces, separations and family tensions, often connected with the fact that 'there's more time to spend less money', with all its consequences. Given the new condition of precariousness and the unbridled flexibility that make it much more difficult to organize a life outside the workplace, it is small wonder that the number of new marriages for Volkswagen workers has plummeted (down 30 per cent between 1993 and 1998). And the tendency, in families, to return to the traditional division of labour between men and women, which to some extent had been called into question – can that be considered progress? It was the women 'for a change', especially women whose children had problems at school, who paid the highest price, with the record for 'voluntary' resignations. And what shall we say about the fall in the rate of unionization, about an 'individual management' of working conditions and hours that are, in fact, unilaterally controlled by management, with its despotic methods?[22] Of course, one may object – as do the union leaders who signed the agreement – that the situation would have been even worse with 30,000 workers sacked on the spot. Well, that's true; and far be it for me to minimize the workers' capacity for resistance. Nevertheless, the crucial point is that the agreement in no way succeeded in preventing the slow, inexorable degradation of the working and existential conditions of workers, individually and collectively.

Six years after the agreement, we can draw the following conclusions. First, no new '7 × 4' model has come into existence, not at Volkswagen or anywhere else. Second, Wolfsburg has by no means been the engine room of a generalized reduction of working hours; it was, and is, a laboratory where a *provisional* reduction of hours is being used in the attempt to increase stably the flexibility and intensity of work, and to break up the labour movement permanently.

Despite the enormous rise in labour productivity obtained in Wolfsburg, the VW management has already set its sights on other 'model plants' where it hopes to do even better: namely, Resende in Brazil and Mosel in Saxony. At Resende, a small plant for the production of trucks, Volkswagen has no factory workers of its own; the assembly line is manned by the workers of subcontractors in competition with one another – with, of course, no shadow of a union. At the Mosel plant this 'new concept of work organization' (largely based on small subcontractor firms) was combined with the latest advances in technology and work intensification experimented in Wolfsburg and Hanover, with the aim of cutting the production time of the VW Golf in half. But, even after the Resende and Mosel 'miracles', Volkswagen is still not satisfied. The personnel manager, P. Hartz, already has a vision of a radical new frontier to conquer: *Programmentgelt*; namely, wages no longer linked to the hours of work done but to the attainment of production goals programmed by the company. The worker, who in the meantime has been linguistically promoted to the rank of 'company co-worker' (*Mitarbeiter*), to obtain the 5,000 marks a month promised as overall pay (no mean sum, but – remember – Henry Ford also started that way) will be obliged to work as long as necessary to reach the production limit set by the company. And while for now the limit of working hours has been set at 48 per week, once the basic principle of this 'revolution in work organization' has been accepted it should not be difficult for companies to go beyond it.[23]

Hartz justifies all this by saying that 'globalization demands it'. Either one takes this new course, exploding all the old limits on working time,[24] or else one has already lost the race to reduce production costs. As things turned out, the way has been winding but rather short. At Volkswagen (and beyond) the introduction of the 28-hour week is paving the way, through the complete deregulation of working time, to… the 48-hour week!

Yes, globalization. As we see, not even Germany can exist in a world of its own, its 'Rhenish capitalism' enclosed in a single country with its eternally pacified 'social market economy', according to the myth made by Erhardt and now embraced by the Social Democrats. In Germany, too, capitalists and workers clash over working time. But what is at stake is not a generalization of the 35-hour week or even its reduction to 32 hours. No indeed, what is at stake here is a *return to the past*, to hours that are not only long but extremely intense and variable, autocratically established by companies and by the state. So far, the intensification of working time and its lengthening appear to have been proceeding separately – but for how long will that be so? So far, the line of defence of the labour movement has not been completely breached; but the movement is clearly on the defensive and in dire straits. It will overcome this crisis only by realizing that the old social and political compromise is finished, and by accepting the consequences – first and foremost, that it must reconquer its *autonomy* of thought and movement from the falsely naturalistic dictates of the market and globalized capitalism. But no less important will be its capacity to reverse the current trend towards division and fragmentation, reweaving a unitary fabric between the unemployed and casualized and the workers who are 'guaranteed', between the workers of the west and those of the east, between German workers and immigrants, between working men and working women. It is just this division and hierarchical stratification of wage labour, astutely encouraged by the economic and political powers that be, that presents the main target for the capitalist offensive – also in terms of working hours.

The French Case

And France? As regards the long-term trends of working hours, we said in Chapter 2 that, compared to the rest of Europe, 'French originality is rife with shadings and accents. Beneath the small numerical variations, however, the basic trends are the same as in the rest of the industrialized world.' A hasty judgement? I don't think so. Despite appearances, this judgement can be substantially confirmed also as regards the most recent evolution of working hours.

But let us begin with the real state of things, not with programmes, intentions or laws, which, in any case, we shall come to later. Well, in this case too the official statistics suffice to give the lie resoundingly to the presumed 'French exception' and the even more presumed 'French model'. They tell us, in fact, that in 1997 average working time in industry was 39.9 hours per week – 1.2 hours *more*, not less, than in 1987; in agriculture it was 40.8

hours, 40.6 in transportation and communications, and 43.6 in the hotel and restaurant sector. The percentage of workers who declare they work more than 45 hours a week has also grown, from 15.4 per cent in 1983 to 22.6 per cent in 1995. Fully 44.2 per cent of the workers report a working week of more than 42 hours. If these are the official figures,[25] on-the-spot reconnaissance presents us with a picture that is all the more clear-cut.

In his book *Le travail jetable non. Les 35 heures oui*, Gérard Filoche gives us a lively and expert (Filoche is a labour inspector) description of the vast area of the French economy in which '5 to 7 million workers are obliged to work as many as 45, 50 or 60 hours a week instead of the famous 39 legal hours.'[26] From call centres to beauty parlours; from showbusiness to cafés and fashionable department stores; from restaurants (700,000 employees), where '50, 60, or 70 hours a week is common practice', to the cleaning sector in which the sum of two or three part-time jobs can often add up to 250–280 hours per month; from luxury leather goods to luxury wristwatches; from truck drivers to taxi drivers, who sometimes do work 35 hours, but... twice a week; from the hospital care, health care, home care, social work sector (743,000 employees) where we find 'hours *à rallonge*, turnover, insufficient teams, working weekends', to the construction sector that employs 1.2 million workers, where 'in building sites working seven days a week, ten hours a day is not unusual' – what a fine picture of long and hard hours! Hours that 'outrageously' exceed and mock the official or legal hours of the 'French model'. And, as is the case elsewhere, also in this France that considers itself 'different' it is in the garment industry – a branch of production that (as we know) wildly exploits immigrant workers – that nineteenth-century working hours reign supreme:

> In the garment industry, the situation in the ateliers of the Sentier district [in Paris] and in other illegal [*clandestins*] ateliers in the big cities is well known. It is not uncommon to find twenty people behind their sewing machines crowded into a 40-square-metre room, where they work 12 or 14 hours a day. It is common knowledge that the textile industry is one of the industries that complains the most, that asks for the most aid, that constantly moans and groans about decentralization, and never stops asking for more deregulation. It even demands the right to work for fourteen-year-old children doing apprenticeships in France! But, above all, after restaurants and construction, this is the sector where we find the greatest number of illegal workers, the *clandestins*, in the very heart of our big cities. The big names, hypocritically, make great use of sub-

contractors; they have the finishing touches done at the lowest possible price by these illegal ateliers where human beings are reduced to slavery. These people are practically sequestered; they have to reimburse the expenses of the illegal machinations that got them into the country, so they work for many years in conditions similar to the ones in the countries they came from... in the very heart of Paris.[27]

The use of this 'imported and "enslaved" labour in France itself' (why the surprise?) is by no means limited to mature production sectors. Right there in the historic Sentier an 'Internet Economy' district has sprung up. And right there, where the suppression of all rules is itself the rule, the owner of one of the brand new companies – named Rosebud – sarcastically declares: I intend to 'launch the 70-hour movement', because 'there is no sense in setting a legal limit on working hours in a sector in full, job-creating expansion'.[28] There is no sense in setting such a limit for the sectors in contraction because of competition with industry of the Third World; nor, obviously, is there any sense in setting it for the sectors in expansion. In sum, the new and the old French capitalists and their friend-enemies in other countries are alike as two peas in a pod. Their favourite activity? Squeezing every possible drop of unpaid working time out of their wage-earning slaves, whom they then – in their magnanimity and incomparable *esprit de finesse* – respectfully refer to as their 'partners' and 'associates'.

These long, or very long, and getting longer working hours concern above all 'the world of small businesses, of subcontractors'; but this world in expansion, which now embraces 50 per cent of private-sector workers, has many organic connections with large corporations. Connections of *dependence*, which oblige small businesses not to content themselves with a so-called 'normal' profit but to go after a profit capable of satisfying not only their own appetites but also the even bigger appetites of the 'masters of globalization'. This accounts for that 'coercion' which induces them systematically to break the law – a coercion coming from the 'upper echelons' of concentrated and 'advanced' capital:

They cheat on overtime. They cheat on wage schedules. They cheat on state 'aid'. It is not a question of 'good' or 'bad' bosses; it is above all the *mechanism of a system* [my stress] of which they are captives. The obligation to seek the greatest profit pushes them into behaving like dictators, 'squeezing the juice' out of their subordinates, making them put in unpaid hours, paying them in dribs and drabs, preventing them from organizing in their own defence, limiting the expenses needed to ensure their health and on-the-job safety.[29]

Other authors, too, insist on this point, speaking of the 'marked degradation of working conditions' in small businesses, which are described as a realm of 'institutionalized casualization' at the service of corporations.[30] In corporations working hours are generally more controlled, slightly more in compliance with laws and contracts; but all the recent studies present a dark picture of the working conditions and industrial relations existing there, in full conformity with what is taking place in smaller businesses and in the other countries of the West.

We note, first of all, an extreme intensification of work. At the Renault Douai plant, one of the car-making factories with the highest production rates in Europe, even micro-breaks are progressively being eliminated, and to avoid any interruption in the production flow a part of the time for breaks has been moved to the end of the shifts. The relentless effort to eliminate all 'dead time' is now pursued according to the strict dictates of Toyotaist just-in-time: 'The aim is to cut down the time it takes to manufacture a vehicle from 18.3 hours to 15 hours next year.' (We recall that at Volkswagen they are already aiming at 7.5 hours.) The race to improve productivity has led to an alarming rise in the number of nervous disorders, accidents, and deaths from overwork.[31]

The intensification of work is not a peculiarity of Renault, but is the general characteristic of the 'new' organization of industrial (and not only industrial) labour, which demands more – and constant – attention on the job, heightened alertness, readiness and concentration, and therefore entails 'a higher degree of psychological compulsion'. Workers are under growing pressure to 'work fast and without mistakes', which combines the old Taylorist methods with the new pressure that comes – it is said – 'from the customer'; the pressure, that is, of the new Toyotaist methods. Work paces and rhythms are constantly stepped up in a framework of work dictated by management that is far more constrained – perhaps a little less painful in terms of muscles, but more painful overall, physically and mentally.[32]

We find the same unbreathable atmosphere at the Peugeot Sochaux-Montbéliard plant, where the effects of the widespread casualization of workers has been heavy. Beaud and Pialoux note that 'the workers feel themselves to be in a situation of objective and subjective vulnerability and work in fear, for themselves and for their children.' This progressive casualization of 'permanent' workers has been aggravated, on the one hand, by the evolution of the labour market outside the factory; and on the other by the difficulties within the factory for workers to move up from the assembly line to higher-category positions, given the reduction of intermediate tasks and a general downgrading of the workers' condition due to a closing of the gap between higher-skilled and lower-skilled jobs.

Those who refuse to see the worsening of workers' conditions produced by the policies of neoliberalism and flexibility will also fail to see why the workers at Peugeot experience the transition to the 35-hour week as a *regression*. For them, the downgrading of Saturday to the status of a normal working day and the exclusion of breaks from the calculation of real working time rank as a greater loss, in material and 'symbolic' terms, than the gain *on paper* of a 1½ or 2 hour reduction of weekly hours.[33] And they are quite right, because the abrogation of these two important basic rules of the old organization of working time is part of that broader deregulation of working hours which is a prelude to the 'suppression of the very notion of legal working time'.[34] It does not bode well for the working class.

Where, then, is the vaunted French originality? Between à la carte hours and time banks, between the widespread annualization of working hours (defined by Filoche as 'the worst system of exploitation') and hours turned topsy-turvy by their increased variability and the increasingly uncertain character of time off,[35] the picture – by no means specifically French – is one of maximum flexibility of working hours geared to company needs, and of the increasingly unilateral management of working time by company bosses. But – one will object – the French originality is not to be sought in the attitude of the French capitalists, who are about the same as capitalists all over the West. No, it is to be found in the positive and active role played by the French state and government in promoting the reduction of working time, in order – as Aubry put it – to 'combat unemployment'. A unique role indeed, since in the last thirty years no other Western government has dared take the initiative in such a way; and *motu proprio* to boot, in the absence of any real proletarian movement.

Just a moment. The initiative taken by the French government, some twenty years after that law on the 39-hour week which had almost no practical effect, is directly connected with a resumption of labour struggles. If the steep fall in workers' agitations and strikes in the period 1979–94 is indisputable, it is equally indisputable that 1995, 'the year of the big strikes', signalled a marked resumption of the struggles, which had significant developments also in the following years.[36] Propagandists of state sociology (or market sociology, which is the same thing) à la Touraine took great pains to deny the movement behind the strikes in the autumn–winter of 1995 not only its working-class character but even its social character.[37] For them, the whole thing was nothing but a jumble of 'individual' initiatives, fundamentally corporative and in conflict with one another, 'without plan, without utopia, without a leading actor, nonpolitical, heterogeneous, and with no expression of their own', and therefore without the slightest influence on the social and political course in France or anywhere else. Well, I don't see it that way. That resumption of the struggle, which began with the railroad workers, the most proletarian section of the public sector, expressed needs that were very strongly felt in the entire universe of wage labour – needs that were still in embryo and incomplete, but *real*. And it set in motion a unifying dynamics capable of bringing this universe back together, in defence of 'social security' and in the refusal to accept a raising of the retirement age. The major strikes of 1995, with the return of the workers to centre stage, encouraged the struggles of the truck drivers, of the *sans papiers*, of the employees of Crédit Foncier, of the unemployed, and contributed to the creation, beyond French borders, of an environment favourable to the Europe-wide Renault strike, to the Europe-wide demonstration for employment in Brussels, to the first European march of the unemployed in 1997.[38]

We are not, of course, talking about a historic turning point, or even a rupture comparable to the one in 1968. Still, the warning sign was quite sufficient to produce a resumption of state intervention in support of 'social cohesion' threatened by a social polarization that, no longer just objective, had become subjective as well. The most significant element of the railroad workers' strike and the others that followed was, in fact, the widespread support of the general public, despite its being 'hit hard' by the strikes. Something quite similar occurred a short time later in the United States with the

UPS strike. This general sympathy, this broad popular support for strikes that in other circumstances would be highly unpopular, can only be explained by the identification with the striking workers of so many apparently disparate social figures (exactly the opposite of what Touraine and company affirm) and, at bottom, by the growing generalization of the working-class condition and its struggle – including, of course, the struggle over working hours. This was particularly clear in the case of the French truck-drivers' strike. In late 1997, when the truckers blocked the entire country demanding reductions in their hellish working hours (over 60 hours a week), despite the turmoil the public opinion of working people was decidedly on their side. And with good reason! Neither can it be said, given the extremely low rate of unionization in France, that this massive solidarity was due to the (absolutely minimal) institutional strength of the trade unions – which, moreover, are constantly bickering among themselves.

Let us begin, then, by saying that in France too, as in Germany, the projection – more apparent than real – towards the 35-hour week is not unconnected with the action of workers. Nevertheless, I agree that it cannot be reduced to this single factor. This affair was also the expression of an ambitious political operation of the Jospin government, a *neocorporative* operation, which Martine Aubry herself presented in the following terms: 'The state has to take initiatives, offer perspectives; in short, get things *going*. The law is not enough. Labour and management have to be mobilized. Social negotiation is indispensable.'[39]

The state, representing the presumed *intérêt général* has to create the best possible conditions to assure 'the greatest possible growth', to 'do everything possible to create jobs', to bring about 'a direct redistribution of purchasing power for those most in need', and 'to re-establish the social bond' between outcasts and society. The state, the state, always and forever the state as stage manager of economic and social life! A perspective that is sub-Keynesian, for the modesty of the goals the state sets itself and of the economic means it can deploy, and at the same time sub-Durkheimian, since it has given up the dream of a general and growing social cohesion and would be happy with just binding up 'social ties' wherever they have been wounded. Still, this is an ambitious perspective, because the state aims, on the one hand, to modernize companies, supporting them in the quest for maximum labour productivity and in their effort to 'close the considerable gap regarding new technologies', and on the other to involve at least a part of the working class in this process of modernization – with a reduction of legal hours as the bait. And all this – note it well – paying no less attention to 'economic constraints' than the attention paid by the 'best of capitalists', and thus taking the greatest care 'not to endanger competitiveness' but, indeed, to increase it. What we have here is a full-fledged squaring of the circle, whose positive effects on employment and on the *real* reduction of working hours all remain to be seen, but whose positive effects for companies can, already, be clearly seen.

The railing of French capitalists against the 35-hour law cannot make us forget that a fundamental objective of the Aubry plan was to urge companies to 'raise productivity, performing the same tasks in less time'.[40] How? In the first place, by promoting and legitimating a total reorganization of working time, beginning with the criteria of its calculation. Already with the advent of the mandatory 39-hour week, and now all the more with its reduction to 35 hours, companies have undertaken a total recalculation of working time, understood – *nota bene* – not as time present in the workplace, and certainly not as time present at work plus commuting time (to which, strictly speaking, vocational training time should be added), but rather as real production time in the strict sense. The Aubry plan, with typically Mitterrandian astuteness, takes a further step in this direction.

Filoche tells us:

> Real working time still depends on article L 212–4 of the Labour Code, which itself depends on a [fascist] Vichy law of 28 August 1942. [Note that in Germany the Goering decree on working hours remained in force until 1990, and in Italy the royal–Fascist decree of 1923 on the 48-hour working week remained in force until the mid 1990s.] This is the law that deducted 'preparation time, snack time, inactive time' from working time. Even the Aubry law of 13 June 1998 refused *in extremis* ... to cut article L 212–4; it just added another paragraph specifying that real working time is defined by the workers being placed 'under the direction of the employer without being able to attend freely to their personal affairs.[41]

A masterpiece of ambiguity that effectively gives management a free hand to do whatever it likes. Filoche continues:

> Thus employers continue to make use of that paragraph written under the Vichy regime; since the law of 13 June 1998 provides for a reduction of working time,

they reduce time by recalculating it. They deduct urination time, lunch time in the factory, commuting time – times the worker cannot eliminate. They even deduct what they call 'contemplative presenteeism', which means that the workers don't always keep up with the work pace 100 per cent! Some of them happen to 'dream' on the job at times, but how can you subtract that from their real working time? The managers who are constantly calling for more flexibility become rigid when it's a question of calculating – right down to the minute – paid working time. The calculation of hundreds of millions of working hours is at stake.[42]

Indeed. Through the simple recalculation of working time, which is apparently technical but in reality fully political and based on class, capital is perpetrating an immense theft of the working time and the living time of the working class and the entire proletariat, in France and everywhere. To say nothing of the profit the capitalists pocket from the annualization of working time! Annualization permits companies to modulate hours freely, expanding or contracting them according to the demands of the market, and thus effectively to do away with overtime, which reduces labour costs and diminishes the workers' average wages, already 'spontaneously' stagnant on their own.[43]

So, the first pillar of the Aubry plan is the rationalization of working time, the maximum closing of the gap between time present in the workplace and time of real work, the maximum productivity of labour obtained by increasing its intensity. The second pillar is the further development of the flexibility of working hours, which means the dismantling of the previous regulation of hours, the greatest possible destructuring (this side of the dysfunctional) of collective hours and collective breaks (it is not only at the Renault Douai plant that they are closing the cafeterias), and the extension of segmented hours, of nightwork, of Saturday work, et cetera.[44] The third pillar is 'wage moderation' – that is, the forced acceptance of a slow decline of real wages; here, too, in full agreement with MEDEF (the French employers' federation) and the policy of the European Central Bank. The decline of the purchasing power of wages obliges workers who want to avoid a fall in their standard of living to lengthen their working time, inside and outside 'their' company. Thus we saw the Jospin government reducing legal hours with its left hand, and with its right hand creating the conditions for an increase in real hours; both with the freeze in wages and with the generalization of casualized jobs – whose greatest 'creators' are none other than the French government and state! The hard life of temporary workers, for whom 'temporary is synonymous with unskilled labour, short-term jobs and "superexploitation",[45] is an ever more present threat to the working conditions and working hours of people with permanent jobs; in France today you will not find a single workplace without 'permanent' workers side by side with 'casuals'. Finally, the fourth pillar of the Aubry plan consists of measures in favour of companies that, with the second Aubry law, are no longer even required to increase their workforce to qualify for aid.[46]

But if this is how things stand, then why have French capitalists been constantly staging protests against the government? The answer: Because they would like to have for themselves this freedom to squeeze workers at will, without even granting them the sop of the reduction of legal hours. And they relentlessly pursue their objective, taking full advantage of the weakening of the working class caused by flexibility, deregulation, casualization. They want everything and right away. This was the reason for their friction with Aubry – who, for her part, while agreeing with them *in toto* on the principles of management of a market economy, asked them for a little more far-sightedness and a certain graduality, to defuse the risk of an explosion of 'labour unrest' through a small formal concession on hours (adequately publicized), a minimal 'relaunching of consumption', and a few 'positive signals on employment'.

This is what the complex manoeuvre on the 35-hour week is all about – a manoeuvre that, far from unifying the condition of workers, homogenizing it at least where hours are concerned, is splitting it up even more. The millions of workers in small businesses, the casuals, the younger workers and most of the immigrants are all excluded. And as for the workers included, in each individual factory they will have to look out for themselves since, with the complicity of the union bureaucracies, in recent years entrepreneurs and the state have established the disastrous practice for the working class of company-by-company agreements, 'articulated' (or rather 'disarticulated') by plant, by department, by task. This is why Aubry's 35-hour week, more than planning the reduction of hours, has served to plan the disorganization of the working class, to plan its hierarchical stratification; as revealed by the fact that, right after the passage of the law, the Jospin government immediately caved in to the protests of truck owners, granting them the possibility of a particular 'adjustment' of the law by which they can have their drivers work up to 56 hours a week and 220 hours a month. For starters, that's not too bad!

So in France, yes, there is a law about a 35-hour week (even if the real working week is at least 40 hours). Still, with the decisive contribution of the Jospin government *all* the social, political, company and union conditions are coming together to create a week far exceeding 40 intense working hours in the near future, *unless* organized proletarian struggle is resumed.[47] The Raffarin administration, which took over from Jospin in September 2002, immediately raised the upper limit for overtime from 130 to 180 hours a year. But French capitalists now demand nothing less than the abrogation of the entire 35-hour law – a demand not heatedly opposed by the majority of workers, who, with good reason, have never been enthusiatic about the Aubry plan.

Apart from Britain, the only European country where this regressive dynamics is more advanced than in France is Italy – the only country besides France where there has been talk in recent years of a law for a 35-hour week. A close look at recent developments there will help bring us back from the presumed exceptions to the true rule.

The Italian Case

In Italy too, as everywhere in the West, along with the diffusion of the 'Toyota system' the 1980s and 1990s witnessed the rise of those neoliberal policies that automatically led – and this time we can say so explicitly – to an overall degradation of the conditions of wage labour also as regards working time.

The liberalization of the labour market did not take place in Italy in quite the same way as elsewhere. Up to now, there has not been the concentrated and frontal attack against the 'institutional limits' to the exploitation of labour power that we saw with the Thatcher policies in Great Britain and the Reagan policies in the United States. In Italy the dismantling of those limits took place gradually and with the participation of union leaders through the method of 'concertation' – a method that was equally devastating for the working class, if not more so. Italian capitalists were obliged to follow this longer road in order to circumvent and demolish the barriers the proletarian struggles of the 'hot autumn' of 1969 had set up against their absolute dominance – barriers constituted far more by labour organization and class consciousness than by contracts, laws and decrees. In a single fifteen-year period the sliding scale of wages was abolished; the rules of the labour market were liberalized; temporary work, fixed-term contracts, and employment agency contracts were introduced; firing practices were liberalized; and as if all this demolition of the workers' defensive guarantees was not enough, in 1993 a first step was taken in the reconstruction of legal rigidity in favour of companies, tying the growth of wages to the level of planned inflation. Thus Italy went from the 'flexible rigidity' of the 1970s (which excluded workers in small businesses) to the inflexible and 'global' flexibility of the 1990s (global, because it included also the workers of large companies). And, as was the case elsewhere, this created an ideal habitat for the intensification and lengthening of working time.

In the Italian case the official statistics are of practically no use; the picture they present of real working hours is just not credible. But in one respect things have improved. Today we do have serious researchers capable of frankly recognizing the state of affairs. Massimo Paci, for example, writes that in Italy

> The adult men are crushed by work ...; their working hours, effectively including overtime, have been practically unchanged for many years, amounting to more than 40 hours a week, and in a great many cases they work second jobs as well. We can say that the life of the Italian adult male is characterized by a 'hyper-participation' in work and by the marginality of the other spheres of his life....
>
> The women, in turn, are crushed by their household activities. And this is true both for full-fledged 'housewives' and for women who hold jobs. They appear to have even more time constraints than the men, often following atypical schedules in their jobs and in their domestic work too (increasingly done in the evenings, on Saturdays, or Sundays). This situation is getting worse today with the generalization of the so-called 'long family' [grown children who continue to live in the family home] .... In this way, working women with a child have no more than 3 hours free time a day, including Sundays (and even housewives have less than 4 hours free).[48]

But there is another side to this coin: the lack of jobs, or at least steady jobs, for young people, especially in southern Italy. So in the 'Italian case', too, we find the contradiction in the distribution of social time – so much work on the one hand, so much unemployment and casualization on the other – that millions of pages against the Marxist theory of the 'industrial reserve army' have not succeeded in banishing from the capitalist economy.

Even though it does make reference to two factors in the lengthening of average hours (second jobs and the 'long family'), Paci's portrait of the situation of working time in Italy is still somewhat static. There are many more factors contributing to the lengthening of the working day. Overtime, for example, which has been on the rise since the 1970s. In big companies, where in 1975 it amounted to 2.8 per cent of the hours worked, overtime shot up to 5.8 per cent in 1989, to a range in the 1990s between around 5 per cent and slightly more than 8 per cent.[49] And we should bear in mind that the highest levels of overtime are in the smaller firms, for which we have no official statistics. Furthermore, we have the continuing expansion of the 'underground economy',[50] which is precisely where illicit working hours are the rule; in many small businesses, in fact, overtime is mandatory and often unpaid. The rate of absenteeism has dropped sharply. Paid vacations have been cut. The first – and predictably not the last – measures have been taken to raise the retirement age. There is a rise in the number of young people who leave school before graduation or, in any event, who start working before – even long before – their eighteenth birthday.

Viewed dynamically, the Italian situation in this brave new 'age of flexibility' reveals a consolidation of the trend towards the *growth* of working time.[51] At the end of the 1980s Sylos Labini claimed that the trend towards the lengthening of hours was due to 'elements of rigidity of the labour market' and to 'workers' fear of losing their jobs'; in short, it was the workers' fault. Fifteen years later, with much of the deprecated rigidity out of the way, hours have grown even longer than before; and since, in the meantime, the blackmail of unemployment has grown heavier, workers are coerced even more than before into accepting overtime, second jobs, flexible hours, and so on. It is a true, perverse, vicious circle.

The fact, moreover, that the Italian northeast is now taken – in Italy and abroad – as a model of capitalism to come tells us that the perversion is no transitory one. And however much it may be hushed up, the fact remains that a fundamental component, if not *the* fundamental component, of the 'economic miracle' of the Italian northeast is constituted by a high tension of work and the notably long working hours – longer than the national and European average – of a labour force that is both abundant and cheap. The competitive success of the Italian northeast shatters all the trite stereotypes of recent years at one blow. This may be the postindustrial age, but the winning model is the area of most rapid industrialization and the highest rate of industrial employment. This may be the age of hyperskilled labour, but in our northeast the average levels of both skills and education are lower than elsewhere. This may be the 'end of work' society, dominated by free (or 'liberated') time, but – as luck would have it – it is also dominated, in capitalist terms, by the area where people work the most and free time is almost optional.[52]

The secret – an open secret – of areas like this one consists precisely in the 'return' not only to an intensive but to an extensive exploitation of the labour force, in the combination of long hours and intense hours. This was already evident several years ago:

> In the first place it is a question, obviously, of the great amount of overtime we find in these areas. But, even more generally, it is a question of the noncontraction of all aspects related to the intensity and length of work.
>
> For vast areas of underground production we are talking about a *working day that is normally 9 to 10 hours long* and a working week that *just as normally includes Saturdays.* We are talking about workplaces without breaks, recuperation, substitution, where there is no slackening of the intensity of work; places where union initiatives regarding the quality of labour are at a primordial stage.[53]

Once again the last word of capitalist competitiveness is the first word of old 'obsolete' Taylorism, and of Ohno's eighth (undeclared) zero: zero organized labour. And since in the meantime the competition from eastern Europe and Asia has become far more direct, the pursuit of flexible working hours is now passing all bounds. The extreme has been reached (for now!) at a small textile factory in the Po delta region, the G&B of Frassinelle, with an agreement between the owner and an autonomous union, the CISAL, that calls for an extension of the working day to 13 hours (breaks not included) and the working week to 52 hours over 6 days; that makes it possible to hire children under 15;[54] and that introduces, with a company contract, wages that are one-third below the minimum prescribed by the national contract. It is easy to predict that the lengthening of daily and weekly hours will be one of the fundamental means of resistance of small businesses that have not been able to equip themselves to compete on the world market.

But let us go down one more step in the scale of businesses, to the minuscule family craft-firms and workshops. Here we find the maximum level of the deregulation of working time and of its capacity to invade living time completely, both for self-employed workers and their employees alike. Here, working time truly knows no limits. And, once again, this does not depend upon the free choice of the workers who are directly involved, be they self-employed or employed, even though it may appear that way to them; no, it is due to the coercion exercised upon them by the ultracentralized capital that rules all the relations of the world market right down to its nooks and crannies.

The lengthening of the working time of self-employed workers, like its intensification, is imposed by outsourcing companies on their subcontractors through two ineluctable mechanisms: the reduction of delivery time (the modern counterpart of traditional Taylorist time reduction) and the fixing of prices for the semi-manufactured products to be delivered. But there is also a form of even greater coercion, which stems from the permanent condition of maximum exposure to the variations of the market that is common to all subcontractors. For them, the possibility of reducing the ever-threatening 'existential risk' of failure depends, of course, on a heightened production effort that the owners of small businesses pass on to wage labour – directly, on to the workers employed in their workshops; and indirectly, on to workers in the larger companies too, who are increasingly threatened by the outsourcing of production from their companies to these tiny subcontractors with practically unlimited working hours.[55]

Benetton is an excellent example of a multinational corporation employing a vast network of subcontractors: 227 in 1981, 507 in 1992, over 600 today. These are all small or very small firms forced to specialize in a single phase of the production cycle, and obligated – by leonine conventions – to produce almost exclusively for Benetton. For the 'mother' company the economic advantage can be expressed as follows: if 100 is the average cost of labour in Italian industry, the average price of labour Benetton pays its subcontractors goes from 65 to 70, a 'saving' of 30 to 35 per cent. And the very low wages typical of these firms is the best incentive to long hours.[56]

But the Italian northeast is not just one big laboratory of long hours; it is also an important field of experimentation in the intensification of working time. If Japanese firms usually grant their workers breaks amounting to 15–20 minutes in an 8–9 hour day, some not-all-that-small firms of our northeast can boast that they do even better! One example: in Scorzé at Aprilia, a well-known producer of motorcycles, breaks amount to 14 minutes per shift, and recently there has been conflict between management and the workers, who are asking for an additional 15 minutes of 'breathing time'. Another example: in Mignagola at De Longhi, a producer of electric appliances, the controversy has been over toilet breaks, after management collectively fined workers for taking more than the 7 minutes per shift prescribed.

At the De Longhi plant a quick survey revealed a density of working time that is simply unimaginable. The minimum number of pieces that pass through a worker's hands each day is 600, more than one per minute. The maximum is regularly between 1,000 and 1,200, two or more per minute, as with the fryers, which are assembled in 29 seconds. But even this is not the extreme limit of speed and physical and psychical effort demanded of workers, the depressing effort of paying the closest possible attention to ultra-fragmented operations that 'even an idiot could perform' (work the Japanese call *baya-yoke* – literally, 'stupidity-proof'). No, there are also periods when, to keep pace with the demands of the market or to make up for lost time, the rhythm is raised to as many as 2,000 pieces per shift, or when workers are ordered to follow the operations of two or three machines at once. In such cases workers have to combine extremely close attention with continuous motion, dashing nonstop from one place to another.

> 'There are times' – a De Longhi worker tells us – 'when they ought to pay me by the mile.' Often the pieces are too small for the robot, the work has to be done by hand, and 'you are blocked there for hours; at the end you can't even remember how to walk'.... The girls on the assembly line have average margins of work of about 12 seconds; if they skip a piece they have to work miracles and make up for it. 'Some of the women [most of the workers, in fact, are young women] have to assemble 4 screws in 10 seconds all day long.' [That means 11,520 screws per full 8-hour day, or 'only' 11,060 if we subtract 15 minutes for breaks.]
>
> The women who assemble the electric coffee-makers have to work at that speed, cutting their hands to pieces. 'You can recognize us right away', Vladia says, and shows me her hands, covered with band-aids. Over the past six years the workers' time for socializing has disappeared; the half-hour lunch break is pure fiction. And the free cafeteria does not exist: 'They've monetized that too.'[57]

Eden of long and intense hours, the northeast is also a territory in which so-called 'atypical' schedules are widespread – that is, shiftwork 24 hours a day, which is presented as short hours because it mistakes nightwork with variable schedules for the 35- or 36-hour week. Electrolux–Zanussi is emblematic. As for the destructive effects of atypical schedules on workers' health, on their possibility of socializing, and on their capacity for organized self-defence of the working class, here is the testimony of someone who speaks from experience:

> One of the very important things we used to have in the old traditional factory were the cafeteria breaks. During those breaks one person talked about soccer, someone else about politics, someone else about the union, everyone had their say. Today the worker gets to the factory, puts in his hours, leaves. There are many workers I don't know at all, because they have closed the relation with what is the everyday world.... Today, unfortunately, even our labour struggles always have to wait 3, 4 or 5 days, when all goes well, because with these schedules, our shifts, it's impossible to get together.
>
> The new work organization imposes these work schedules that are alienating. At Zanussi in Susegana the overwhelming majority take pills to sleep and pills to keep calm. This is the everyday situation. We have an infirmary that is frequented by workers all the time. There are fewer injuries, but there are always the little (or big) illnesses that lead to nervous breakdowns. We have lots of cases of people like that ..., people who are nothing but robots, and this is the fruit of this new modern company.[58]

So, the Italian northeast of the 1990s fully confirms the ongoing trends we have seen throughout the West, with its long hours, almost 100 per cent saturated and increasingly variable. But the northwest, too, is holding its own. Lombardy is competing with the eastern regions for primacy in the casualization and flexibilization of labour, with its continual increase in irregular and 'atypical' work (which in Milan now covers more than 60 per cent of new hiring); with the expansion of work done at home and craftwork; with night shifts and working Saturdays and Sundays; with 'a universal rise in hours worked'; with a fall in average real wages; in short, with an overall 'regression of the working condition' of proletarian wage labour and with greater 'misery both socially and of the forms of cohabitation'.[59]

The phenomenology of the 'post-Fordist' exploitation of labour is no less striking if we consider the more industrialized areas of central Italy, in particular as regards working hours. Over against a certain number of firms, especially in Emilia–Romagna, which have bartered continuous-cycle work for a small formal reduction of hours, we find a far greater number of firms where working hours are far indeed from the legal and contractual limits. In the textile district of Prato, one of Italy's most flourishing, many people are working over 50 – and over 60 – hours a week.[60] In the larger firms industrial relations are less fierce but the basic trend is the same, even if it takes more sophisticated forms. At Fiat–Piaggio in Pontedera the lessons of Toyotaism are no less evident than in Treviso or Melfi; the company cut breaks by 20 minutes, obligating workers to devote 10 of them (later reduced to 5) to discussions about how to improve product quality and another 10 directly to production. And what shall we say about the Upim department store in Florence, which in 1997 declared 1 May a working day for its own employees... so that other workers could do their shopping!

Moving further south presents us with an even bleaker picture, as is to be expected in areas of high unemployment. We have already seen the situation at Melfi. Elsewhere, however, we find things that are even worse – if not in terms of full-cycle plants,[61] then most certainly in the small subcontractor workshops ancillary to them, where from time to time certain situations 'just happen' to come to light. Thus in Martina Franca, in Catania, in Nereto, in Gravina, a chance inspection 'discovers' shops with unlimited and arbitrary hours, fourteen-year-old children working for less than 250 euros a month, physical violence against workers – situations that are immediately swallowed up by the darkness of the *legal* 'illegality' from which they emerged. But the most successful southern industrial district is no Keynesian kingdom 'of leisure and of abundance' either. In the Santeramo furniture industries seeing is believing. The Natuzzi corporation, quoted on the New York Stock Exchange, is a record holder in structural overtime (with workdays of up to 12–13 hours), in the control of working time, in the outlawing of any union and political activity by the workers, while the company newspaper has launched a campaign with prizes for anyone with an absentee rate of less than 2 per cent and publishes solemn praise of model workers capable of not missing a day of work in 6 years.[62]

As for the 'service' economy, in Italy too, as everywhere in the West, working time closely follows the variations in industry: both regarding its length, with the liberalization of hours in the wholesale and retail trade, which will entail their lengthening and the expansion of shiftwork; and regarding its intensity, with just-in-time systematically applied in the transportation sector, or with the extreme intensification of work at Telecom.[63] It is a unitary process where 'flexibility' leads to 'flexibility', valorization leads to valorization, in an intersectorial and international crescendo in which capital strives to remove all obstacles to its quest for profit while assimilating new methods for the extraction of surplus value.

And in Italy too, as in the rest of Europe, immigrant workers – subjected to harassment, discrimination and 'special' forms of exploitation – are systematically used as human guinea pigs for experiments in 'squeezing' methods that can later prove useful with the native workers as well. The latest gem of this differential treatment for 'races and nationalities of colour' is represented by the so-called 'pact for Milan' between the CISL and UIL trade unions and the city administration, which provides for wage differentiation for immigrants and the complete liberalization of their temporary employment. But with no 'Aryan' intent! On the contrary, with noisy proclamations against any theory of racial inferiority. So be it, but the fact remains that the immigrant workers are being used as test cases for all the pejorative innovations in the condition of *all* workers.[64]

By the same token, the south of Melfi acts as a field of experimentation for the north of Mirafiori, the northeast for the northwest, the craft shop for the corporation, industry for 'services', and vice versa. Each new day brings us some (negative) news.[65] And in a context of power relations that, for now, are unfavourable to the working class, the legal regulation of working time is increasingly distanced and mocked by the true reality of the material power relations between capital and labour, between the capitalist class and the working class. Indeed, if it is true that *legal* weekly hours have fallen from 48 to 40, that *contractual* hours actually range from 38 to 34, it is also true that *real* working hours – the only ones that really count – are sharply higher and on the rise. Real working time – depending on your estimate – ranges from 43 to 45–46 hours a week.[66] And all this is such common knowledge that the only ones who seem not to know about it are our 'experts' in economics and the sociology of labour – expert indeed, in closing their eyes before all the 'disagreeable' aspects of the workers' condition. That is to say, expert in closing their eyes before the workers' condition *tout court*.

Thus the 'Italian case' too brings us right back to our starting point. The difficulties may be great but the accumulation of capital goes on. The quantity of capital per employee, which is a good indicator of labour productivity, is increasing. The quantity of labour power in relation to the fixed capital accumulated continues to decrease. The rate of profit is once again on the rise. Yet neither technical–scientific progress nor the rise in profits is translating into a reduction of working time. On the contrary. Against all forecasts, except ours, while the chatter in Italy about a 35-hour week has vanished without trace, working time is proceeding towards... the 45-hour week. These are the facts, and not only in Italy.

In the final chapter it shall be incumbent upon us to offer some sort of explanation of this enigma.

6

Modern Times, Ancient Hours:
An Enigma?

I. THESES OF NEOLIBERALISM

In the most developed capitalist countries, as we have seen, capital forcefully opposes the reduction of working hours; indeed, there is a growing trend towards the lengthening, intensification and variability of the working time of wage labour. In this concluding chapter we shall attempt to individuate the causes of this phenomenon, which is not conjunctural.

Today's leading socio-economic doctrine is neither capable of nor interested in ascertaining these causes. For this doctrine, in all its schools and shadings, one axiom holds: within the framework of the market economy, the advances in science, technology and labour productivity must necessarily translate into free time for the mass of workers. William Grossin, expressing the dominant opinion, states: 'In the long run the effects of technology are indisputable: they translate into a decrease of the time devoted to work.'[1] But on this basis the issue of working hours as we have presented it does not exist; or, if its existence is recognized at all, the phenomenon is taken to be as anomalous as it is contingent. And doubly so since neoliberalism has prevailed over Keynesianism in the field of political economy, today the self-proclaimed 'queen of the social sciences'.[2]

Neoliberalism is the modality of political economy that has brought the 'naturalization' of the market economy to a level of radicality never attained before; where by naturalization we mean the transformation of a particular, transitory, historical form of the economic organization of society such as capitalism into an eternal, metahistorical entity, directly descending from 'human nature'. For its prophets, the market is the natural solution of *all* – not only economic – human problems, so long as it is left free to operate in its spontaneity. If this condition is met, individual freedom and social development will know no bounds. This is why submission to 'the impersonal forces of the market' (as Hayek quite rightly defines them) must be full and unconditioned, a sort of act of faith.

For neoliberalism 'free enterprise' is the visible incarnation of the market. Freedom of the market, of capital, demands absolute freedom of enterprise. This shall be the source of all good. But Heaven help us if we coerce or constrain it! No end of evils shall rain down on our heads! Unhappily, the enemies of free enterprise and the free market are legion. And one of the worst – for its senselessness (given that the Market is Reason, and something more) and immorality (given that the Market, by definition, is ethical) – is the labour movement, with its programs, its organizations, its trade unions. Crisis, debt, unemployment, inflation, all the disorders of social life – these are the scourges that the class of infidel workers brings down on society and on itself when it hinders or denies the free play of the market. But, indeed, these 'collectivist' workers are by no means the only enemies of the Free Market. What about the people who make concessions to 'collectivism', even just in the sense of 'solidarism' – which in bourgeois neoliberal opinion is equivalent to blind 'corporatism'. The market may not be absolutely perfect, perhaps, but any alternative to it will bring disaster.

If this is the theoretical framework, we can easily imagine how much room it leaves for discussion of the conditions of wage labour in general, and of the weight, length and intensity of working time in particular. For neoliberalism, the only problems of wage labour are, by definition, the problems it makes for itself, with its unjustified and irrational demands. The way, then, really to help the workers is by helping them free themselves of their sick fantasies. This is the only real problem. For twenty years now, and with some success, neo-liberalism has been engaged in this work of 'liberation', with an intensification of the competition between industrialists, between countries, between the North and South of the world and between proletarians all over the world, that has already done so much to make working hours long and heavy, and that tomorrow will lead to even fiercer forms of intercapitalist competition.

For neoliberalism, freedom of the market, freedom of capital, the freedom and well-being of society, and thus also of workers, are all the same thing. Rings of the same… chain. The improvement of working conditions can come only through the workers' total subjugation to the market and to capital – obtained with their consent or, if need be and without hesitation, with violence. We may recall that the first full-scale application of neoliberal theories took place in Pinochet's Chile – a 'horror film' produced and directed by US-American supercapitalism.[3] And some of the very first material consequences of that 'production' were the 'precariousness and instability of the source of work' and the 'disproportionate increase of the work pace, of hours, of shifts, in conditions of greater industrial insecurity'.[4]

From this quarter, then, we shall find no solution of the problem that concerns us. With the naturalization of the market, the contradictions experienced by the workers are minimized. For neoliberalism, it is *natural* that 'free enterprise' and the 'competitive order' infinitely elevate the living conditions of all 'open' societies and of all their members, workers included. It is equally *natural* that, in given conjunctures, these conditions, and especially working conditions, grow worse – due to causes extrinsic to the market, of course.[5] In either case, the freeze of hours or the intensification and lengthening of working time are *nonproblems*, destined to take care of themselves; one has only to leave, or restore, full freedom to the market. There is nothing to worry about. But *struggling* to reduce working time – against the 'moral imperatives' of the market – would, indeed, be counterproductive.

The anti-labour stance of neoliberalism is heir to a long tradition in political economy. From the opposition of the Manchester 'philanthropists' Cobden and Bright to the introduction, in 1847, of the 10-hour day, to Alfred Marshall's livid hostility to the engineering workers struggling for the 8-hour day,[6] to Luigi Einaudi's 'lessons', in 1933, to Giovanni Agnelli Sr on the disastrous character of the general reduction of working hours,[7] the message has been unwavering and unmistakable.

Things are not all that different in the ideas of Keynes and Keynesianism, whose faith in the system of the market economy is not, at bottom, less than that of neoliberalism. As Keynes tells us, 'the problem of want and poverty and the economic struggle between classes and nations is nothing but a frightful muddle, a transitory and an *unnecessary* muddle'; 'the resources and the technique' for a definitive solution are already available to capitalism, if only it 'could create the organization to use them'.[8] As for the reduction of working hours, Keynes certainly does not champion the cause; but in the ground rules of the market economy he sees no structural impediment to such reduction. In the long run, the only serious impediment to the drastic cut of working time and to its egalitarian redistribution (the 'three-hour shifts or a fifteen-hour week') is, in his view, psychological. And it does not come from capital, but from our 'old Adam' pathologically attached to his overdose of toil, who will have to be re-educated, detoxified from that morbid attachment to work, so that 'we can reach our destination of economic bliss.' The general reduction of working time thus becomes an essentially psycho-pedagogical question.

Keynes, moreover, is able to predict the real possibility of this drastic reduction of working time on the basis of the extraordinary evolution of technology. The problem, however, is that he abstracts – fatally – from the *capitalistic use* that will be made of such technology within the framework of capitalism; and thus he abstracts from the fundamental factor that keeps this real possibility from becoming reality.[9]

'Our grandchildren' of 1930 – the ones whom Keynes reassured – have white hair today, and still have caught no glimpse of anything remotely resembling that promised land of 3-hour working days. So now, thanks to Paul Samuelson, we have some fresh reassurance (even if slightly less reassuring) for 'our grandchildren' of the 1970s and 1980s:

> Historically, working hours have been progressively shortened, as we have already seen. Saturday work will no doubt become rarer and rarer in American industry. Probably there will be a trend towards increased vacations with pay – not so much because the vacation will improve workers' productivity as that people get enjoyment from summer and winter vacations. Taking more time off will probably be one of the ways in which we shall choose to enjoy the fruits of technological progress. No doubt, too, our grandchildren will choose to work a shorter week; but that should reflect choice, not necessity.[10]

These few lines, roving between the certain and the probable, give us a sample of 'social science' in the pure state. Everything is slippery, or inexact.

By what mechanism, by what social power, and in what circumstances have working hours 'been progressively shortened' in the past century? How come, in the United States since World War II, working hours have *not* been reduced, Saturday work has *not* become rarer, annual vacation days have *not* increased, either in winter or in summer, but instead have decreased? And what does it mean that our usual 'grandchildren' 'will choose' a shorter week? (No more talk here of '3-hour *days*'; note how Keynes's promise has been reduced!) Does it perhaps mean that those who 'choose' to do so may take part-time jobs, with equally partial wages? Is this what the further certain– probable 'reduction' of working time boils down to? Well, who knows? In such haze it is useless to look for more definite answers. Let us just rest assured that in the future we will all work less than today. Certainly. Indeed – probably.

Many of our contemporary 'experts' on working time, especially the sociologists, flaunt an even more carefree optimism and, at the same time, a capacity to avoid the real crux of the issue that is not less than Samuelson's. Just as an example, let us take Roger Sue (but if, limiting ourselves to France, we took Aznar or Gorz or de Foucauld, the result would be about the same). Sue is convinced we have already entered an age in which 'free time has become, by far, the new dominant time' of human existence – but we are not prepared to realize it yet. In his view, the contradiction we are faced with is *cultural*. It is only a conditioned reflex that makes 'society, in its self-representation, cling desperately to the ancient order', in which work and working time were still central.

So, if through cultural backwardness 'postindustrial' society refuses to see that there is no need to toil and moil, then one can and one must release it from its fixation with a suitable work of illumination. A new cultural paradigm – this is the cornerstone! And, along with it, a policy of promoting sectors of 'social utility'.[11] But what Sue and his ilk totally fail to consider is the fact that their indeed 'inviolable' market economy absolutely cannot stop taking immediate working time as the 'measure of all things', even if and when the measure has become obsolete historically; that it cannot do so for reasons that are organic to its social being, and not for some mental backwardness that can be taken care of with a postmodernization of people's heads. And that the law of 'utility' that rules in today's society – and accounts, indeed, for our 'high-tech' sector − is the law of the *private* utility of the accumulation of capital. No, Sue − and a host of sociologists and intellectuals like him − are not concerned with any of this.

Juliet Schor stands apart from this company of illusionists and, if I may coin the word, 'elusionists'. She sees the seriousness of the problem, and understands that resistance to the reduction of working hours comes from the entrepreneurial class and not from American workers, a vast majority of whom are in favour of such reduction.[12] Still, Schor sees the industrialists' opposition as due to their lack of trust in the workers (again, an exclusively psychological factor), or to their narrow-mindedness (again, a cultural factor), or to their having forgotten (a lack of historical consciousness?) that 'each time the working day was reduced − first to 10 hours and then to 8 − productivity rose'.[13] But the cultural, or psychological, attitudes of the owners and managers of capital do not spring *ex nihilo* into their more or less narrow minds; they are generated by the current relations of production and competition. If the capitalists and their managers so vehemently reject further reductions of hours, it is because they fear they will not be able to compensate for such reductions with a new rise in productivity capable of keeping profit levels intact.

It is true that Schor does attempt to individuate the *structural* foundation of long hours, which, she concludes, can be ascribed to the structural coercion of 'consumerism'. But then the *origin* of such coercion must be explained; instead, it is at this very point that her critical investigation breaks off. In spite of everything, she ultimately fails to extricate herself from the logic of neo-classical economics, which expelled the moment of production from its field of study. She thus ends up by individuating the cause of the lengthening of hours *outside the process of production* and outside the laws by which commodity production is governed, in an irrational consumerist craving whose rationality and *necessity* for the accumulation of capital and the social stability of late capitalism she does not see.

But Juliet Schor deserves credit for seeing what so many others have not: namely, that resistance to the reduction of working hours comes not from all of society but rather from one part − the capitalist class. And this class makes no bones about it, but justifies itself with the constraints now placed on even the most advanced countries by international competition in a globalized market. In France, in Italy, everywhere in the West, the opposition of the capitalist class to the reduction of working time even 'just' to 35 hours a week has indeed been fierce.

For a crystal-clear explanation of the by no means contingent character of this opposition, consider these words of Innocenzo Cipolletta, a leading Italian industrialist, former Secretary of the Confindustria:

> In the debate on the reduction of the legal working week to 35 hours, the stupidest thing being said is that the reduction of working hours is an inexorable historical trend that it is not worth resisting. Instead, precisely because it is a historical trend, it *tends to diminish until it peters out altogether!*
>
> In fact, a process of reduction obviously has its limit, represented in this case by the zero-hour working week. Now, I do not think anyone really believes it is possible that all the workers become rentiers who earn without working [this place is already occupied by Cipolletta and his friends], and it is even less possible to believe that on average one can work zero hours ….
>
> It is clear, then, that there is an absolute limit that we can never reach. This means that the historical trend towards the reduction of working hours (legal and *de facto*) is destined to come to a halt. When?
>
> It is hard to say; but it is sure that, before coming to a halt, the process of reduction of working hours will tend to slow down considerably. This means, for example, that if it took us forty years to go from the 48- to the 40-hour week [to be precise, it took not 'us' but the workers fifty years], then to go from the 40- to the 35-hour week *will take much longer, perhaps eighty or a hundred years.* So it is clear that the people who pay attention to historical processes and assert that the reduction of working hours is a historical trend ought to say that *by now we are not far from the lower limit* and that any further reduction will be a *very slow* process.[14]

We really have to hand it to Cipolletta for his plain speaking. Of course, his 'historical argument' isn't worth a plugged nickel. If any historical trend worthy of the name is absolutely obliged to a halt at half-mast like the trousers of a clown, then history is full of antihistorical trends, and we had better revise the very concept of history. What shall we say, in fact, about the Roman Empire's trend towards decline, which instead of stopping with Diocletian (its 35th hour) pressed right on to its zero point (with Romulus Augustulus)? And how about the trend towards decline of feudalism, which, perhaps, would have been quite happy to stop at the Reformation, the first of the bourgeois-popular civil wars, but instead went right on, very slowly for a time, before suddenly falling to its zero point with two and a half centuries of bourgeois revolutions? Cipolletta's 'historical argument' has zero force.

Yet his words reflect a solid sense of reality. Unlike all our 'experts' in sweetening bitter pills, he *knows* that the historical trend towards the reduction of working time has, in the framework of capitalism, progressively ground to a halt. We do not ask him to subscribe to our analysis, which has already been turned upside down. We realize that, being a practical man, he does not mince words; to reduce the working week even just from 40 to 35 hours will take, if all goes well, 80 to 100 years. Entrepreneurs throughout the West agree. Those of the Third World might agree too – if we add another zero, and make it 800 to 1,000 years.

It is crystal clear. And on the *causes* of this 'slowdown', once the very stupid 'historical argument' has burst? Here, we are given just one hint: surely the workers cannot live without working, as do the owners of the means of production and the catechists of private property. And they certainly cannot become rentiers, because we already have a sea of rentiers, and it is the wage labour of workers that has to maintain them. Up to here, it is still crystal clear. It is from here on that things get muddled – extremely muddled. Cipolletta continues:

> In particular, again with reference to my 'historical' observation, the reduction of average and legal working hours has always come about when there was a sharp increase of capital per employee, or, in other words, a substitution of labour with capital. This substitution made it possible to increase the productivity of labour, attenuating the implicit costs of the reduction of working hours....
>
> Today we are no longer in those conditions. Our labour market is one of the most rigid in the world ... and technical progress does not generate a sharp growth of jobs; it reduces them.

In this statement not a single term is in its proper place. Both in 1917–19 and in 1968–69, the two periods of this century in which the reduction of working hours was concentrated, the reduction *derived* from the struggle of the working class. In neither case did it derive from a sharp increase of capital per employee. Indeed, in the first case, it came in the wake of a great destruction both of capital and of 'employees'. It is true, vice versa, that the reduction of hours stimulated (as it had in the nineteenth century, with the introduction of the 12- and then the 10-hour day) a reaction of the entrepreneurs aimed at recouping – by increasing the productivity and intensity of labour – that profit margin which had been lost with the reduction of labour (of *surplus* labour) time. The increase of fixed capital per employee is far more a consequence than a cause of the reduction of working time. In any case, if the increase of fixed capital were truly the prime and automatic cause of the reduction in hours, then it would be impossible to understand why the reduction of hours has come to a halt while fixed capital continues inexorably to increase.

The second aspect of the question: empirically, it is true that technical progress does not generate sharp growth (any more), either of the economy in general or of jobs; but this occurs *everywhere*, not just in Italy, unless one resorts to doctored statistics. After 1974, the growth rate of the economy fell everywhere in the West. It would really take a colossal stretch of the imagination to blame an international phenomenon on such a scale to the 'rigidity' of the Italian labour market. There are other reasons indeed, of a general order. Furthermore, it is totally untrue that the only possibility of reducing hours is through flexibility, because – it is said – only flexibility makes higher development rates possible. The two countries of the West with the greatest flexibility, the United States and Great Britain, are the countries where hours are increasing the most. They are now on the verge of the industrial hours of the 1920s, with the 43-hour week in the United States (45 in the metalworking sector) and the 44.4 official (48 real) weekly hours in Great Britain. Indeed, these Western 'leaders' have inspired our Italian industrialists to compose a slogan: 'Work more so everyone can work.'[15]

We are left, then, with one statement of fact: Within the framework of the current social system, technical progress is no longer capable of increasing employment, or of reducing hours. What are the reasons for this harsh response of history to the promises of political economy and of the market economy? Why, right now when technical progress is enjoying such an extraordinary acceleration, is the historical trend towards the reduction of working hours braking, and at some points going into reverse? Why has it become impracticable for capital to lower the costs of production and reduce hours at the same time? In the mid nineteenth century this combination was common practice, even if the class struggle for the reduction of working hours was harsh. And it was still common – even if the social conflicts were even harsher – in the early days of Taylorism. It was even common in the last period of the thirty-year cycle of post-war development. Why, then, at least as a general solution, is it categorically denied today?

Current socio-economic thought can give no convincing answers to these questions. Indeed, in most cases it is not even capable of posing the questions themselves, precisely because it refuses to take the capitalist mechanism, the capitalist social system of production, for what it really is. Even when it makes reference to the 'laws' that regulate the movement of capital, without hiding the fact that they are well and truly laws,[16] they are seen as laws of prices, of wages, of personal consumption, of monetary circulation, or of competition between companies, never as laws regulating the specific social relation that connects capital and labour – as laws of the capitalist mode of production. But one must go back to this very relation and this very level in order to explain adequately the enigma of a working time that can no longer be substantially reduced – indeed, that often grows longer – in spite of the new technological revolution now under way.

II. FIRST ELEMENTS OF A CRITICAL ANALYSIS

Social Labour, Private Appropriation

'My' thesis – which derives entirely from Marx, if I have understood him correctly – is that the fierce resistance today of the capitalist class and the capitalist states to the reduction of working time and the international trend towards its freeze, and even its lengthening, have a very solid structural foundation. This foundation is constituted by the increased complications of the process of valorization[17] of capital; complications which are due, at bottom, to the relative reduction of the part constituted by living labour – the only source of surplus value – in commodity production, compared to the increasingly larger part constituted by technology, science and machinery (used capitalistically). It is precisely this 'progressive' reduction – which is not in contradiction with the numerical increase of the industrial proletariat on a world scale – that heightens the necessity for capital to squeeze the 'residual' labour to the utmost, in intensity as well as in duration. This necessity, in its turn, and the widening gap between the capitalist (for-profit) use of technical–

scientific progress and the reduction of working time, are rooted in the basic contradiction of the capitalist mode of production; namely, the contradiction between the *social character* of the productive labour power developed by capitalism and the *private character* of its application.

Let me say that in these few pages I shall not fully develop 'my' thesis, and thus shall not furnish a detailed explanation of the dynamics of the socio-economic processes that have led to the current situation. I shall limit myself to a presentation of the categories that, in my view, are indispensable for putting the situation into perspective and understanding it. What follows, accordingly, will be no more than the schema of a theoretical exposition of the question. It has been my aim here to let the facts speak for themselves, so that unbiased readers can get some idea of the gap between the *reality* and the current *representation* of this decisive issue for social life – the issue of working time. Living as we do in times of leaden conformity, I shall be satisfied if I can raise a few doubts and arouse some criticism with regard to the 'unquestioned and unquestionable truths' of the moment; to stir up some reaction against the status quo. But despite the priority given to the description and analysis of real processes, I certainly do not intend to shirk the duty of indicating the basic causes of the enigma 'modern times, ancient hours'. After all, the phenomenon in question is not something inexplicable, to be ascribed to the 'unfathomable mysteries of the economy' or to the 'feminine caprice' of social interaction. By no means.

In this schema I shall attempt to bring the essence of the capitalist market economy to light; any discussion about 'oddities' of working time that prescinds from this essence is pointless. One may object that this places undue weight on objective, structural, economic factors, to the detriment of subjective ones. Well, I have no difficulty in admitting the *partial* character of this treatment. Indeed, let me say that also in my examination of economic questions I shall follow a selective criterion; I shall not deal with prices and circulation, but rather with value and production. These categories, of course, are not equivalent. Value is not equal to price, nor is production equal to circulation. Yet price depends on value, just as circulation depends on production, despite more than a century of (unsuccessful) attempts to demonstrate the contrary and to substitute (unsuccessfully) the conflict between capital and labour, judged 'illusory' (by Jevons and others), with one between producers and consumers. Neither shall I deal, consequently, with the relation between value and price, or with that between individual value and social value, or with the average of the conditions of production that determine the market price, or with the role of competition in this sphere. This indispensable self-limitation is consistent with the theoretical logic underlying the investigation, and with the aim of focusing attention on the most concealed, neglected, mystified – and also most decisive – factors that combine to produce the trend towards long and heavy hours.

Consider this, then, a schema reduced by half – an A–B instead of an A–B–C of the question. I think, however, that a first reconnaissance of the material – structural – foundations of the trend that concerns us will help us understand its subjective, psychological and cultural components as well. For they are not something other than those foundations, just as the branches of a tree are not something other than the tree itself, or than its trunk or its roots.

The essential trait of capitalist production that distinguishes it from previous forms of production can already be grasped in its historical beginnings.[18] Capitalist production only really begins, Marx tells us, when an individual capitalist has enough money to bring together a large number of workers and to have them produce a large quantity of commodities – masses of money, masses of labour power and masses of commodities for a production that has to expand continually in order to make accumulation possible. The action of this 'ideal' pioneer and of his emulators, protracted in time and extended over growing spaces – the action of 'primordial' capitalism – broke the isolation of the 'private labour' proper to the forms of precapitalist production, while lending the means of labour, the labour process, and human labour power, an increasingly social character. This does not mean, however, that the socialization of labour – the development of human cooperation in the labour process – was born with capitalism, but rather that the capitalist socialization of labour, which rests on the millenary development of its precapitalist socialization, marks an extremely important historical leap. It was capitalism that showed human labour the unlimited possibilities of its own collective power, both past and present. It did so by collecting, combining and fusing many labour powers into a single collective social labour power, creating what Marx called the combination of labour powers as a collective force.[19]

This force is a result of the concentration, first of labour powers, then of the conditions and instruments of production, and, 'finally', of the incessant technical and social revolutionizing of these objective conditions of the labour process that the growing socialization of labour makes possible. Within these dynamics of the concentration–socialization of labour powers, from the ashes of handicraft production with its specific type of workshop-labour based on the production of use value, rises what Marx calls *average social labour*. This is labour for the production of exchange value (for the production of commodities, and not only of use values), which is such insofar as it is an integral part of a vast social collective combination of labour powers (whose emblem is the factory). Together with average social labour arise an average social *quality* of labour and a *quantity* – a time – of average social labour, expressions of the social working day and of its productivity in the different stages, sectors and points of capitalist development. In particular, the capitalist socialization of labour gives rise to an exponential growth of the productive force (productivity) of social labour – which is now, precisely, a *social* productive force of labour.

The effects of this cooperation between a growing number of labour powers spread in successive waves, over all forms of social production, and on all 'levels' are: division of labour within manufacturing; differentiation and competition between the different spheres of manufacturing production; upsetting of the old forms of the division of labour between city and countryside; creation and incessant perfecting of machinery; absorption into production of natural forces; separation of science and technology from the labour that generated them; continual revolutionizing of the means of labour and labour processes; scientific analysis of production and of its planning; creation of systems of machinery. The capitalist socialization of labour is a cyclone that for five centuries has been widening the scope of its demolition of old social relations and old methods of production to the four corners of the world, while arousing – in a manner *uneven and combined* – the productive capacities of associated human labour, through the centralization of capital and the reduction of the working time necessary for commodity production.

This process of the socialization of labour and expansion of the scale of production is a process that is 'possessed by a devil' – the profit of capital. Its distinctive trait is that of tending to create a 'single' mode of production on a world scale, of becoming universal, giving rise to a world market that in its various stages of development is the base and the accelerator of the *global-ization* of capitalist social and productive relations, and thus also of capitalist exchange, trade, credit, circulation – and crises.

But this formidable heightening of the power of universal social labour harbors a *genetic contradiction*. This social power is not at the disposal of society as a whole, but of one 'private' part of society – namely, capital. And what drives it is not the conscious satisfaction of human needs, but rather the chaotic satisfaction of the need of self-expansion of capital. Capital, which takes possession of the conditions of social labour accumulated over time, uses them as if they were its own qualities, its own powers, and fetters them to the particular private purpose of its own valorization – that is, of profit. This genetic contradiction of the capitalist social system, which presents itself as an objective antagonism between capital and labour (even when, on the surface, there is no shadow of such conflict), is fraught with antithetical consequences. These start with the production process, which is at the same time a process of social labour and a process of 'private' valorization, and finish with the creation of time 'free from work', which takes the opposite forms of mass unemployment and the idleness of our rentier classes, via a working time that is itself subjected to opposing tensions.

There is, then, a fundamental contradiction between the socialization of labour and the private appropriation of the conditions and products of social-ized labour. This does not mean that there is an equivalence, a permanent stalemate between the two forces; no, in the framework of the capitalist economy, capital commands (exploits) socialized labour. Collective social labour is forced to serve a private end: namely, to expand capital according to the despotic law of profit. Unless, of course, it rebels against this 'destiny'.

Capitalism, Production for Profit

The essence of capitalist production is, in fact, to be a production for profit – for a profit 'ever growing into larger quantities, ad infinitum'.[20] Profit – nothing other than profit, nothing above profit – is, under capitalism, 'the main motive force of the economic machine',[21] whose one and only factor of production (along with mother nature, which offers the raw material) is living wage labour.

Capitalist production is like an underground volcano inhabited by immense collective forces (the subterranean city of Fritz Lang's *Metropolis*). Everything is in motion. But this realm of perpetual motion is by no means a realm
of freedom, as is claimed. The class of the workers themselves, of the men and
women 'at the machines' on whose labour all social life depends, although
juridically free, are in a state of de facto subjugation. This class is engaged in
production, but neither the conditions nor the means of this production
belong to it. The only good that belongs to these former craftsmen, or former
peasants expropriated of their means of production, or their more or less
distant descendants, is the energy of labour. This is what they put – what they
have to put – at the disposal of those who possess the conditions and means
of social labour as their 'property'. 'Putting at the disposal' is equivalent to
selling their labour power, their labour time, which means their living time,
if it is true that time is 'the root of human development'.[22]

Day after day this vital human energy has to look for employment in the
market in order to reconstitute itself. It has to look for 'someone' who has the
monetary and the technical-organizational means to purchase and employ it.
And it finds this means in the class of the possessors of capital, who purchase
it (but never in its entirety, lest it put on airs as rare goods do) and put it to
work: in order that it produce commodities, and above all in order that it
produce profits. This is the purpose of the perpetual motion of capitalist
production: to expand, make fruitful, and valorize capital.

This same labour process interests capital not as a production of 'things' that
are useful for the satisfaction of genuinely human needs, but only as a means
to the process of valorization. For capital *what* is produced makes no difference
– aspirin or ecstasy, spring chickens or mad cows, copies of *Anna Karenina* or
biographies of Sarah Ferguson, delicious marmalades or napalm bombs. All
product-commodities are equivalent. What counts is that they be usefully
sellable, and that the sales make profits for the capital that produced them. And
the psycho-anthropological type of the individual capitalist – be he formal
proprietor or actual manager or both together – is the materialization of this
mode of being, of being-for-profit, of capital and of capitalist production.

> The self-valorization of capital – the creation of surplus value – is therefore the
> determining, dominating and overmastering purpose of the capitalist, the absolute
> driving force and content of his action.[23]

The individual capitalist, the individual company director, is not free to 'will' this or that, to 'do' one thing or another as he likes, any more than individual workers are free to sell or not to sell the energy of their labour. The capitalist is not free, since he is himself an instrument of the 'impersonal forces of the market' that have but a single purpose, even when they are devoted to philanthropy or to the 'nonprofit sector'. That purpose is profit, under capitalism 'the main motive force of the economic machine'.

Profit, Unpaid Working Time

What we have said thus far is, to a certain extent, self-evident. But it has brought us to the heart of the key question that concerns us: What is the substance of profit, and what is its origin?

Profit is remuneration for innovation; profit is a reward for 'entrepreneurial risk'; profit is the just gain conquered in the market by an entrepreneur who obtains a special price for his commodities; profit is the gain produced by commodities of superior quality. All are nothing but tautologies, based on two groundless premises: that profit arises in the market; and that, in one way or another, it springs from the relation between the shrewd (or informed) capitalist and the foolish (or uninformed) capitalist, or from that between seller and consumer. Instead, the commodity market is nothing but the place where profit is *realized*, not the place where it is *produced*. In the relations between capitals, considering not the individual transactions but rather their sum, gains and losses balance out; as is the case in the relations between the sellers and the buyers of commodities.[24] The only nontautological explanation of profit given by social science is that it is labour, unpaid labour, *unpaid working time*, collectively taken from the working class by the class of the proprietors of the means of labour.

The 'surplus' of (monetizable) value in which profit consists is a 'surplus' of labour, surplus labour, which wage labour (the working class) has surrendered, within the production process, to capital (to the capitalist class). This is 'surplus' with respect to the labour, the quantity of labour, the quantity of working time, that capital actually paid. An economist of the nineteenth century ingenuously depicted this 'surplus' as the last hour of the working day, which is worked for free. But for all his ingenuousness he had a sharp sense of reality. He knew the ground in which the plant of profit grew – the very thing that, for economists today, it is a point of honour to have forgotten.

Profit refers us, then, to the production process. It is here that the funda-mental social operation of capitalist society takes place, the *appropriation of unpaid working time*. How is such an operation, in open conflict with the (juridical) principle of equality, possible? It is possible because, given the material relations in force, the exchange between capital and labour is not an exchange between 'free and equal' parties. It is a socially uneven exchange, since it takes place between a class that has monopolized the means and conditions of social production and another class that is without them; be-tween a class that can buy all the working and living time it needs to expand its capital and another class that, to live, is forced to sell its working and its living time for wages; between a class proprietor of social time, of 'everyone's' time, of time *tout court*, and the class whose time has been dispossessed, the class of those 'without time'. This is the heart of the entire matter of time and of working time in society today; namely, *time is a commodity*, an object of cash transaction.

In this transaction capital is in a position of dominance with respect to labour, in social and political life in general and on the labour 'market' (a typical buyer's market) specifically. This position permits it to lay its hands on that very special commodity called 'labour power'. It is special because, while normal commodities are worth what they cost, labour power, besides having a given value, is itself a source of value. The capitalist who purchases it on the market, paying for x amount of value, in addition to that x also appropriates a power capable of producing value permanently (apart from its physical limits, which, as we have see, are elastic). This power is unique because it is capable of adding to whatever passes through its 'hands' in the production process a 'surplus' of value, a new value. The word 'hands' is placed in quotation marks because, if it is true that there is no wage-earner who is not obliged to do some form of manual labour (even working at a computer keyboard is one such form), the reference to labour power is a collective reference, to 'collec-tive social labour'. This includes both low-skilled and highly skilled workers, even if in this book attention has been focused on the great mass of 'lower echelon' industrial workers.

The 'surplus' we are speaking of is a surplus of working time.[25] Working time, the working day (be it individual or social), may be divided into two parts. The first is composed of the section that corresponds to the value of the wage. It is the working time that the wage labourer works 'for him/herself' and for his/her family, the working time that is necessary for reproduction. This is also true on a social and on an international scale. The second part is composed of the section of the working day that exceeds the value of the wage. It is unpaid working time (supplementary, or of surplus labour). In it wage labour, the working class, works for the 'other' without payment[26] – for the capitalist, or, more precisely, for capital. It is this unpaid working time that maintains the nonworking classes of society, and the capitalist class in particular. Capital would go out of business – as indeed it does – if and when this unpaid working time is lacking or even just insufficient; but it prospers when such time is abundant and grows.

The content of profit, then, is nothing other than the unpaid labour, the unpaid working time (surplus labour, labour exceeding paid working time) of the working class. And capital, which lives only to make profit, has distinguished itself from the very beginning by its relentless pursuit of unpaid working time – a pursuit that has been enriched, in the twentieth century, by its highly perfected methods of the organization and intensification of work.

Let us make this first point clear. If, under capitalism, 'the main motive force of the economic machine' is the pursuit of profit; if capital lives to make profits; if profit is composed of unpaid working time; then it follows that capital lives only to appropriate supplementary – unpaid – working time. It lives to extract – and on the condition of extracting – as much unpaid working time as possible from wage labour (and without it, capital 'dies'). That is why it absolutely cannot abandon the reference to *immediate* working time as the measure of its valorization. This it why it reacts 'growling and struggling' to any attempt by the proletariat to obtain reductions of working hours.

The Capitalist Use of Science and Technology

Today many people think such 'growling and struggling' is no longer necessary, because science and technology have become more important in the production process than the immediate labour of workers. In their opinion (take, for example, the banker–essayist Attali) it is time to shout 'Hurrah! Robots and computers have liberated the working class!' But this is both false and foolish. With the introduction of robots and computers in the workplace, the necessity of capital to appropriate as much unpaid working time as possible has by no means been superseded; neither have we seen any capitalists making new, drastic reductions of working hours. This is because, *in the context of capitalism*, science, technology and machinery do not act as powers that spread their benefits throughout society, and certainly not as powers favourable to labour; they act insofar as they are forced to do so by the powers of capital. Put in this condition, they have no possibility of giving the working class the gifts of living time of which they are capable; especially in light of the fact that the amount of living labour in relation to 'dead' labour incorporated in machinery is, in relative terms, decreasing.

Indeed, science and technology are *powers of labour*. It was universal social labour, both manual and intellectual, that created them, and it is social labour that fuels them. But these labour powers, too, have been appropriated by capital, which has transformed them into its own powers.[27] The first bourgeois philosophers of industry enthusiastically assigned to machinery, a product of science, precisely the function of dispossessing and disciplining what Andrew Ure called 'the refractory hand of labour' – the workers.[28] In exalting this 'higher' function of science and technology, in fact they were exalting the subjugation and incorporation of science and technology by capital itself, as its technical component (in fixed capital) and its arm of domination over the proletariat. This is the 'higher function' that gives the organization of the factory the despotic and autocratic stamp so familiar to the people who work there.

A century and a half after Ure, Babbage and their ilk, there has been practically no change either in the subordination of science and technology to the imperatives of profit, or in the consequences of this subordination on workers, and in particular on working time:

> Technology paves the way to the society of abundance; hence everything that is necessary to its functioning, and in particular the *subordination* of human time to that of machinery, represents the *ineluctable* price of progress.
>
> It is in the name of this [socially dominant] principle that we have accepted the negative influence of technology on working hours – the development of

shiftwork, of nightwork, of work on Sundays and holidays. The entire structure of working time has, likewise, become tighter. The paces and rhythms have accelerated. Mental fatigue has been added to physical fatigue or, in any case, has increased, which means that the greater time available outside working hours due to rises in productivity is utilized in part for recuperation and hence cannot completely be considered a benefit. Whether the workload has been increased or diminished is open to debate; but it is an indisputable sociological fact ... that almost all the workers complain about the working time currently in force.[29]

Even today the working time of wage labour, in its extension and in its intensity, is entirely subjugated to the time of machinery, to the presumably 'objective' time of technology. Before the iron necessities of this time, dictated by the iron necessities of the pursuit of profit, all the negative consequences for workers – and the 'indisputable' (and indisputably ignored) fact that the workers 'complain about the working time currently in force' – have no weight. The workers express a 'growing request for time', but this request 'clashes with the logic of the capitalist system, where the pursuit of profit presupposes an ever-growing production and sale of products'.[30]

This is how things stand. Within the current relations of production, science and technology are tools of capitalist valorization, tools for the extraction of unpaid working time. These powers of production, while indeed the offspring of intellectual and manual socialized labour, which generated and continues to regenerate them,[31] are in the hands not of the working class but rather of the fraction of society that has appropriated social capital in its entirety (including the 'capital' of knowledge that has been accumulated all over the world for centuries). This is why these powers militate against labour as extraneous and hostile forces, as regards both the *quality* of work and the *quantity* and *intensity* of working time.

As regards the quality of work, science and technology oppose living labour, setting themselves up as 'intellectual powers of production' that downgrade manual and even 'nonmanual' labour to mere appendages of machinery. This is why, as Marx tells us, 'all our inventions and all our progress seem to have no other result than that of giving life and intelligence to material powers while lowering man to a material power.'[32]

In the capitalist mode of production, machines, these '*organs of the human brain, created by the human hand*',[33] serve to mutilate human capacities of knowledge and work, making workers into 'partial men', broken into pieces like the work they do, and 'partial machines', cripples reduced to 'insignificant appendages of machines', who may be considered, at most, virtuosi of unilateral specialization. What we have said about the Taylorist and the Toyotaist factory is unequivocal confirmation that this aspect, too, is still with us today. The representation of so-called 'post-Fordist' industry as a universe made up of machinery, engineers, technicians, and just a very few superskilled workers in surgeons' spick-and-span white coats, is sheer humbug. By the same token, the microelectronics revolution, far from abolishing the standardization of mass-production operations typical of mechanization, has extended – or transferred – them to the 'logical modalities' of common labour, while radicalizing the separation between ideation and execution:

> This, in our judgement, is the least transitory and most enduring character, the real *trend*, of the microelectronic society. An increasingly widespread and high-level modelling of the labour processes, which in the capitalist mode increasingly separates the planner of new models and the operative who works within them, and which Marx called 'the separation of the mental powers of labour' [from living labour].[34]

And as regards the duration and intensity of working time, then, nineteenth-, twentieth- and twenty-first-century capitalists all ask science, technology and machinery for the very same thing: 'Shorten necessary labour time as much as possible, and lengthen surplus labour time all you can.' This request is in keeping with the logic of profit, because it asks for a saving of work, a maximum 'slimming down' of the quantity of labour power to be employed, a *substitution* of living labour. Moreover, and always with an eye for profit, it asks for a *rationalization* of the squeezing both of 'residual' labour and of the new labour that the continual expansion of production to new branches and new countries brings into the production process. First in the extensive sense, with the lengthening of hours; then in the intensive sense, with the increased density of working time; finally – and this 'finally' has lasted a century and a half – by combining the two.

This is why, today as yesterday, machinery is 'the most powerful means … for shortening the working-time required in the production of a commodity', and, simultaneously, 'the most powerful means … for lengthening the working day beyond all bounds set by human nature' and for giving it the greatest intensity possible.[35] As an agent of modern industrial production, machinery would operate perpetually and at unlimited velocity if 'it did not meet with certain natural obstructions in the weak bodies and strong wills of its human attendants'. Nevertheless, 'endowed, in the person of the capitalist, with intelligence and will', the automaton 'is therefore animated by the longing to reduce to a minimum the resistance offered by that repellent yet elastic natural barrier, man'.

But do not think, reductively, just of the 'old', and still very topical, assembly lines that went, and go, if all goes well, from eight in the morning until five in the afternoon. Think of the new continuous production cycles, 24 hours a day (and night), which are moving into all branches of industry and, even, of 'services'; or of the endless chain for the transit of commodities and people composed of supertechnological trucks, ships, airplanes, in perpetual motion and at breakneck speed, which mimics factory time in every way; or of the brand new production line of the global industry of information and telecommunications that by definition has continuous hours and functions according to that time – 'real time' – which is 'speed itself'.

Science and technology, as powers of capital, have thus come to play a decisive role in the process of the production and circulation of commodities. As a consequence, the alienated work performed by production engineers, technologists, scientists and top-echelon technicians constitutes, for capital, an important direct source of surplus value, since, however well paid they may be, they render to the purchasers of their time far more than what they cost. But the maximum of their added value is in the contribution they make to perfecting the means and methods by which capital takes unpaid working time from the muscles, hands, nerves, and (even) brains of the army of common workers. Even today, the unpaid working time of the great mass of factory labour (75 to 80 per cent of the half-billion people employed in industry, to say nothing of the workers in other sectors of production) is, in quantitative terms, capital's prime source of profit. If – hypothetically – there should ever be an industry without human beings (after two and a half centuries of industry, there is not a single plant of the sort), an industry that proceeds from beginning to end by pure input from research centres to a fully automated system of machines with no need of any control or supplementation, this dream of a few doctrinaires would be transformed into a nightmare for the owners and managers of capital. The auriferous vein mined by capital so long and so 'well' would be exhausted. At *this* point, even if capital paid hordes of scientists and technologists two-bit wages[36] and lashed them twenty-four hours a day with whips and stimulants, it could not put its golden egg back together again.

The Paradox of Labour Productivity

With the enlistment of science,[37] the capitalist class has appropriated all the benefits of technical–scientific progress, and has made working time increasingly more intense and more productive of surplus value. Nevertheless, for a certain period this progress was in fact not incompatible with the reduction of working hours. Paradoxically, it seems to have become so with the passing of time, precisely in relation to the protracted exponential growth of labour productivity. But this is to be expected in a market economy. If technical–scientific progress is ever to give its plentiful gifts of social free time to the entire society, it will have to extricate itself from the law of profit. Otherwise, it cannot but hinder the reduction of working hours even more. The reason, once again, is not enveloped in the mists of the unknowable.

Consider the historical course of capitalism. Capital started out on a local scale and with a low organic composition,[38] while its vocation is to realize itself as a *worldwide* mode of production, expanding its form of fixed capital 'ad infinitum', along with the productivity and socialization of labour. In the early stage of capitalism living labour directly supplied by workers overwhelmingly prevailed over the dead labour incorporated in machinery. Machinery was still 'alongside' living labour, a helper for the worker. The amount of surplus labour time was rather small. In *Capital* Marx hypothetically, and not arbitrarily, supposed that the working day of wage labour was divided in two halves: 50 per cent necessary labour, 50 per cent surplus labour.

Precisely because the unpaid part of this working day was relatively limited ('just' 50 per cent of total working time), the length of the working day was still particularly long (10 to 12 hours, or more), and the intensity of labour was still rather bland, capitalists had ample margins to increase the section of working time that contains their profit. Indeed, the margins were so ample that, despite fierce social conflicts, while the overall duration of the working day diminished the surplus labour time of workers increased.

Marx himself observed how British industry went from the unlimited working day to the 12-hour day, and then after 1848[39] to the 10-hour day, with no fall in production. In a certain sense, the transition from a furious plundering of labour power to a plundering 'in instalments' could in fact be to the advantage of the capitalist class (even though the individual capitalists opposed it), since '[the] lengthening of the working-day becomes compatible only with a lower degree of intensity, and a high degree of intensity, only with a shortening of the working-day.'[40]

The last major reduction of the working day was obtained by the working class in 1917–19, with the conquest of the 8-hour day. Since then, there has been an enormous concentration–centralization of capital, an unequalled rise in the degree of intensity of labour, a relentless perfecting of production machinery (now it is living labour that stands 'alongside' the machine), and a universal diffusion of capitalism; and despite all of this, the epoch of the 8-hour day gives no sign of fading. The historical course of the working day is thus highly irregular. At least in Britain, the transitions from unlimited hours to the 12- and then to the 10-hour day were relatively rapid. By contrast, the transition from the 10- to the 8-hour day was much longer and more arduous (it took a cycle of revolutions to make it possible). And nearly a century later the 'less ambitious' transition from the 8- to a 7-hour day, still incomplete and far from the goal, has again been branded as rank folly.

The problem lies in what we said earlier: The more the part of the working day that corresponds to wages has been compressed, and the more the length of the working day has been reduced, the more difficult it becomes for capital to recoup in labour productivity and intensification (now extremely high) any further contraction of nominal working time. The solution of the paradox is in the conflictual relation between the productivity of labour (which is *social*) and profit (which is capitalistic, and therefore *private*). In the socio-economic conditions of today labour productivity has to serve profit, but it comes up against a serious objective barrier: namely, the amount of working time of wage labour that has already been expropriated; or, expressed differently, the immense quantity of fixed capital compared to variable capital.

Marx summarizes, in theoretical terms and with extraordinary foresight, the decisive question of the relation between labour productivity and profit (surplus value), between capital already accumulated and its further valorization:

The larger the surplus value of capital *before the increase of productivity*, the larger the amount of presupposed surplus labour or surplus value of capital; or, the smaller the fractional part of the working day which forms the equivalent of the worker, which expresses necessary labour, the smaller is the increase in surplus value which capital obtains from the increase of productivity. Its surplus value rises, but in an ever smaller relation to the development of the productivity. Thus the more developed capital already is, the more surplus labour it has created, the more terribly must it develop the productivity in order to valorize itself in only smaller proportion, i.e. to add surplus value – because its barrier always remains the relation between the fractional part of the day which expresses *necessary labor*, and the entire working day. It can move only within these boundaries.... The self-valorization of capital becomes more difficult to the extent that it has already been valorized.[41]

Let us take an example. Suppose that the fraction of the average (8-hour) working day corresponding to wages is, today, 2 hours (1/4), that another 2 hours are taken by the state,[42] and that capital is left directly, on average, with 'just' 4 hours of labour per day per worker. All other conditions being equal, if there is a sharp rise in labour productivity, say, 100 per cent (approximately the rise in Italy over the past twenty years), the increase in unpaid working time will by no means amount to 100 per cent but to just 25 per cent; the rise will 'only' be from 4 to 5 hours. And things would be 'even' worse, for capital, in the case where the value of the wage and of the part taken by the state had already been cut in half; reduced, that is, from 2 hours to 1 hour each (it is quite probable that the average situation in Western countries today is close to this threshold). In this case, a second 100 per cent rise in labour productivity would increase unpaid working time by a 'paltry' half-hour ($\frac{1}{16}$ more, instead of $\frac{1}{8}$).[43] In sum: there are big problems about raising a labour productivity that is already high, and even bigger problems about translating this rise into a rise in profits, with *falling* gains of unpaid working time, since in general the value of capital rises in far lower proportions than does the productive force (the productivity) of labour.

Perhaps Ohno's obsession with reducing to zero the part of total work that is not 'value-added work', a goal that Taylor himself could never even have conceived of in this form, can now show itself, in its structural foundation, for what it really is: namely, a universal – not merely 'Japanese' – response of the monopolist proprietors and the managers of 'added value' to the increased difficulties of valorization.

Some 'physical' data regarding Fiat Auto. In 1900 fifty Fiat employees produced 24 cars per year, just under half a car each. It took thirty-five years to reach the threshold of one car per year per employee. In 1949 the figure was still only 1.3 cars each, but it rose to 3.3 in 1955, 5.7 in 1960, 8.4 in 1970. In 1980 it shot up to 19, and in 1993 to 44 (at Mirafiori). But just three years later at Melfi over 64 cars per employee were produced. In physical terms, the rise in the productivity of factory labour since 1890 was 8,800 per cent if based on Mirafiori/1993, and 12,800 per cent if based on Melfi/1996. Compared to 1949, we have *circa* +3,400 per cent for Mirafiori and just below +5,000 per cent for Melfi. Even though the calculation in terms of value cuts these percentages considerably down to size, it can still give us an idea of how much the part of the working day in which Fiat employees work exclusively for the company has grown. Of course, their real wages have also grown, but even today, for an unskilled factory worker, they amount to 800 to 1,000 euros a month (for shiftworkers), not far above survival level. But if there has been no exponential growth of wages, company output (just in the postwar period) grew from 150 billion lire in 1950 to 50,550 billion lire in 1997, while the number of employees rose slightly more than 50 per cent (71,000 in 1952, 118,000 today) and the product per employee skyrocketed from 2.5 million lire in 1950 to 420 million lire in 1997.[44]

This represents bloating of fixed capital, resulting from the capitalist use of science and mechanization, and from the rise in labour productivity. As we have seen, the growth of fixed capital (plants, machinery, raw materials, amortization, etc.) is never proportional to the growth of labour productivity; nevertheless, over time it has been enormous. The centre of gravity of the accumulation of capital has shifted from living to objectified labour (since – note it well – fixed capital too is the fruit of labour; it is *accumulated labour*). This change in the composition of capital heightens the potentialities of social production on one hand while heightening its contradictions on the other, since, in any case, the profit of capital continues to be measured in terms of the profitability of the 'subjective' factor of production, i.e. of living labour, whose objective weight within capital is in (relative) *decline*.

This has had a series of consequences, denied by today's dominant economic theory but inexorably highlighted by the reality of the global economy: above all, the progressive fall in the general rate of profit (fully documented for the period 1950–82 even by the official statistics, and to which capital reacted with its neoliberal policies); then the widening gap between production and consumption, and thus the increasing possibility of overproduction (countered by the monetary authorities with systematic curbs on development); then, the heightening of the conflict between our increased knowledge of nature and the use of that knowledge for the private plunder and consumption of nature itself. And so forth. At the root of it all, inescapably, there is a heightening of the antagonism between the forces of social labour and the increasingly antisocial force that privately appropriates them.

This also accounts for the tendency of capital systematically to compress (in 'lean' production) employment levels in order to produce more with less labour. The latest fashion on Wall Street, the soaring of a stock price at the first hint of 'corporate killers' preparing for mass firings, just shows how important it is for the market that a company be capable of squeezing an increased quantity of surplus value from a decreasing (in relation to accumulated capital) mass of labour power. And it is in the newest sectors, where technological innovation is most rapid, that this process has greatest dynamic force; it is there that companies are particularly loath to reduce hours and do what they can to lengthen them, in order to compensate for the reduced number of employees and to amortize their large capital investments as quickly as possible.

The growth of mass unemployment in the past twenty-five years is so glaring that it is the only one of the phenomena we have considered that almost everyone empirically admits. Thus the functionaries of the Bureau International du Travail speak of years of 'rarefaction of the possibilities of regular employment'; Dahrendorf speaks of 'underemployment' as the 'true scourge of the late society of work' (I would say 'of late capitalism'); economists and sociologists note a rise in the rate of 'physiological unemployment', even if, simultaneously, many of them caution against 'dramatizing' the 'unemployment experience';[45] Leontiev goes so far as to consider the long-term rise in unemployment to be an almost natural effect of the diffusion of labour-saving technology; Rifkin predicts the imminent 'end of work'. None of them says, however, that this growing mass of unemployed and casual workers, from the First to the Third World, is the result *not* of technical–scientific progress as such, but of its subjugation to the profit motive. None of them says, or says with sufficient clarity, that the expansion of worker overpopulation and of pauperism is the other side of the intensification of work and the extremely high productivity of labour, and – also – of the trend towards longer working hours. None of them says that the logic of the market economy produces a twofold dissipation of the labour power of society. On the one hand, it squeezes to the utmost everyone employed in the production process; on the other, it consumes in total or partial inactivity everyone who is excluded.[46] While it saves labour, it destroys, in two different ways, human labour power.

This is the paradox of the growth of labour productivity under capitalism. The more the function and the quantity of living labour in the immediate process of production are reduced to a minimum (reduced, not eliminated!), the more working time approaches maximum density, the more the part of the working day that corresponds to wages is reduced – the more the further growth of labour productivity hinders the increase of profits, on the one hand, and the reduction of working hours and of mass unemployment, on the other.

While capitalist society is an extraordinary producer, in general, of time free from work,[47] it has certainly given the lie to Keynes when it comes to making 'what work there is still to be done to be as widely shared as possible' (his 'three hours a day' for everyone). Indeed, it has moved in the opposite direction. With the increase in the productive power of social labour, 'worker overpopulation' (the mass of workers who cannot find steady employment) also increases, and in the working class the division between the overworked and the out-of-work tends to become chronic. On a social scale, by contrast, we find an enormous rise in unproductive consumption, destructive consumption, and gilded and empty idleness typical of the rentier. Thus the society of maximum rationality in the use of human labour is also a society in which the waste of human labour is taken to the extreme (in the circulation of commodities, in the stifling domestic life of women, in excess production, in the many forms of harmful and antisocial production, in militarism, etc.). And the society of hyperproductive (hyperprofitable) labour and long working hours is also a society in which two phenomena typical of decadent feudalism are making their reappearance: namely, rampant social parasitism[48] and rampant unemployment–casualization.[49] All this, while the length of the working day has been frozen for nearly a century, and the length of the working week for over twenty-five years.

This 'irrational' distribution of time free from work generated by technical–scientific progress is itself also an effect of the law of profit. The systematic propensity of capitalists to encourage consumption rather than a reduction of working hours[50] can be explained by their need to expand incessantly the mass of production (the mass of surplus labour) while compressing, in relation to it, the number of workers employed (the total time of necessary labour). If they did the opposite, they would raise the costs of production while compressing both the mass of profits and – even more – the rate of profit, exactly 'that for which and by which they live'. The expansion of the consumption of commodities – which, again, is not free but is determined from outside the individual,[51] industrially organized and planned – is an extremely important factor of social stabilization, of reconfirmation of the social order by means of the apparent – alienated – fulfilment of the human expectations and needs that are compressed or denied in working life.[52] However, that general and growing difficulty of valorization whose genesis and portent we have attempted to show is beginning to affect the very possibilities of consumption itself. The 'rewards' of growing consumerism are no longer beyond dispute. Indeed, our superconsumer, the USA, foresees a 'mean season' for the working class, and a pretty mean one for a fair slice of the middle class as well.[53] The only way to avoid reducing consumption, we are told, is by *more* people working more and in conditions of greater casualization.

Globalization and Working Hours

So, our friend Innocenzo Cipolletta is quite right when, unwittingly eavesdropping on our Marxist vocabulary, he says that the historical trend in the reduction of working hours '*tends* to diminish until it peters out altogether'; or that 'we are not far from the lower *limit*' of the historical process of the reduction of working hours, which, if it continues, will be 'very slow'.[54] Things *tend* to approach a *limit*...

This is perfectly true. In the West resistance to the reduction of nominal daily working hours, and subsequently of weekly hours, has *tended* to increase for several decades, and, on an ever greater scale, to turn into its opposite.

And the structural causes of such resistance become all the clearer if we observe the so-called process of the globalization of capital, which is just another name for that process of the accumulation of capital which we have considered up to now from the side of labour productivity and technical–scientific progress.

Capital's impulse towards globalization is far from new. From the very beginning it has been an organic characteristic of capitalism to tend to produce a growing mass of commodities so that the 'surplus' value that results (with respect to the capital advanced) is large enough to ensure its at least partial reinvestment as added capital. In fact, the unlimited enlargement of the scale of production is no less constitutive of capitalism than is the socialization of labour. Creating a world market and expanding it continually is an 'immanent necessity' of capital,[55] a compulsory stage of its development and, at the same time, the end point of its evolution.

The international division of labour produced by this impulse of capital is the basis for the global (neither harmonic nor complete) socialization of the forces of production – the *capitalist* basis, of course, marked by the contradictions typical of this mode of production. Accordingly, this has never been a process of universal cooperation between 'free and equal' parties, but rather an antagonistic process of subjugation, expropriation and exploitation of 'backward peoples' by the most concentrated Western capital – European capital in particular. Skimming the centuries and skipping over the most distant period of primordial European accumulation, we can distinguish two phases of this process.

The first phase was the one of historical colonialism. In that phase, Western capital provoked the universal ruin of the small independent producers of the colonial countries, thus securing a market for its own industrial production while using these countries as a source of agricultural and industrial raw materials and, in part, of low-cost labour power. This phase concluded with the great democratic revolutions of 'peoples of color' throughout the world, culminating in the birth of modern bourgeois nations and the inception, even on the 'periphery' of the world market, of capitalist socio-economic relations.[56]

The second phase is the one (in progress) of financial colonialism, in which ultracentralized capital in the West (multinational corporations, the

IMF, Western states, stock exchanges, etc.) permits and, to a certain extent, stimulates the development of capitalism in the rest of the world; apart, of course, from keeping it strictly subordinate to its own priority interests, and nipping in the bud any ideas of full independence from the 'centre.' For Western capital *direct* recourse to the plentiful and low-cost labour power of the dominated countries serves to fuel, with its overprofits, a valorization that is beginning to gasp for breath.

In the course of this process of the expansion of capitalist accumulation and capitalist social relations on a global scale, a phenomenon that characterized the development of Western capitalism in the past is constantly renewed with different protagonists. That is, the countries that come from behind have the advantage – as the United States did with respect to Great Britain, then Japan and Germany with respect to the United States, and today China and the other Asian countries with respect to the West. This is so because they start out with a lower degree of organic composition (less fixed capital, more variable capital), and also because, with great efforts, they can reap the benefits of the peak that has been attained by labour productivity and technical–scientific progress.

The overall result of this twofold drive to industrialization, from the 'centre' and from the 'periphery', is, in the first place, to swell the ranks of the industrial proletariat; and, in the second, to integrate the two extreme poles of the global market. This, moreover, is an increasingly competitive integration in which, if the more centralized capital can wield the formidable arm of its accumulated technical–scientific knowledge,[57] the younger capitalisms of the Third World can, in turn, respond with their own powerful arm of a huge mass of living labour (the source of all surplus value). Obviously, then, the great Western powers that dominate the global market will use all the economic and non-economic means at their disposal to appropriate the competitive advantages gained by these 'newcomers', driving them back while benefiting from the progress they have made.[58]

At first, the *two* working days that correspond to the 'centre' and to the 'periphery' are very different from one another. The first is shorter and, due to its enormously greater intensity, produces on average more surplus value, despite the second's far greater length.[59] In time, however, the difference tends to diminish, due to the rapid rise – together with the rate of accumulation –

in the intensity and productivity of the working day on the 'periphery', while its length contracts only slightly. China, South Korea, and the other most dynamic Asian countries in particular have forged ahead, accomplishing in fifty years what in Europe took over two centuries.

This new drive linked to the global expansion of capitalism, on the one hand, has managed to resolve certain difficulties of the process of accumulation, but, on the other, has come up against new and greater difficulties of capitalist valorization. A greater productive drive, in fact, cannot fail to produce a new rise in the organic composition of capital, which entails a relative reduction of the part that living labour has in production. And, as we have seen, the only (provisional) way out of this situation for capitalism as a system, be it in the 'centre' or on the 'periphery', is to squeeze wage labour even more systematically, imposing a working time of even greater density and duration.

Looking at the present situation, it would be impossible to overestimate the consequences that the globalization of financial flows (the latest aspect and degree of the globalization of capital) is having and will have on working conditions and hours. Consolidating the 'systemic unity' of global capitalism, a 'differentiated and hierarchized' unity,[60] such globalization goes on, simultaneously and on the same scale, to reorganize all the sectors of international social production in the interest of the greatest concentrations of capital. From the textile to the metalworking sector, from electronics to accounting services for corporations,[61] to the production of tourist ships, the oligopolistic power of transnational corporations does everything possible to increase the mass of its profits and raise its profit rate. It aims to bring, under its control, manufacturing production to countries of the Third World where an extremely high rate of exploitation of labour is possible, and on the condition that it be possible. At the same time it uses this expansion to cudgel the 'guarantees' of industrial workers back in the West, bludgeoning them into accepting the fact that the 'good old days' are gone forever.

Thus the distance between the 'marginal' and the 'central' areas of the global economy is shrinking. The working conditions and hours in Western industry (and, gradually, in services too) increasingly *depend* on the working conditions and hours that globalized capital manages to impose on the workers of the 'periphery'. And vice versa.[62]

The textile sector was the first branch of production to have this experience, due to the degree of international integration it had attained. It is certainly not fortuitous that this is the sector of Western industry where we find the lowest wages, the most 'atypical' hours, extremely intense work rates, an extremely high percentage of female workers, and, in the larger firms, the most widespread recourse to craft workshops, to subcontractors, to work done at home, to payment by piecework. And the entrepreneurs of the sector 'want to go even further in their attempt to attain greater flexibility, demanding more weekend work, more continuous shiftwork, more nightwork for women, and more planning of part-time work.'[63]

Despite its incomparably greater technical rigidity, the Western automobile industry is rapidly moving in the same direction, both on the 'periphery' and in the 'centre'. In the vanguard we find a corporation from the 'different' Europe – Volkswagen, the most 'different' of them all, our model of 'short hours', which created at Resende, in Brazil, a 'dream factory', organized as follows. Out of 1,000 employees, only 200 – in quality-control, marketing, and research and design – are directly employed by Volkswagen. The other 800 (the totality of the production workers) work for their many subcontractors. A single assembly line is divided into a number of sections, operated by different firms, so that these firms (and their workers) may compete with one another to see who is best at lowering costs while raising the reliability of the product. The pay is 'about a third of what the auto workers get in São Paulo'. In short, 800 workers now have to produce what 2,500 workers were producing before. Working time – in shifts, of course – follows the criterion of just-in-time, with one innovation: whatever the reason for which the line stops, the time has to be made up at the workers' expense, without overtime.[64] This dream factory *for dream profits* was inaugurated in the autumn of 1996. 'Just by chance', less than a year later at 'far away' Fiat Mirafiori, subcontractors for work previously done by Fiat workers and outsourcing of new work first made their appearance.[65]

The rebound effects of the worsening of working conditions and hours from the 'periphery' to the 'centre' do not stop here. They have now hit electronics, optical manufacturing, the iron and steel industry, work in the ports, tourism, and so forth. But what particularly interests us is the fact that this process is taking the shape of a double spiral. It is true that Western capital is trying to make the Western working class pay the consequences of the 'competition' of Third World workers, but the more it succeeds in doing so, the less it is satisfied with the 'natural' conditions of exploitation it finds today in the Third World. Thus with the eager cooperation of the 'peripheral' capitalists and their respective states, it is attacking the progress that has been made by the working class of the dominated countries – in all fields, working time included. Examples? Take your pick; since the crisis of the 1970s they have been countless. Pinochet's Chile (and post-Pinochet Chile), post-Peronist Argentina, post-*Intifah* Algeria, Mubarak's Egypt (where, according to the official statistics, the working day is an hour and a half longer than in Nasser's day),[66] the post-Stalinist regimes of eastern Europe – all of them have been responsible for an exponential worsening of the conditions of the exploited masses.[67] And no small part of this has involved the abolition of any real, and sometimes any legal, limitation of working hours. And then, what shall we say about the 'globalization of poverty' policies of financial institutions such as the IMF and the World Bank?[68] What about the new crusade of these 'humanitarian organizations' against the workers of state-owned companies in China or in Vietnam, because they earn too much and work too little?[69]

There is, indeed, a great deal still to be said. But suffice it to say, for now, that if we widen our field of observation from the West to the entire world, as is only right, since we live in an entirely globalized economy, then the enigma of ancient hours in modern times proves even less enigmatic.

Notes

Introduction

1. See J. Seager, *The State of Women in the World Atlas*, London: Myriad, 1997, comment on Plate 20 (my stress).
2. Just one example: in Milan and its hinterland, the centre of Italian industry, 92 per cent of firms have fewer than ten employees. What do the official statistics know about the working hours in these firms?
3. See *Croissance*, no. 428, July–August 1999, pp. 34–5 (the article is by C. Besson). Note how there is not the slightest hint of possibility that workers in their free time may take part in union, social or political activities. For the same general picture, with some additional detail, see the article by M. Hunter, 'US workers demand "quality time"', *Le monde diplomatique*, November 1999 (English edition).
4. We owe this foolish commonplace, and mystification, to D. Mothé, *L'utopie du temps libre*, Paris: Esprit, 1997, who nonetheless, unlike Gorz, Aznar, Sue, Méda and friends, at least knows that 'free' time by no means has an automatically 'civilizing' and egalitarian effect, in the context – I add – of the market economy.
5. See L. Mishel, J. Bernstein, and J. Schmitt, *The State of Working America 1996–97*, Armonk and London: Sharpe, 1997, pp. 131–239; and *The State of Working America 1998–99*, Ithaca and London: Cornell University Press, 1999, pp. 121 ff., 380 ff.
6. See E. Luttwak, *Turbo Capitalism*, London: Orion, 1999, p. 188. This author goes so far as to write: 'It is a fact that US wages have been slowly converging with Third World wage rates, having long since fallen much below German and Japanese wages' (p. 62). As recently as 1971 Nixon could boast that the real wage of a US worker was approximately double that of the wealthiest competitor.
7. It is interesting that McDonald's is defined by one of its executives as a company that 'bases its organization on the flexibility of hours' (M. Resca and R. Gianola, *McDonald's. Una storia italiana*, Milan: Baldini & Castoldi, 1998, p. 103). At

McDonald's working hours can be modified at the discretion of management 'even without the written consent of the worker' (*il Sole 24 ore*, 15 July 1998). More generally, as R. Sennet has noted, in flexible capitalism common labour has no 'quality' (see *The Corrosion of Character*, New York and London: Norton, 1999).

8. K. Moody has pointed out that in the United States 'overtime and downsizing have gone hand-in-hand in the 1990s' (*Workers in a Lean World: Unions in the International Economy*, London and New York: Verso, 1998, p. 95).

9. K. Moody, *An Injury to All: The Decline of American Unionism*, London and New York: Verso, 1998; C. Sauviat, 'Un syndicalisme affaibli', *Chronique internationale de l'Ires*, no. 58, May 1999, pp. 24–32.

10. See H.P. Martin and H. Schumann, *Die Globalisierungsfalle. Der Angriff auf Demokratie und Wohlstand*, Hamburg: Rowohlt, 1996.

11. See European Foundation for the Improvement of Living and Working Conditions, *Second European Survey on Working Conditions*, ed. P. Paoli, Dublin, 1997.

12. As reported by J. Goytisolo and S. Nair in *El Pais*, February 2000, thousands of Moroccan labourers at El Ejido, in Andalusia, are forced to work as many as 16 hours a day for extremely low wages and in terrible working conditions (in continuous direct contact with pesticides). And when they went on strike they were, literally, threatened with lynching.

Chapter 1

1. See A. Toffler, *The Third Wave*, New York: William Morrow, 1980; J. Gershuny, 'La répartition du temps dans les sociétés post-industrielles', *Futuribles*, no. 165–166, May–June 1992, p. 215 ff.; R. Sue, *Temps et ordre social*, Paris: PUF, 1995.

2. See, for example, the chapters by G. Olini in *Tempo di lavoro e flessibilità dell'orario*, Rome: Cnel, 1993, pp. 15 ff., 69 ff., 105 ff. Nearly all the literature coming from the unions may be placed within this school, or alongside it – and it contains a great many contradictions. We find quite an assortment in the afterword by A. Lettieri, '…ma i tempi di lavoro sono cambiati', to the book by B. Ugolini, *I tempi di lavoro*, Milan: Rizzoli, 1995, pp. 127 ff. The author recognizes how in the past fifty years 'legislative and contractual progress' regarding working hours has been '*next to nothing*'; he sees a trend, not only in the USA, towards longer hours; he sees the 'undeniable contradiction' between the stagnation or even growth of industrial hours and the new industrial revolution that took place in the meantime, but takes no pains to explain it. Indeed, he makes the question all the thornier, maintaining that in any case there has been a reduction of hours, which, however, took place 'outside the rules', with… an increase in the periods of part-time work and 'full unemployment'. A curious way of squaring the circle.

3. For a lively description of the 'overwork fever' that pervades the high-tech world of Silicon Valley, see *Le Nouvel Observateur*, 30 April–6 May 1997, pp. 14 ff. The article tells, among other things, of an executive who, to test 'his' middle managers' degree of company devotion, sent them an email on Saturday at two in the

morning, and received an immediate reply from every one of them. Here the 'love of work, but also of money' has already transformed all living time into potential working time. It is not hard to imagine how middle managers (technical or not) with this sort of training must treat 'their' white-collar and blue-collar workers.

4. The cultured conformist, reading this, will exclaim: 'But how can one possibly claim to *explain* social phenomena and – no less! – to individuate the *causal relations* that determine them?' It is not in my power to prevent such questions, nor do I wish to. This, however, is not the place to give a full reply. I have, rather, to confirm the conformist's impression: this, in fact, is no conformist book. And if, as a consequence, the conformist reader wishes to bid us adieu, how, indeed, shall we stop him?

5. See J.B. Schor, *The Overworked American: The Unexpected Decline of Leisure*, New York: Basic Books, 1991.

6. This is the case with the monograph of *Politica ed Economia*, February 1994, pp. 39 ff., dedicated to working time, which includes an essay by Schor, 'Come redistribuire il dividendo della tecnologia', dealing in part with the themes of *The Overworked American*.

7. Schor, *The Overworked American*, p. 4. She goes on to say, in amazement, *'Despite the fact that worktime has been increasing for twenty years, this is the first major study to explain or even acknowledge this trend'* (p. 5, author's stress). It should be remarked, however, that several authors, from different points of view, had previously noted the stability of working hours in the United States since World War II. Besides the authors and studies cited in Chapter 2 below, see, among others: S.B. Linder, *The Harried Leisure Class*, New York: Columbia University Press, 1970; J.D. Owen, *Working Lives, Working Hours: An Economic Analysis*, Lexington MA: Lexington Books, 1979.

8. Schor, *The Overworked American*, p. 5.

9. See ibid., pp. 1, 29–30, 163, 217 n. 4. The author refers to the total amount of hours worked ('market plus nonmarket'), which for full-time employees in 1987 came to 2,837 for the year, 162 more than in 1969. If we add 162 hours to that figure for the following twenty years, we come up with 2,999 hours (60 hours a week for 50 weeks). For the figures on the previous rise in working hours, see L. Leete-Guy and J.B. Schor, *The Great American Time Squeeze: Trends in Work and Leisure, 1969–1989*, Washington, DC: Economic Policy Institute, February 1992, p. 2. It should be emphasized that this total also takes, correctly, the hours of household work into account as working hours (indeed, as *unpaid* working hours); as a result, a woman's part-time job is taken for what it really is – namely, an *increase* in her overall working time. Usually, instead, the diffusion of part-time work is taken, the wrong way round, for an aspect of the trend towards a reduction of working hours, and is used statistically for that purpose.

10. Schor, *The Overworked American*, p. 163.

11. Ibid., p. 15. Stress due to overwork is such a common experience in the USA

that it has become a popular theme in comic strips. One of them (S. Milzer, *Going Postal*, New York: Random House, 1997) became a bestseller, and with no need of any great promotional campaign; to launch it into orbit the universal experience of everyday work was quite sufficient.

12. See Schor, *The Overworked American*, p. 107.

13. See ibid., in particular chs 3 and 6.

14. Ibid., p. 153.

15. 'The sovereign image of time is that of the quantitative time of industrial production, the time of wage labour, organized according to the logic of productivity' (S. Tabboni, *La rappresentazione sociale del tempo*, Milan: Angeli, 1984, p. 81).

16. See V. Capecchi, 'Flessibilità e rigidità dei tempi sociali: un primo confronto tra Giappone ed Europa', in M.C. Belloni, ed., *L'aporia del tempo*, Milan: Angeli, 1986, pp. 170–71. For the USA, see D. Costa, *Less of a Luxury: The Rise of Recreation since 1888*, NBER Working Paper no. 6054, June 1997, which examines the long-term trends. Costa reports that for male workers expenditure has fallen for reading material (it reached its peak in 1917), for the cinema and 'light entertainment' (which peaked in the mid 1930s), and for (nonspectator) sports (the peak was in 1972). On the other hand, since World War II the expenditure for home entertainment (television) has literally exploded. In 1985 television absorbed 47 per cent of the 'recreation' time of the low- and medium-low-income social classes. Costa's triumphalistic reading of this process is, evidently, worlds apart from mine.

17. P. Bourdieu speaks of 'predigested cultural food' – a pretty heavy metaphor (*Sur la télévision, suivi de L'emprise du journalisme*, Paris: Liber–Raisons d'agir, 1996).

18. See *ISTAT Notizie*, Year II, no. 14, 31 July 1997, pp. 1–3, which gives a full report of the figures regarding 'shadow employment' furnished by the president of ISTAT in the course of a parliamentary hearing. From 1980 to 1996 the section of social production in which 'undocumented' (i.e. illegal) employment increased the most was industry, where it rose from 16.5 to 20.1 per cent (one employee out of five).

19. See F. Schneider, 'Empirical Results of the Size of the Shadow Economy of OECD Countries Over Time', unpublished working paper, September 1997 (text received directly from the author, whom I thank). Germany went from between 3.6 and 4.3 per cent in 1970 to 13.1 per cent in 1994, France from 3.9 to 14.3 per cent, the United States from between 2.6 and 4.6 to 9.4 per cent. The criterion of calculation is the one based on currency demand. The area of 'shadow' is even broader in the Eastern European countries: 32.8 per cent in Poland, 31 per cent in Hungary, 28.6 per cent in Croatia, 22.3 per cent in Slovakia (cf. Table 1.2; in this case the calculation is based on the consumption of electricity).

    The four reasons identified as the causes of this growth are: direct taxation and (of decreasing importance) the complexity of the fiscal system, indirect taxation and (of increasing importance) the 'intensity of the system of regulations'.

Of course, it is to be expected that in the transition from a 'regulated' to a deregulated economy certain legal and contractual limitations of working hours break down.

20. See *Futuribles*, no. 165–166, pp. 37–8 and 113, which provides a wealth of information, even if it is uncertain and contradictory as far as our basic problem is concerned.

21. See ISTAT, *Rapporto sull'Indagine pilota' – 7° Censimento dell'industria e dei servizi 1991* (edited by the Census Division for Industry and Services), Rome, 1990, which reports that 49 per cent of the companies included in the census gave no answer to the questions concerned with working hours.

22. For the most part I shall deal with industry in the strict sense, without taking into consideration construction, public works, transportation, and that series of services *for* industry which is camouflaged in the statistical category 'services'. I find the block of data relating to the manufacturing industry sufficiently meaningful. Furthermore, the fact that the data concerning manufacturing is compiled in different countries with somewhat homogeneous criteria makes it less complicated to use. On the effort to harmonize European statistics on working hours, see L. Frey, 'Verso l'armonizzazione delle statistiche sul tempo di lavoro con altre informazioni economico-sociali comparabili nei paesi dell'Unione Europea', in L. Frey, ed., *Le statistiche sul lavoro in Europa, Quaderni di economia del lavoro*, no. 56, 1996, pp. 31 ff.

23. See World Bank, *Workers in an Integrating World*, Oxford: Oxford University Press, 1995, pp. 2–7.

A study in the journal *World Economic Outlook*, April 1997, places two-thirds of the responsibility for the decline of industrial employment in the OECD nations on the growth of labour productivity, and a great deal of the remaining one-third on the fact that a series of jobs, from book-keeping to cleaning, that companies used to have done by their own employees have been transferred in recent years to outside concerns that the statistics usually classify as nonindustrial. It should also be noted that the outsourcing of segments of industrial production not infrequently gives rise to the 'miracle' of their statistical disappearance.

24. Consider the ongoing revolution in the organization of health care in the United States with the creation of chains of 'for-profit hospitals' based on the reduction of costs (especially of labour costs); or the longer banking hours that appear to be in the offing in Italy and other European countries.

25. See W. Rybczynski, *Waiting for the Weekend*, New York: Viking, 1991, pp. 222–4. That it is a fallacy to take nonworking time as equivalent to a time that is 'free from any form of constraint' is affirmed also by J. Dumazedier, 'Le temps libre, cet inconnu', *Futuribles*, pp. 227 ff.

26. The study in the IMF journal *World Economic Outlook* cited in note 23 estimates that from 1960 to 1994 the contribution of the Western manufacturing industry to gross national product in the OECD nations has been constant. Even though the criteria of evaluation and of the calculation of value added used by the IMF

cannot be ascertained, the data is indicative nonetheless. The decline of industrial employment in the OECD nations is by no means due to the presumed decline of industry; it is a consequence of the growth of labour productivity connected with the automation and informatization of the processes of production and with the intensification of labour.

27. William Shakespeare, *Henry IV*, Part I, Act V, Scene ii.

Chapter 2

This chapter is an almost exact reprint of the essay (written in 1990, and revised the following year only as regards the statistical data) 'L'orario di lavoro nell'industria occidentale nell'ultimo mezzo secolo' [Working hours in Western industry in the last half century], published in *Ventesimo secolo*, Year II, no. 4, 1992. In addition to a few minor changes, the first part of the text, on Keynes, has been slightly enlarged.

1. See J.M. Keynes, 'Economic Possibilities for Our Grandchildren', in *Essays in Persuasion*, London: Macmillan, 1931, pp. 321–32.

2. Ibid., p. 321.

3. See J. Fourastié, *Les 40.000 heures*, Paris: Laffont-Gonthier, 1965. The author posed two conditions: that labour productivity continue to grow at the same pace as in the 1950s and 1960s; and that the increase of productivity be transferred in its entirety to the reduction of hours.

   H. Kahn and A.J. Wiener, in an essay in the volume *Toward the Year 2018* (ed. E.G. Mesthene, Washington DC: Foreign Policy Association, 1968), made their claim in the late 1960s, when average working hours in the USA (by their own estimate) amounted to about 2,000 hours per year; in 1989 the exact figure was 1,904 hours.

4. See R. Dahrendorf, *Die Chancen der Krise. Über die Zukunft des Liberalismus*, Stuttgart: Deutsch Verlags-Anstalt, 1983; P. Sylos Labini, *Nuove tecnologie e disoccupazione*, Rome and Bari: Laterza, 1989, p. 22; A. Gorz, 'Pourquoi la société salariale a besoin de nouveaux valets', *Le Monde diplomatique*, June 1990, p. 22; V. Valli, 'Tempo di lavoro e occupazione: il caso italiano', in V. Valli, ed., *Tempo di lavoro e occupazione*, Florence: La Nuova Italia, 1988, pp. 36–7.

5. The present book just begins to broach the issue. To get some idea of industrial working hours in countries of the Third World, see Bureau International du Travail, *Annuaire des statistiques du travail*, Geneva, 1988, pp. 729–91. Some realistic estimates of the phenomenon are presented in A.G. Frank, *Crisis: In the Third World*, London: Heinemann, 1981, pp. 157 ff.; and, limited to the textile industry, in L. Frey, 'La gestione del tempo di lavoro', in N. Cacace, L. Frey and R. Morese, *Lavorare meno per lavorare tutti*, Rome: Ed. Lavoro, 1978, pp. 91 ff. As for the mass of workers employed in industry and in the building trade in dominated countries, in the case of Asia alone (Japan excluded), on the basis of figures

furnished by the *Asia 1987 Yearbook*, edited by the *Far Eastern Economic Review*, the total amounts to 186 million workers, or about three times the number of the industrial employees in the major Western nations. (See Chapters 4 and 6.)

6. See, for the various countries, E.H. Carr, *A History of Soviet Russia: The Bolshevik Revolution 1917–1923*, London: Macmillan, 1950; P. Broué, *Révolution en Allemagne (1917–1923)*, Paris: Editions de Minuit, 1971; G.A. Ritter and S. Miller, eds., *Die deutsche Revolution 1918–1919*, Frankfurt am Main: Fischer Bücherei, 1968; G.D.H. Cole, *Communism and Social Democracy (1914–1931)*, London: Macmillan, 1958; E. Ragionieri, 'La storia politica e sociale', in *Storia d'Italia*, vol. IV, Turin: Einaudi, 1976. Clearly, there is a great deal to be said about the particular circumstances in each individual country and about the real meaning of the introduction of the 8-hour day.

7. The agreement was approved in application of Article 47 of the Versailles Treaty. On the reasons that led to its passage, see V.-Y. Ghebali, ed., *La réglementation international du travail*, Paris: La Documentation Française, 1986, p. 7.

8. D.R. Roediger and P.S. Foner, *Our Own Time: A History of American Labor and the Working Day*, London and New York: Verso, 1989, p. 259.

9. Liesner's *One Hundred Years of Economic Statistics* cited in Table 2.1 gives us the following figures: in the USA the average working week throughout the 1930s was constantly less than 40 hours; in Great Britain, instead, as of 1938 it was between 46.3 and 47.7 hours; in Germany it fluctuated between the 44.2 hours of 1930 and the 48.7 of 1939; while in France, from the 48 hours of 1930, it had already fallen below 40 hours (to 38.7) by 1938; and in Italy too – but here we have some doubts about the reliability of the figures – it had already stabilized at less than 40 hours. We must not forget, of course, that all these countries had been hit by the Great Depression, albeit to different degrees. The situation was quite different in Japan, where in the 1930s monthly hours amounted to between 266 and 276, far more than they are today. As a matter of fact, both on the structural level (the transition to intensive development), and in the socio-political arena (in particular, the high degree of labour conflict, with a rate of strikes forty to fifty times higher than today), it was only in the period just after World War II that Japan experienced something comparable to what Europe and the US did in the first two decades of the century. Indeed, in that same period Japan made its (belated) transition from 'nineteenth century' to 'Tayloristic' hours.

10. The figure given in the table is among the lowest of the available estimates; other sources give between 42 and 43 hours per week.

11. This publication, which is the most complete compendium of historical statistics for the economies of Great Britain, the United States, Australia, Canada, France, Germany, Italy, Japan and Sweden, is quoted here in its second edition, revised and expanded to 1987. A further updating of the data to 1989 gives only small differences from the figures in Table 2.1. To be precise: 41 weekly hours for the United States, 43.4 for Great Britain, 179.3 (monthly) for Japan, 39.9 for Germany and 38.8 for France (cf. United Nations, *Monthly Bulletin of Statistics*, March

1991, p. 16; The Bank of Japan, *Economic Statistics Monthly*, February 1991, p. 185).

12. G. Rosa and V. Siesto, *Il capitale fisso industriale*, Bologna: Il Mulino, 1985, pp. 40, 58, 67–9, 77–9, 82. For a survey of the same trend in the major Western nations, see A. Maddison, 'Comparative analysis of the productivity situation in the advanced capitalist countries', in J.W. Kendrick, ed., *International Comparisons of Productivity and Causes of the Slowdown*, Cambridge MA: Ballinger, 1984, pp. 59 ff.; A. Maddison, 'Crescita e slowdown nelle economie capitalistiche avanzate: tecniche di valutazione quantitativa', *Economia & Lavoro*, no. 1, 1989, pp. 3–51.

13. W.W. Leontief, 'The distribution of work and income', *Scientific American*, September 1982, p. 152 ff..

14. B.K. Hunnicut, *Work Without End: Abandoning Shorter Hours for the Right to Work*, Philadelphia: Temple University Press, 1988, pp. 2–3.

15. See D. Owen, 'Workweeks and leisure: an analysis of trends, 1948–1975', *Monthly Labor Review*, August 1976, pp. 3–8; see also US Department of Labor, Bureau of Labor Statistics, *Handbook of Labor Statistics 1975 – Reference Edition*, Washington DC, 1977, pp. 176–86; US Department of Labor, Bureau of Labor Statistics, *Employment and Earnings*, Washington DC, March 1990, pp. 79–81.

16. See Roediger and Foner, *Our Own Time*, p. 270; P.O. Flaim, 'Work schedules of Americans: an overview of new findings', *Monthly Labor Review*, November 1986, pp. 3–6. The spread of second (or more) jobs continued in the second half of the 1980s, and at an even faster pace: see J.F. Stinson, Jr, 'Multiple jobholding up sharply in the 1980s', *Monthly Labor Review*, July 1990, pp. 3–10.

17. The 1987 Harris report comes to similar conclusions: a sharp increase in average weekly hours (40 in 1973, 43 in 1976, 47 in 1980, 49 in 1986), a sharp decrease in the hours workers spent in recreation (27 in 1973, 23 in 1976, 18 in 1980, 17 in 1986). It needs to be specified, however, that, first, the definition of working time used by the Harris Institute includes commuting time to and from work, or school, as well as household work; and, second, the Harris Institute survey – considered the most reliable in the United States – concerns both workers and students. Thus its figures cannot be compared with the official figures, which, interestingly enough, also confirm the rise in working hours.

18. See the special report 'Can Americans Compete?' in *Business Week*, 27 April 1987.

19. See B.K. Hunnicut, 'The End of Shorter Hours', *Labor History*, vol. 25, no. 3, Summer 1984, p. 378; Hunnicut, *Work Without End*, p. 3. On the decline of leisure time, in particular for women with jobs outside the household, see also I. Illich, *Shadow Work*, Boston and London: M. Boyars, 1981.

20. See *Japan Statistical Year Book 1988*, Tokyo: Statistics Bureau, Management and Coordination Agency, 1989, pp. 110–13; Bank of Japan, *Economic Statistics Monthly*, February 1991, pp. 151–2; A. Maddison, 'Crescita e slowdown', p. 23 (Table 13) and pp. 40–41 (Tables A-9, A-10, A-11); H. Nohara, 'Le syndacalisme japonaise à la croisée des chemins', *Travail et Emploi*, no. 2, 1989, pp. 65–77; and *Sociologia*

del lavoro, no. 34, 1989. It should be kept in mind that the Japanese government statistics refer to firms with more than thirty employees and, even here, only to 'regular workers', which thus effectively excludes the employees of small businesses as well as the 'irregular' workers in larger firms, whose working conditions are considerably worse than those of the workers surveyed. On the 'rigidly dualistic' character of the Japanese labour market, see V. Capecchi, 'Organizzazione e politiche del tempo: un primo confronto tra Giappone ed Europa', *Economia & Lavoro*, no. 1, 1986, pp. 45–76; T. Shigeyoshi, 'Alcuni recenti sviluppi nelle relazioni industriali giapponesi, con particolare riferimento alle grandi imprese private', *Sociologia del lavoro*, no. 34, 1989, pp. 75–89.

21. K. Dohse, U. Jürgens, and T. Malsh, 'Dal "fordismo" al "toyotismo"? L'organizzazione sociale dei processi di lavoro nell'industria automobilistica giapponese', *Sociologia del lavoro*, no. 34, 1989, pp. 113 ff.

22. See B. Moore, Jr., *Social Origins of Dictatorship and Democracy*, Boston: Beacon Press, 1966; E.H. Norman, *Japan, and the Uses of History*, New York: Random House, 1975; the essays by K. Taira, 'Lavoro e rivoluzione industriale in Giappone' and by K. Yamamura, 'L'industrializzazione del Giappone. Impresa, proprietà e gestione', in *Storia Economica Cambridge. L'età del Capitale*, Turin: Einaudi, 1980, vol. 7, part II, pp. 241 ff. and 267 ff. respectively.

23. See J. Halliday, *A Political History of Japanese Capitalism*, New York: Pantheon Books, 1975; J. Moore, *Japanese Workers and the Struggle for Power, 1945–1947*, Madison: University of Wisconsin Press, 1983.

24. Dohse, Jürgens and Malsch, 'Dal "fordismo" al "toyotismo"?', pp. 120–21. It is obvious that, like all definitions, this one is also unable to 'contain' the totality of the 'manifold determinations' of the phenomenon; nonetheless, it does give its essence. Its two principal limits are the lack of any reference to the more complex and flexible technological context within which Toyotaism developed, and the failure to dig more deeply into the authoritarian process of 'auto-activation' of 'Toyotaized' workers.

25. N. Masami, '"Modello Giappone"? Le caratteristiche delle relazioni industriali nell'industria automobilistica giapponese', *Sociologia del lavoro*, no. 34, 1989, p. 32.

26. On the methods used for organizing and guaranteeing 'spontaneous cooperation' in the firm between labour and management, and on the advantage – for management – of entering into the private life and 'inner nature' of employees, see the ground-breaking research of E. Mayo, *The Human Problems of an Industrial Civilization* and *The Social Problems of an Industrial Civilization* (President and Fellows of Harvard College), 1933 and 1945; and the work of H. Munsterberg, the father of 'economic psychotechnics' (cf. W. Volpert, 'Die Lohnarbeitswissenschaft und die Psychologie der Arbeitstätigkeit', in P. Groskurth and W. Volpert, *Lohnarbeits Psychologie*, Frankfurt am Main: Fischer Verlag, 1975).

27. Trades Union Congress (TUC), *Review of Working Time in Britain and Western Europe*, December 1988, p. 9; TUC, *Europe 1992: Progress Report on Trade Union Objectives*, London: TUC, 1989, p. 22.

28. 'Basic' hours are nothing more than a 'theoretical' point of reference of actual hours (which, of course, does not mean it is unimportant); but even in this 'theoretical' sphere the TUC warns 'there is a definite risk of a new 39 hour barrier developing' that may be even more resistant than the old one around the 40-hour week (see TUC, *Review of Working Time*, p. 8).

29. See Cole, *Communism and Social Democracy*; and Liesner, *One Hundred Years of Economic Statistics*, p. 44.

30. See IG Metall, 'Il documento delle 35 ore', *Azimut*, no. 11, 1984, p. 15. It should also be noted that in Germany the comprehensive volume of overtime, whose average level is far lower than levels in Japan or Britain, in 1982 was nonetheless the equivalent of additional jobs for 1.2 million potential employees.

31. O. Negt, *Lebendige Arbeit, Enteignete Zeit*, Frankfurt am Main: Campus Verlag, 1984, p. 32; for a detailed examination of the problem, see *Der Gewerkschafter*, no. 7, July 1983, pp. 20 ff.

32. IG Metall, *Il documento delle 35 ore*, p. 12.

33. United Nations, *Monthly Bulletin of Statistics*, March 1991 (New York: UN), p. 16. On the other hand, an 'appreciable rise' in overtime in Germany (still West Germany) was recorded in the course of 1989; see M. Silveri and P. Pessa, 'Orario: in Germania va meglio', *Nuova Rassegna Sindacale*, no. 5, 1990, p. 46.

34. Italy is the only major European country whose statistics on working hours in the manufacturing industry are not given regularly in the *Monthly Bulletin of Statistics* of the United Nations, and are given incompletely in the publications of Eurostat and the Bureau International du Travail (for the latter, see the *Annuaire des Statistiques du Travail*, Geneva, 1988, pp. 738, 744, 768).

35. See Silveri and Pessa, *Orario: in Germania va meglio*, pp. 44–51 (the firms in question are Fiat and Volkswagen); A. Cucchiarelli, 'Con meno ore quali risultati?' in *Nuova Rassegna Sindacale*, no. 12, 1990.

36. See F. Sabbatucci, 'La durata del lavoro nei principali Paesi industrializzati', in Quaderno no. 26 of *Rassegna Sindacale*, June 1970, p. 94.

37. P. Garonna, 'Le politiche sul tempo di lavoro e il sistema di relazioni industriali in Italia', in Valli, ed., *Tempo di lavoro e occupazione*, p. 155; G. Bodo, 'Ore contrattuali, orari di fatto e occupazione nella recente esperienza italiana', in *Ivi*, pp. 118–54; A Cucchiarelli, ed., *L'orario di lavoro in Italia e in Europa*, Rome: Datanews, 1990, pp. 33 ff.

38. See ISTAT, *Lavoro e retribuzioni – Anno 1988*, Rome: ISTAT, 1990, pp. 17–20 (Tables 1.3, 1.5, 1.6); ISTAT, *Annuario statistico italiano 1989*, Rome: ISTAT, 1990, pp. 250–51 (Tables 7.24 and 7.25); F. Barca and M. Magnani, *Fra capitale e lavoro: piccole e grandi imprese industriali dall'autunno caldo al risanamento*, Bologna: Il Mulino, 1989, pp. 116, 128. The estimates for de facto weekly hours at Fiat Mirafiori and Alfa-Lancia at Pomigliano are from the trade-union press.

39. See United Nations, *Monthly Bulletin of Statistics*, p. 16.

40. See Trades Union Congress, *Review of Working Time*, pp. 34–5; G. Cavezzali, 'In Francia l'orario diventa più flessibile', *Conquiste del Lavoro*, 3 June 1987.

41. See *Juin 36. 'L'esplosion sociale' du Front Populaire*, presentation by G. Lefranc, Paris: Gallimard–Julliard, 1966, p. 276.

42. Sylos Labini, *Nuove tecnologie*, p. 131.

43. Even if, as P.L. Berger and T. Luckmann write, the objective reality of a thing one never speaks of gradually begins to waver (see *The Social Construction of Reality*, Garden City NJ: Doubleday, 1966), which means that the subjective repression of a historical process is not absolutely impossible.

44. In Italy average life expectancy in 1875 was 36 years, and the average working day in industry, according to the factory survey of 1877, was between 11 and 12 hours (see R. Mainardi, 'Popolazione e politiche demografiche in Italia', Appendix to J. Verrière, *Troppi o troppo pochi?*, Milan: Mondadori, 1980, pp. 216–17; S. Merli, *Proletariato di fabbrica e capitalismo industriale. Il caso italiano 1880–1900*, Florence: La Nuova Italia, 1972, pp. 143 ff.; 195 ff.). Take the case of a worker who begins his life of toil at the age of 12 and exhausts it at 36 (24 years of work), working 305 days a year, 6 days a week (with very rare exceptions), and 12 hours a day. In terms of hours worked, the 'entire life span' of this worker amounts to $12 \times 305 \times 24 = 87,840$ hours.

Now let us see how his sybaritic grandchildren are doing. In Italy as of 1987 average life expectancy had risen to 72.9 years for men and 79.4 for women (see ISTAT, *Le regioni in cifre*, Rome: ISTAT, 1990, p. 152, Table 17.3). Let us say that the long-lived contemporary worker puts in 40 years, and let us take as our point of reference not the hours in the small factories and workshops but those in our biggest company, Fiat, which in 1988 amounted to 1,878 annual hours worked (1,788 'ordinary' hours plus 90 hours of overtime). The sum of contractual hours plus overtime is evidently higher than the sum of average real hours, which is why we take it as our general point of reference. We should bear it in mind, however, that the difference between the two sums has been decreasing in recent years due to the sharp reduction of absenteeism in the course of the 1980s, and that our sum in fact does not include a number of phenomena that were unknown to the workers of a hundred years ago (such as lengthy commuting time, second jobs, etc.). The hours worked in an 'entire life span' by our present-day worker amounts to 75,120 hours ($1,878 \times 40$). At Volkswagen the lucky worker only puts in $1,758 \times 40 = 70,320$ hours. Assuming in all this, of course, that our workers do not work for more than 40 years.

45. Sylos Labini, *Nuove tecnologie*, pp. 132–3, 144.

46. See J.-Y. Boulin and D. Taddei, 'Les accords de réduction-réorganisation du temps du travail. Négotiation et conséquences économiques', *Travail et Emploi*, no. 1, 1990, p. 44.

47. In a recent report in *L'Unità* on the condition of workers, V.R. (Vittorio Rieser) described conditions in small factories:

> Wages are low, often at the national contractual minimum, and thus (especially for women and young people) less than a million lire a month. However, an 'exchange between wages and hours' is possible almost everywhere,

through which the worker (at a high cost, in terms of sacrifice of his own time) considerably augments his wages with overtime hours. This mechanism reaches extreme limits in the tannery, where wages can amount to more than 2 million lire a month, which 'pay' not only for a very high number of overtime hours but also for the extremely harmful environment the worker has to bear. *Hours are thus almost always lengthened*, to satisfy the needs of the boss but also the wage-needs of the worker. And, apart from paid overtime, 'unpaid lengthening' of hours is common custom (for women in garment-making, for example), so that the 8 hours 'normally' become 9.

L'Unità, 'Dentro il lavoro', Supplement to no. 128, 2 June 1989, pp. 40–41.

48. The restructuring of hours is, if you will, one aspect of the more complex and general phenomenon of 'flexibility'; see M. Regini, ed., *La sfida della flessibilità*, Milan: Angeli, 1988, and the introductory essay by the editor in particular ('La sfida e le risposte', pp. 13–38), for its attempt to distinguish between the various aspects of the question.

49. D. Taddei, *Des machines et des hommes*, Paris: La Documentation Française, 1986.

50. Ibid., pp. 55–58, 76–80.

51. Ibid., p. 32.

52. See, for Italy, Cucchiarelli, ed., *L'orario di lavoro*, pp. 19–21, 61.

53. The IG Metall statement continues:

We cannot accept this. There are exceptions, where it is necessary to work also on Saturdays (and also at night and on Sundays) in certain circumstances: above all for health care, as in hospitals, and where technology demands it, as in blast-furnaces. In such cases weekend work is indispensable and the unions have always taken the necessities deriving from these jobs into account. But today we are talking about a *general extension of work to Saturdays and later also to Sundays*, which we no longer accept.

See Cucchiarelli, ed., *L'orario di lavoro*, p. 114.

54. See *Lavorare di domenica*, ed. Filta-CISL of Lombardy, Rome: Ed. Lavoro, 1988.

55. On the spread of 'non-compliance agreements' on the nightwork of women, see the dossier 'Gli "accordi" della notte', *Nuova Rassegna Sindacale*, no. 32, 1989, pp. 32–44. Then we have the interesting case (will it be the only one?) of a Bavarian firm that operates 'practically only at night' to 'reduce energy costs thanks to the preferential rate' (see C. Teiger, 'Nuove tecnologie e condizioni di lavoro: di cosa, di chi, a chi si parla? Il punto di vista dell'ergonomo', *Sociologia del lavoro*, no. 33, 1988, p. 135).

56. C. Tuchszirer, *La réduction et l'aménagement du temps de travail en Belgique et en RFA*, Paris: La Documentation Française, 1986, p. 25.

57. Boulin and Taddei, 'Les accords de réduction-réorganisation', p. 34.

58. Ibid., p. 33.

59. Tuchszirer, *La réduction et l'aménagement du temps*, p. 131.

60. Negt, *Lebendige Arbeit*, pp. 97 ff.

61. On the position of labour in the automated and informatic factory, see K.H. Ebel, 'L'usine automatisée a besoin de la main de l'homme', *Revue International du Travail*, no. 5, 1989, pp. 589–608, and Teiger, 'Nuove tecnologie', pp. 149 ff. For Italian industry on the whole, see the findings of the Lama Commission in the comments by R. Greco, 'L'Italia a rischio', *Nuova Rassegna Sindacale*, no. 25, 1989, and by C. Sircana, 'Altrimenti ti licenzio', *Nuova Rassegna Sindacale*, no. 35, 1989.

62. See K. Marx, *Grundrisse: Introduction to the Critique of Political Economy* (1857–58), trans. M. Nicolaus, London: Penguin Books, 1993, pp. 333–41, where Marx expresses (in 'abstract form') the relation between productivity and surplus labour (or surplus value) – a relation fraught with 'concrete' consequences.

63. See Iovane and Pala, *Lavoro salariato e tempo libero*, pp. 141–5.

64. See Maddison, 'Crescita e slowdown', pp. 16–17. In the mid 1960s the Max Planck Institute in Munich affirmed that in the transition from the 8-hour to the 7-hour day the improved productivity of labour would have a compensation effect of no more than 36 per cent. Around the same time, the French study group on working hours of the 'Commissariat général au Plan' calculated that the threshold of compensation was even lower, no more than 20 to 25 per cent. This means that, given a reduction of working hours of 10 per cent, only 3.6, or in the second case 2 to 2.5 per cent, could be recouped with a greater productivity of labour; the remaining 6.4, or 7.5 to 8 per cent, would translate into an increase in employment. (See the chapter by J. Fourastié and J.P. Courthéoux in H. Janne, ed., *La civilisation des loisirs*, Verviers: Editions Gérard, 1967.)

Chapter 3

1. See P. Basso, 'Mondialisation et temps de travail', *Page 2*, no. 11, May 1997, pp. 42–52.

2. See J.P. Womack, D.T. Jones, and D. Roos, *The Machine that Changed the World*, New York: Macmillan, 1990, p. 13.

3. Ibid., p. 103 (my stress).

4. See F.W. Taylor, *The Principles of Scientific Management*, New York: The Norton Library, 1967 (1911), p. 46. This, Taylor says, is how Schmidt, his first-class, 'high-priced worker' has to behave; his ideal pig-iron handler is 'a man of the mentally sluggish type' – 'a man of the type of the ox' (p. 62).

5. See T. Ohno, *Toyota Production System: Beyond Large-Scale Production*, Cambridge MA: Productivity Press, 1988, pp. 6 ff. With the concept of 'autonomation', or 'auto-activation' of production, which he indicates as the 'second pillar' of the Toyota system (the first is 'just-in-time'), Ohno refers, on the one hand, to the auto-activation of 'human operators' who are ready and able to intervene in real time on the production line (in particular, to 'stop the line') when they discover

defects or errors in the production process; and, on the other, to the auto-activation of the machines themselves, i.e. to the introduction of 'intelligent' machines equipped with automatic stopping devices for all the cases in which the machine itself detects an 'abnormality'.

6. Systematicity is an essential characteristic of Toyotaism, which in fact is con-stantly on the lookout for 'a systematic one best way, applicable not to the motions of the individual worker but to those of the entire factory and, beyond that, to the entire and articulated system that revolves around the production of a certain good' (see M. Revelli, in the 'Introduction' to the Italian edition of Ohno: *Lo spirito Toyota*, Turin: Einaudi, 1993, p. xxiv). The 'one best way' is the Taylorist principle that 'among the various methods and implements used in each element of each trade there is always one method and one implement which is quicker and better than any of the rest', and 'this one best method and best implement' have to be 'discovered or developed' (see Taylor, *The Principles of Scientific Management*, p. 25).

It is thus extremely superficial to see Toyotaism as a system designed to super-sede the assembly line. This system, even if and when it rationalizes the indi-vidual assembly line, physically detaching it from the rest of its department, works to construct – and has in fact constructed – the most extended and com-plex assembly line between departments, between plants, between companies, between production and distribution, that has ever been built. The permanent point of reference of the Toyota production system is the activity of the company as a whole. The trouble is that this effort to socialize and multiply the productive force of associated human labour, while extraordinary in many respects, is ulti-mately geared to competition (of one firm against others) and to the accumu-lation of private wealth (of only one part of society – the part that lives off the labour of others), and thus works *against* the associated human labour it pretends to foster. The system saves time and labour, on the one hand, and dissipates it, on the other – both on the social scale and within the immediate production process.

7. Ohno refers to it as 'visual control or management by sight.'

8. Ohno, *Toyota Production System*, p. 58; the French translation gives *mon obsession* ('my obsession') rather than 'my greatest concern', which may well be closer to Ohno's real spirit (see *L'esprit Toyota*, Paris: Masson, 1989, p. 67).

It is funny that, while from Jevons and Walras onward official 'economic science' pretends it has liquidated any sort of objective theory of value, and therewith the question of value itself, the most celebrated (by this very 'science') of the contemporary producers of goods should have written a little treatise on the organization of labour with an extremely objective, structural, impersonal lust for 'added value' – Marxian surplus value – oozing from its every pore. By the same token, look at the bustle about the question of the creation (or destruc-tion) of value on the part of those 'practical' economists who are asked by com-panies to come up with increasingly precise indicators on the subject ('economic value added', 'revised income', etc.), or who, with reference to the links between firms, do not hesitate to talk about a 'chain of value'.

And it is no less amusing that the text with which Ohno's alter ego, Shigeo Shingo, presents the 'Toyota system' – a text that is thoroughly dialectical, in so far as it reflects with particular vigour the impetus to an incessant *revolutionizing* of the means and procedures of production – should conclude with nothing less than an explicit panegyric on the dialectical process as a 'method of reasoning' that eliminates contradiction and reconciles opposites. 'The Toyota production system', Shingo tells us, 'comes into clearer focus once it is understood that this dialectic is applied throughout.' (See S. Shingo, *A Study of the Toyota Production System from an Engineering Viewpoint*, Cambridge MA: Productivity Press, 1989, pp. 235–6 – a felicitous and genuine interpretation.)

Ohno, too, has some cutting things to say about the frequently hidebound and sclerotic outlook of the world of industry, and even comes to advocate 'reverse common sense or inverse thinking' (Ohno, *Toyota Production System*, p. 115) – as long, of course, as it is confined to production techniques. Heaven help us if we apply the dialectical method, and the historical method (which, at bottom, coincide), to social relations and to history!

9. See Y. Hippo, 'Japon: la réduction du temps de travail. Une révolution culturale inachevée', *Futuribles*, no. 165–166, May–June 1992, p. 114; K. Ohmae, *The End of the Nation State*, New York: The Free Press, 1995. In *Japon illustré*, no. 4, 1991, we read that in Japan 'sixty percent of the suburban-dwellers spend more than two hours a day commuting by means of mass transportation'.

Naturally, long working hours are the rule for white-collar workers as well: 'the office workers leave the workplace in the evening only when the boss's coat has disappeared from its peg' (A. Mauriello, *Il Giappone dalla A allo Zen*, Rome: Theoria, 1996, p. 65).

10. See S. Kamata, *Japan in the Passing Lane: An Insider's Account of Life in a Japanese Auto Factory*, Introduction by R. Dore, New York: Pantheon Books, 1982, p. 108.

11. R. Dore, Introduction to ibid., p. xii; M. Burawoy, *Manufacturing Consent: Changes in the Labour Process under Monopoly Capitalism*, Chicago: University of Chicago Press, 1979. It may also be said, using Ouchi's terminology, that at Toyota, and in Japanese companies in general, bureaucratic control, 'market' control and 'clan' control are welded together; and in all three cases the controller (management, and above it the owners, the shareholders) and the controlled (the workers) are the same, even if 'clan' control is distinguished by the fact that the controlled (an assistant foreman, for example, or the worker who just aspires to be one, or even the 'common' worker with no such ambition) acts as a controller of his fellow workers: see W.G. Ouchi, 'La progettazione dei meccanismi di controllo organizzativo', in R. Nacamulli and A. Rugiadini, eds., *Organizzazione e mercato*, Bologna: Il Mulino, 1985, pp. 576–96.

On the link between military discipline and industrial discipline, see P. Naville,

'Travail et guerre', in G. Friedmann and P. Naville, *Traité de sociologie du travail*, Paris: Librairie Colin, 2nd edn, 1964, vol. 2, ch. 22, where Naville recalls Max Weber's opinion that military discipline is the ideal model for the modern capitalist factory, as it had been for the ancient agricultural estate. This view was reaffirmed in recent years by R. Reich, *The Work of Nations: Preparing Ourselves for 21st Century Capitalism*, New York: Random House, 1993, p. 51.

12. See T. Tagaki, 'Le relazioni industriali in Giappone e in Italia', in G. Fodella, ed., *Giappone e Italia. Economie a confronto*, Milan: Etas Libri, 1982, pp. 251–2.

13. See S. Hill, *Competition and Control at Work*, Cambridge MA: MIT Press, 1981, p. 53. Hill describes the big Japanese companies as a unique synthesis of paternalism and bureaucracy, pointing out that the 'quality circles' do involve the workers in some questions of organization (or, more precisely, of execution), but basically leave the company's management structure intact.

14. See J. Fucini and S. Fucini, *Working for the Japanese: Inside Mazda's American Auto Plant*, New York: The Free Press, 1990, pp. 37, 148, 178. At the Flat Rock plant, as an exception, Mazda did seek some union involvement in the firm.

15. See P.S. Adler, 'Time-and-motion regained', *Harvard Business Review*, January–February 1993, pp. 97 ff.; the article sings the praises of Toyotaist methods.

16. See C. Deutschmann, 'L'organizzazione giapponese, la sua influenza sul management e sulle relazioni industriali dell'Europa occidentale', *Sociologia del lavoro*, no. 41–42, 1990, pp. 137–60, and the entire issue no. 51–52, 1994, of *Sociologia del lavoro*, in particular the essays by P. Turnbull and by R. Delbridge on Great Britain, and by J.P. Durand on the 'French way' to the 'new production model'. On working hours in Japanese auto factories in Europe, see G. Bosch and S. Lehndorff, 'Working time and the Japanese challenge: the search for a European answer', *International Contributions to Labour Studies*, no. 5, 1995, pp. 1–26.

17. I am not only referring to H. Kern and M. Schumann, *La fin de la division du travail? La rationalisation dans la production industrielle*, Paris: Maison des Sciences de l'Homme, 1989 (French translation from the German), but also to the so-called 'Harzburg model' developed in Germany in the 1950s, which already foresaw the 'delegation' of technical responsibilities to common workers as well as a certain 'auto-control' of working operations, and to which the criterion of flexibility was not unknown (see Volpert, 'Die Lohnarbeitswissenschaft').

18. See V. Rieser, 'La fabbrica integrata "realizzata"', *Finesecolo*, Anno II, no. 3–4, December 1996, pp. 27–99.

19. A recent report of the interparliamentary Committee on safety in the workplace also noted this phenomenon, describing it as (no more than) an 'abnormality'.

20. See A.L. Kalleberg, 'Coinvolgimento e flessibilità: i cambiamenti delle relazioni di lavoro nelle società industriali', *Sociologia del lavoro*, no. 41–42, 1990, p. 27.

21. Ibid., pp. 27–8.

22. The British government refused to endorse the directive, judging it to be excessively restrictive for companies.

23. The two figures are neither altogether inclusive nor exclusive of one another,

since there are shiftworkers who do not do nightwork, just as there are (a smaller number of) workers who regularly work nights (see European Foundation for the Improvement of Living and Working Conditions, *Statistics and News*, *BEST*, no. 6, 1993 (Dublin), pp. 9–11). This European foundation in Dublin estimates that in the West approximately 20 per cent of the workforce are shiftworkers.

24. K. Marx, *Capital*, Volume 1, trans. S. Moore and E. Aveling, ed. F. Engels, Moscow: Progress Publishers, 1965, part III, ch. X, sec. 4, p. 256.

25. On the fall in the rate of profit in the period between 1960 and 1982, which involved all the OECD countries, see J.H. Chan and Lee-H. Sutch, 'Profits et taux de rendement', *Revue économique de L'Ocde*, no. 5, Autumn 1985, pp. 143–89. That the policies of flexibility in companies, in the labour market, in working hours, do indeed promote the recovery of the profitability of capital is demonstrated by the fact that the rate of profit showed its first signs of recovery, in the 1980s, in the countries where these policies were adopted first and most radically, i.e. the United States and Great Britain.

26. Some specialists in the field believe that *all* physiological processes can be traced back to circadian cycles or rhythms: see W.N. Dember and J.J. Jenkins, *General Psychology*, Englewood Cliffs NJ: Prentice-Hall, 1970. D.S. Landes affirms that biological circadian rhythms (recurring, that is, at 24-hour intervals) and approximately annual rhythms are stamped in our flesh and in our blood (*Revolution in Time*, The President and Fellows of Harvard College, 1983).

27. See A. Ferraris and A. Oliverio, *I ritmi della vita*, Rome: Ed. Riuniti, 2nd edn, 1991, pp. 107–9 (my stress). E. Mott (with his study group) was among the first to speak of a full-fledged 'shiftwork syndrome' in *Shiftwork: The Social Psychological Consequences*, Ann Arbor: University of Michigan Press, 1965. On the interrelations between human biological rhythms and the nervous system more generally, see A. Oliverio, *Biologia e comportamento*, Bologna: Zanichelli, 1982; The Open University, *Ritmi biologici*, Milan: Mondadori, 1980.

28. See T.H. Monk, ed., *Shiftwork International Newsletter*, vol. 12, no. 1, May 1995, dedicated to the abstracts selected for presentation at the Symposium. The most interesting of the abstracts deal with the consequences of shiftwork on sleep (pp. 23, 24, 48, 64), fatigue (pp. 15, 49, 128), the risk of cardiovascular disease (p. 13), gastrointestinal disturbances (pp. 75, 83, 102), impotence (p. 138), mood (pp. 15, 56, 96), work accidents (pp. 2, 57, 58, 89), motor vehicle accidents (pp. 125, 129), multiple and combined damage to health (pp. 36, 37, 47), participation in family and social life (pp. 27, 30, 64, 73, 76, 102). The extremely particular harmfulness of nightwork is confirmed (pp. 20, 26, 31, 35, 43, 54, 58, 70, 71, 79, 84, 86, 88, 99). Not more than 10 per cent of the over 130 studies are inclined to rule out or greatly minimize the harmfulness of shiftwork. But not a single one of them is concerned with studying whether shiftwork hinders participation in political life and trade union activity: this, apparently, is either taken for granted, or considered of no importance. After all, we are talking about wage labour, almost exclusively about manual workers. We certainly do

not want to consider them capable of governing.

29. Ibid., pp. 32, 103.

30. See R. Fontana, *Vivere controtempo. Conseguenze sociali del lavoro a turni*, Bologna: Il Mulino, 1992, pp. 168–9 (my stress); European Foundation for the Improvement of Living and Working Conditions, *Compensation for Shiftwork*, BEST, no. 4, 1991 (Dublin), pp. 7–9, which notes, in addition to the biological, medical and social costs and the price paid in fatigue, also specific financial costs paid by shiftworkers (for transportation, for soundproofing and lightproofing the home, etc.); M. La Rosa, ed., 'Qualità del lavoro e lavoro a turni nelle esperienze europee', *Sociologia del lavoro*, no. 13, 1981; and the essay by A. Maasen, 'Vita domestica nelle famiglie dei turnisti e carriera scolastica dei figli', cited in Fontana, *Vivere controtempo*, pp. 51–52, which emphasizes how the educational performance of the children of shiftworkers is inferior to that of the children of the other workers.

31. See European Foundation for the Improvement of Living and Working Conditions, *Guidelines for Shiftworkers*, BEST, no. 3, 1991 (Dublin), p. 5 (my stress). At first, the 'political philosophy' of this Foundation was based on a 'humanization of the shiftwork system', but even this hazy 'idea' has gradually faded. Taking the concept literally could have obliged the Foundation to draw some radical conclusions (after all, the concept implies that such a system violates human needs that have to be defended). It was advisable to take a lower-profile position: 'Shiftwork is not naturally beneficial to family and social life, but with imagination, hard work, and some compromises, it can be made highly flexible and much more acceptable' (European Foundation for the Improvement of Living and Working Conditions, *Social and Family Factors in Shift Design*, BEST, no. 5, 1993 (Dublin), p. 35). Is that low enough for you?

32. See European Foundation for the Improvement of Living and Working Conditions, *Statistics and News*, BEST, no. 9, 1996 (Dublin), pp. 34–6; M. Melbin, *Night as Frontier*, New York: Macmillan, 1987; Fontana, *Vivere controtempo*, p. 52.

33. See the fine study by L. Corradi, *Il tempo rovesciato. Quotidianità femminile e lavoro notturno alla Barilla*, 2nd edn, Milan: Angeli, 1994, pp. 21–2. On the other hand, for a publication that contributed to legitimating the (even formal) suppression of the prohibition of nightwork for women see European Foundation for the Improvement of Living and Working Conditions, *Women and Nightwork*, BEST, no. 2, 1990 (Dublin).

34. See M. Lallement, 'La fine di un tempo? Flessibilità e differenziazione del tempo sociale in Francia', *Sociologia del lavoro*, no. 58, 1995, pp. 81 ff.; Fondation européenne pour l'amélioration des conditions de vie et de travail, *Statistiques et nouvelles*, BEST, no. 9, 1996 (Dublin), pp. 25–7.

35. See G. Cerruti, 'Il tempo di lavoro tra fordismo e post-fordismo: dall'orario standard all'orario variabile', in M. Bergamaschi, ed., *Questione di ore*, Pisa: Biblioteca Serantini, 1997, p. 173; Lallement, 'La fine di un tempo?', p. 95; J.Y. Boulin, 'Les politiques du temps de travail en France: la perte du sens', *Futuribles*,

no. 165–166, May–June 1992, pp. 41 ff., in which Boulin notes how in the past ten years or so the policies of 'aménagement et reduction du temps de travail' have lost their original sense and been transformed into policies of 'aménagement et de réorganisation du temps de travail dictée par les impératifs de la compétitivité.' In point of fact, the sense, the class nature of those policies was not in doubt in the late 1970s either, the only difference being that, at first, they had to confront the (very modest) requests of workers and their unions for 'compensation' in terms of a reduction of hours.

36. See Cerruti, 'Il tempo di lavoro', p. 183. Cerruti comes to the following conclusion: 'After so much talk about a generalized reduction of working hours and about "chosen time" [i.e. working hours *chosen by workers*], the labour movement finds itself faced with an *increase in the length of working hours*, with a process of segmentation of working time between long hours and short hours, with a "chosen time" *chosen by management*, with a deregulation of industrial relations, and with a *total disempowerment of the regulations on the saturation of working time*' (p. 193; my stress).

37. See H. Schauer, 'La lotta dei metalmeccanici tedeschi', in *Il giusto lavoro per un mondo giusto. Dalle 35 ore alla qualità del tempo della vita* (collected papers from an international conference), Milan: Ed. Punto rosso, 1995, p. 50, my stress.

38. On the particularly long hours of craftsmen, and of the self-employed in general, see S. Bologna, 'Orari di lavoro e post-fordismo', in *Il giusto lavoro,* pp. 57–74 (an EC study estimates that in 1992 51 per cent of self-employed male workers in industry and in services and 32 per cent of the females 'regularly worked 48 hours or more per week'); P. Bourdieu, ed., *La misère du monde*, Paris: Editions du Seuil, 1993, pp. 155 ff.; Eurostat, *Work Organization and Working Hours 1983–1992*, Brussels–Luxembourg, 1995, pp. 38–9, 43.

For the contractual limits to overtime, which vary from sector to sector, see G. Olini, 'La contrattazione nazionale e decentrata in materia di tempo di lavoro', in Cnel, *Tempo di lavoro e flessibilità dell'orario*, pp. 80 ff. (there is an upper limit, for craftwork ceramics, of 280 hours a year).

For daily working time structurally exceeding 8 hours, see European Foundation for the Improvement of Living and Working Conditions, *Compressed Working Time*, BEST, no. 10, 1996 (Dublin); while for the first important labour struggle against the forced introduction of a 12-hour day at Staley's Decatur plant, see T. Frank and D. Mulcahey, 'Gli scioperi duri degli operai americani', *Le Monde Diplomatique* (Italian edition), October 1996, pp. 4–5.

The annualization of hours has also begun to exert pressure for the lengthening of working hours instead of simply for their reorganization. Recently, the British television network Independent Television News presented its employees with three alternatives for annual hours, two of them longer than present hours: the first of 1,836 hours (standard contract), the second of 2,044 hours (standard plus contract), and the third of 2,214 hours (see European Foundation for the Improvement of Living and Working Conditions, *Statistics and News*, BEST, no.

9, 1996 (Dublin), p. 21). Just a few years ago a relation between annualization and lengthening was not even taken into consideration; if anything, the opposite relation was emphasized: see European Foundation for the Improvement of Living and Working Conditions, *Negotiating Shorter Working Hours in the European Community*, *BEST*, no. 1, 1989 (Dublin), ch. 7.

39. See J.F. Marquis and C.-A. Udry, 'Les heures s'étirent, le travail se densifie', *Page 2*, no. 2, June 1996, p. 12.

40. See European Foundation for the Improvement of Living and Working Conditions, *Stress Prevention in the Workplace: Assessing the Costs and Benefits to Organizations*, Dublin, 1996, p. 4, which reveals, among other things, that out of 13,000 European workers interviewed in 1991 in an EC study, fully 48 per cent considered their work harmful or potentially harmful to their health, and 42 per cent considered it stress-producing (p. 5).

41. See J.F. Marquis and C.-A. Udry, 'L'hopital malade du travail', *Page 2*, no. 2, June 1996, p. 17; the authors remark that in Switzerland 'the hospital is henceforth considered a business.' Not only in Switzerland.

42. See Lallement, 'La fine di un tempo?', p. 94.

43. In Ugolini, *I tempi di lavoro*, p. 54, Lecher, a German economist, predicts that by the year 2000 in large companies there will be a permanent nucleus of steady 'central' employees of around 25 per cent, a second 25 per cent of 'peripheral steady' employees, with the remaining 50 per cent employed 'in precarious, occasional and unskilled external or peripheral jobs'. Voilà the 'postindustrial' paradise!

44. The document of FIOM–FIM–UILM of the province of Venice is from February 1997. I have actually seen 'pay envelopes' (actually, pieces of paper of absolutely no legal value) of workers with these subcontracting firms showing 245 to 250 hours for one month (equal to 60 hours a week on average, 10 hours a day for 6 working days); but it is taken for granted, among the workers and in the union, that there are workers – almost always immigrants – who put in as many as 400 hours a month, which means over 13 hours of work on average per day, without one single day off in the entire month. The 'chosen people' of cruise passengers must not be kept waiting!

45. See J. Rifkin, *The End of Work: The Decline of Global Force and the Dawn of the Post-market Era*, New York: G.P. Putnam's Sons, 1995; A. Chassagne and G. Montracher, *La fin du travail*, Paris: Stock, 1978; M. Drancourt, *La fin du travail*, Paris: Hachette, 1978. But Hannah Arendt had already spoken of the prospect of a society of workers without work (in *The Human Condition*, Chicago: University of Chicago Press, 1958), and Norbert Wiener had had the same idea even earlier (in *The Human Use of Human Beings*, Boston: Houghton Miffin, 1950).

46. See the report presented by the IMF in September 1993 and published in *Il mondo economico*, 2 October 1993, with the title 'Emergenza disoccupazione' ('Unemployment Emergency'). This phenomenon points up the perfectly antithetical character that the creation of time free from work assumes: on the one hand the

part of society that *can* afford to 'live' in a parasitic condition of uncreative, 'absolute' idleness, living off the labour of others, swells up like a diseased bladder; on the other, that part of society which is unable to sell its labour power 'usefully', because of the excessive labour supply, is eaten away in *forced* inactivity.

47. Generally three exceptions are given, purportedly with low unemployment rates, one of them permanent (Japan) and the other two more recent (the United States and Great Britain). But if the unemployment rates of these countries are purged of the restrictive criteria with which they are calculated (in the USA it suffices to have done 1 hour of work in the previous 2 weeks to be considered employed, and it suffices not to have actively looked for work in the previous week to be crossed off the list of the unemployed and 'vanish' from the statistics), or of other particular circumstances that lower them statistically (in Great Britain, the mechanism for granting unemployment benefits that ties them to the 'job seekers' allowance'), there is not much left of our exceptions. See K. Taira, 'Japan's low unemployment: economic miracle or statistical artifact?' in *Monthly Labor Review*, July 1983, pp. 3–10; J. Freyssinet, 'Etats-Unis: une nouvelle mesure du chômage', in *Chronique Internationale*, no. 26, January 1994, pp. 9–12; 'Les nouveaux maîtres du monde', in *Manière de voir*, supplement to *Le Monde diplomatique*, no. 28, 1995, pp. 59–61, which furnishes the following estimates of the *real* rates for 1995: for Japan 9.6 rather than 2.7 per cent, for Great Britain 12.3 rather than 9.8 per cent, for the United States 9.3 rather than 6.4 per cent.

As for the United States, Schor's estimates are even higher, especially if unemployment and underemployment are considered together (J.B. Schor, *The Overworked American: The Unexpected Decline of Leisure*, New York: Basic Books, 1991, pp. 39–41). L. Thurow's estimates give a real unemployment 'closer to 10 than to 5 percent' (see his interview in *Le Nouvel Observateur*, 9–15 October 1997). Finally, economists such as J. Rifkin and M. De Cecco have pointed out that just by adding to the US unemployment lists the 1.6 million people in US prisons (their number has quadrupled since 1980), the official index would rise by more than one point.

For the (also graphic) documentation of the notable differences between the various unemployment indices and the increase of these differences over time in the United States, see J.E. Bregger and S.E. Haugen, 'BLS introduces new range of alternative unemployment measures', *Monthly Labor Review*, October 1995, pp. 19–26.

The criteria of calculation of the unemployment rate have recently been made more restrictive in France, where, to be considered employed, it now suffices for someone to have 'quelques petits boulots' (some odd jobs) at the moment of the survey (see *Liberation*, 1–2 November 1997).

48. See G. D'Aloia and M. Magno, eds, *Il tempo e il lavoro. Gli orari di lavoro in Italia e in Europa*, Rome: Ediesso, 1994, p. 163, Fig. 2; European Foundation for the Improvement of Living and Working Conditions, *Statistics and News*, Fig. 3.3; *Le Monde*, 10 October 1997, which speaks of between 200 and 400 million hours

of overtime in France, equivalent to between 110,000 and 230,000 full-time jobs.

49. See Eurostat, *Labour Force Survey: Results 1995*, Brussels and Luxembourg, 1996, pp. 206 ff.

50. See L. Mishel and J. Bernstein, *The Jobless Recovery: Deteriorating Wages and Job Quality in the 1990s*, Economic Policy Institute, September 1993; B. Bluestone, 'Che ve ne sembra dell'America senza lavoratori organizzati?', in *Politica ed economia*, April 1994, p. 33; E.B. Kapstein, 'Workers and the world economy', *Foreign Affairs*, May/June 1996, p. 22, which notes how the trend towards income polarization is underway 'even in that most egalitarian country, Sweden'; B. Berberoglu, *The Legacy of Empire: Economic Decline and Class Polarization in the United States*, New York: Praeger, 1992, chs 4 and 5; and the dossier 'Clinton, le rêve républicain', with texts by H. Sklar and R. Brenner, in *Page 2*, no. 1, May 1996, pp. 23 ff.

The reduction or stagnation of the purchasing power of wages is one moment of a broader social polarization underway in Western societies; for the best comprehensive documentation of the situation in Italy, see M. Paci, ed., *Le dimensioni della disuguaglianza. Rapporto della Fondazione Cespe sulla disuguaglianza sociale in Italia*, Bologna: Il Mulino, 1993.

51. See the article by P. Krugman in the *New York Times Book Review*, 20 October 1996, and the virulent article by L. Thurow, 'The Birth of a Revolutionary Class', in the *New York Times Magazine*, 19 May 1996, where the author states, unequivocally, that the elderly are demolishing the welfare state and threatening the future of the United States.

52. See D'Aloia and Magno, eds., *Il tempo e il lavoro*, pp. 153–66; D.E. Herz, 'Work after early retirement: an increasing trend among men', *Monthly Labor Review*, April 1995, pp. 13 ff.; M. Eisenscher and P. Donohue, 'The Fate of Social Security', *Z Magazine*, March 1997, p. 28.

The 'manifesto' of all the pension counter-reforms of the 1990s is the document of the World Bank, *Averting the Old Age Crisis: Policies to Protect the Old and Promote Growth*, Oxford: Oxford University Press, 1994. But the true trailblazing counter-reform was the one launched in 1981 in Chile by the Pinochet regime that, even in the view of nonradical critics, penalized low-paid workers, those without steady jobs, and a vast majority of the women – in short, almost 100 per cent of Chilean workers, forcing them to work *longer*, if they still have it in them (see A. Barrentios and L. Firinguetti, 'Individual capitalisation pension plans and old-age pension benefits for low-paid workers in Chile', *International Contributions to Labour Studies*, no. 5, 1995, pp. 27–43).

53. See L. Mishel and J. Bernstein, *The State of Working America 1992–1993*, Washington DC: Economic Policy Institute, 1992, p. 157.

54. See the statement by the Veneto secretary of the CGIL, 'Basta ragazzi in fabbrica sotto i sedici anni', in the newspaper *Il Gazzettino*, 16 October 1996 (in the Veneto the school-leaving rate in vocational high schools is above the national average, as high as 30 per cent in the first year); B. Garet, 'L'apprentissage en

France. Enquête sur le terrain', in B. Schlemmer, ed., *L'enfant exploité. Oppression, mise au travail, prolétarisation*, Paris: Karthala–Orstom, 1996, pp. 367 ff. On the rise in teenage labour in Western countries, see C. Bellamy, *The State of the World's Children 1997*, published for UNICEF by Oxford University Press, 1996; on the rise of the phenomenon in the United States in open violation of child labour laws, as reported in 1989 by government inspectors, see Schor, *The Overworked American*, pp. 26–7.

55. See P.L. Rones, R.E. Ilg and J.M. Gardner, 'Trends in hours of work since the mid 1970s', *Monthly Labor Review*, April 1997, pp. 3–14 (note that a more thorough study of working hours, also by the US Bureau of Labor Statistics, concluded that – in 1994 – 76.9 per cent of employed men and 55.7 per cent of employed women worked 40 hours or more); H.B. Pressner and A.G. Cox, 'The work schedules of low-educated American women and welfare reform', ibid., pp. 25–34.

For the Harris Institute the average working week in the USA was – in 1997 – 50.8 hours against the 40.6 hours of 1973 (see *The Harris Poll*, no. 31, July 1997, Table 2), which means *a 25 per cent increase* in the past twenty-five years.

56. See Rifkin, *The End of Work*, and 'Le nouveaux modèle américain', *Manière de voir*, supplement to *Le Monde diplomatique*, no. 31, 1996.

57. See European Foundation for the Improvement of Living and Working Conditions, *Statistics and News*, passim; *Le Nouvel Observateur*, 17–23 April 1997, p. 22.

58. See B. Ugolini, *I tempi di lavoro*, Milan: Rizzoli, 1995, ch. 16 (the judgement is expressed by the ex-secretary of the UGT, J.M. Zufiaur); C. Velasco Murviedro, 'Argomenti sociali e viabilità economica della riduzione della giornata di lavoro di fronte alla disoccupazione. Idee e proposte spagnole', *Sociologia del lavoro*, no. 58, 1995, pp. 102 ff.; C. Tuchszirer and C. Vincent, 'Espagne. Les partenaires sociaux s'imposent une nouvelle forme de flexibilité', *Chronique Internationale*, May 1997, pp. 25–9. It is worthy of note that the unemployment rate in Spain is over 20 per cent.

59. See European Foundation for the Improvement of Living and Working Conditions, *Statistics and News*, p. 24.

60. *Il sole 24 ore*, 9 October 1997.

61. The average weekly hours of a full-time German worker, for example, were 39.2 in 1992, just one hour less than a British worker (see C. Meilland, 'Le temps de travail dans l'Unione Européenne: une analyse sexuée dans six pays', *La Revue de l'IRES*, no. 22, Autumn 1996, pp. 124, 160). Furthermore, in calculating the real hours of German workers, one has to consider that Germany has an absentee rate of about 2 per cent, by far the lowest in Europe (see Eurostat, *Work Organization and Working Hours*, pp. 93–4).

62. See Eurostat, *Work Organization and Working Hours*, p. 28; Eurostat, *Labour Force Survey*, p. 168. We have to remember that these Eurostat estimates include overtime hours, but do not include breaks for meals (so the figures do not give us the total hours spent in the workplace) and commuting time (so we do not have

the total hours directly or indirectly consumed by work): see European Foundation for the Improvement of Living and Working Conditions, *Statistics and News*, p. 17.

Eurostat also estimates, for 1995, that 18.6 per cent (about one out of five) of the full-time workers in Europe regularly work between 41 and 50 hours a week, with a maximum in Great Britain (52.6 per cent work over 41 hours) and a minimum in Holland (2.7 per cent), while 10.8 per cent of the workers (one out of nine) regularly work over 51 hours a week: see Eurostat, *Labour Force Survey*, pp. 174–5, 192–3.

63. See L. Frey, 'Verso l'armonizzazione delle statistiche sul tempo di lavoro con altre informazioni economico-sociali comparabili nei paesi dell'Unione Europea', in L. Frey, ed., *Le statistiche sul lavoro in Europa* (*Quaderni di economia del lavoro*, no. 56, 1996), p. 42, Table 5.

64. See Bank of Japan, *Economic Statistics Monthly*, May 1989, p. 113; Bank of Japan, *Economic Statistics Monthly*, September 1994, pp. 11, 211; Bank of Japan, *Economic Statistics Monthly*, March 1997, pp. 11, 223.

65. See C. Molteni and C. Zucca, *Rapporto Giappone. Quale ruolo nei nuovi equilibri dell'area Asia-Pacifico?*, Turin: Edizioni della Fondazione Agnelli, 1996, p. 5; Bank of Japan, *Economic Statistics Monthly*, March 1997, p. 11.

66. See T. Ken, 'Are the Japanese workaholics? Their consciousness has begun changing', *Japan Quarterly*, vol. 28, no. 4, October–December 1981, pp. 510 ff.; Hippo, 'Japon: la réduction du temps de travail', p. 119. The 'seven enigmas' are: the lack of reduction of hours and overtime; the low rate of absenteeism; the workers' not taking all their vacation days; the acceptance of prolonged hours especially by the older workers; the acceptance of the practice of unpaid overtime; the lack of sharp borders between working time and leisure time; the less prolonged working hours of women.

67. See Bank of Japan, 'The Japanese Employment System', *Quarterly Bulletin*, May 1994, pp. 52–85, a general policy statement of great importance.

68. See C. Leblanc, 'Le nuove paure dei lavoratori giapponesi', *Le Monde Diplomatique* (Italian edition), May 1994, p. 19. Interviewed by Leblanc, S. Kamata points out that the first 'victims of the reduction of personnel are workers over fifty, women, the disabled, and anyone who "lacks spirit of conciliation" (*kyochosei*) – that is, workers who do not submit to the rules imposed by the company.'

69. See Bank of Japan, *The Japanese Employment System*, p. 60, Table 7.

70. In the current examination of this type of competition, this, naturally, has been its most concealed dimension: see J.D. Blackburn, ed., *Time-Based Competition: The Next Battleground in American Manufacturing*, Homewood IL: Business One Irwin, 1991; Boston University and Insead Waseda University, 'Fabbriche del futuro', *L'impresa*, no. 3, 1991, pp. 101 ff.

71. So argues M. Husson, 'Du relentissement de la productivité', *La Revue de l'IRES*, no. 22, autumn 1996, pp. 98 ff.

72. Although Husson speaks of an 'institutional rupture' that took place in Great

Britain with the adoption of 'a policy aggressively aimed at labour market flexibility' (ibid., p 99), he then appears to underestimate the consequences of this policy on the intensification and on the productivity of labour when he fails to include it among the factors that can transform 'latent autonomous technical progress' into real gains in productivity (p. 113).

Vice versa, the increasing attraction that Britain – and some regions in particular, such as Wales – exerts on international capital derives precisely from its having the lowest cost of labour in Europe, hours that are among the longest (practically without legal limits) and vacations among the shortest, and a degree of 'difficulty in industrial relations' that Ernst & Young places, on a scale of zero to ten, at zero (see M. Maggi, 'Com'è bello fare il padrone in Galles', *L'Espresso*, 9 January 1997). On the working conditions and industrial relations in Japanese-owned companies in Wales, see J. Morris, M. Munday and B. Wilkinson, *Working for the Japanese*, London: The Athlone Press, 1993, in particular chs 4 and 6.

Chapter 4

1. See A.M. Chiesi, 'I dati sulla riduzione dell'orario di lavoro sono soltanto un'opinione?' in Centro Ricerche G. Di Vittorio–Istituto milanese per la storia della Resistenza e del movimento operaio, *Tempo, orario, lavoro. Prospettive storiche e dibattito attuale* (papers from a conference), 1992, pp. 16 ff.
2. See European Foundation for the Improvement of Living and Working Conditions, *The Changing Use of Time: Report from an International Workshop*, Dublin, 1991. The report, coordinated by J. Gershuny, concerns the period 1965–85 (and thus the same considerations must be made as those regarding Sylos Labini in Chapter 2). Consider also the fact that in several cases the last years of reference fall between 1974 and 1981, with the shortest working hours since World War II.
3. See Chiesi, 'I dati sulla riduzione', p. 19.
4. As S. Tabboni maintains; see *La rappresentazione sociale del tempo*, Milan: Angeli, 1984, p. 129.
5. Figure 4.1 is from S. Bullock, *Women and Work*, London: Zed Books, 1994, p. 31; its source is the United Nations document *The World's Women: Trends and Statistics, 1970–1990*, New York: United Nations, 1991. For an updating of the UN data, see *The World's Women 1995: Trends and Statistics*, New York, United Nations, 1995, pp. 132 ff., Table 8 – a table that, in any event, is full of dubious figures (such as the average weekly working hours of male employed Italians given as 27.9 hours).
6. See Chiesi, 'I dati sulla riduzione', p. 16.
7. As an anonymous Ricardian put it, quoted by Marx in *Theories of Surplus Value* (1861–63), in *Collected Works*, vol. 32, London: Lawrence & Wishart, p. 390; this Ricardian also affirms that 'a nation is really rich if the working day is 6 hours rather than twelve'.

8. See Gershuny, 'La répartition du temps dans les sociétés post-industrielles', *Futuribles*, no. 165–166, May–June 1992, p. 222 (my stress).

9. See T. Treu, 'Nuove tendenze e problemi del tempo di lavoro', *Stato e mercato*, no. 18, December 1986, p. 377 (my stress).

10. See O. Marchand, 'Une comparaison internationale des temps du travail', *Futuribles*, no. 165–166, May–June 1992, p. 34.

11. See A. Ure, *The Philosophy of Manufactures: or an Exposition of the Scientific, Moral and Commercial Economy of the Factory System of Great Britain*, London: C. Knight, 1835; reprinted in 1967, New York: Kelley, p. 15.

12. See M. Sahlins, *Stone Age Economics*, Chicago: Aldine, 1972, which describes the existence of the Australian Bushmen as decidedly not centred on work: 'Reports on hunters and gatherers of the ethnological present … suggest a mean of three to five hours per adult worker per day in food production. Hunters keep banker's hours, notably less than modern industrial workers (unionized), who would surely settle for a 21–35 hour week' (pp. 34–5). See also P. Clastres, *La société contre l'état: Recherches d'anthropologie politique*, Paris: Editions de Minuit, 1974, which sets the average length of the 'workday' among the Yanomani at about three hours; and M. Harris, *Cultural Anthropology*, New York: Harper & Row, 1987, ch. 4.

13. The laws against (labour) combination were not repealed in England until 1824, five centuries after their introduction; in France they were abolished in 1864, and in Italy in 1889. It may be useful to recall that the French Revolution, the champion of the rights of man, *confirmed* the prohibition of workers' combination with the Le Chapelier law of 14 June 1791, just as it conserved slavery in the colonies and the civil and political nullity of women: see A. Soboul, *Précis d'histoire de la Revolution française*, Paris: Editions sociales, 1962, ch. 3; M. Wollstone-craft, *A Vindication of the Rights of Woman* (1792), London: Penguin, 1975; C.L.R. James, *The Black Jacobins*, New York: Random House, 1963.

14. O. Negt, *Lebendige Arbeit, Enteignete Zeit*, Frankfurt am Main: Campus Verlag, 1984, p. 183. F. Novara writes: 'Historians believe that in the Middle Ages work took up about one half of the days of the year. (In France there were 141 official holidays.)' ('Il tempo di lavoro tra cronobiologia e cultura', *Sociologia del lavoro*, no. 58, 1995, p. 28).

15. See J. Le Goff, *Time, Work, and Culture in the Middle Ages*, Chicago: University of Chicago Press, 1980, pp. 29 ff., 58 ff.; E.P. Thompson, 'Time, Work-Discipline and Industrial Capitalism', *Past and Present*, no. 38, 1967 (Oxford: The Past and Present Society); Landes, *Revolution in Time*, which relates the birth and evolution of the clock to the birth and evolution of the modern world, described as a civilization based on the measurement and on the notion of time; C.M. Cipolla, *Le macchine del tempo (1300–1700). L'orologio e la società*, Bologna: Il Mulino, 1981 (on the same question, but over a shorter time span). E. Zerubavel's work, *Hidden Rhythms: Schedules and Calendars in Social Life*, Chicago: University of Chicago Press, 1981, proves, however, to be of very little use, on this point at any rate;

while it is concerned with the 'rational elements of temporal organization', it places the process of rationalization of time outside time itself, outside its real historical sequence, while giving short shrift to the 'rational temporal organization' par excellence – that is, the factory. It is as if Zerubavel wished to do everything possible to confirm Fernand Braudel's judgement on the tendency of the social sciences to 'eschew the historical explanation' of time, plunging, on the one hand, towards a punctual time, the time of the 'occurrence', and projecting themselves, on the other, above social occurrences, towards ethereal 'almost atemporal structures' (see Braudel, *Écrits sur l'histoire*, Paris: Flammarion, 1969).

16. Le Goff, *Time, Work, and Culture in the Middle Ages*, p. 44.

17. Ibid., p. 50.

18. Thompson, 'Time, Work-Discipline'.

19. K. Marx, *Capital*, Volume 1, trans. S. Moore and E. Aveling, ed. F. Engels, Moscow: Progress Publishers, 1965, Part III, ch. X, Sec. 5, pp. 264–5. The stress is all in the original text.

20. See J.B. Schor, *The Overworked American: The Unexpected Decline of Leisure*, New York: Basic Books, 1991, p. 45. Note, here, how the zero point is actually set at zero, and not at 1,500 hours as in the 'objective' Figure from *Futuribles*.

21. See P.A. Samuelson, *Economics*, New York: McGraw-Hill, 1973, p. 81 (author's stress).

22. See D.R. Roediger and P.S. Foner, *Our Own Time: A History of American Labor and the Working Day*, London and New York: Verso, 1989, chs 7–11. There is a photographic documentation of these labour struggles in P.S. Foner and R. Schultz, *Das andere Amerika. Geschichte, Kunst und Kultur der amerikanischen Arbeiterbewegung*, Berlin: Elefanten Press, 1983.

23. R. Luxemburg, *Einführung in die Nationalökonomie* (1925), Reinbek bei Hamburg: Rowohlt Taschenbuchverlag, 1972, p. 160.

24. Some essential works: B.K. Hunnicut, *Work Without End: Abandoning Shorter Hours for the Right to Work*, Philadelphia: Temple University Press, 1988; Roediger and Foner, *Our Own Time*; M.A. Bienefeld, *Working Hours in British Industry*, London: Weidenfeld & Nicolson, 1972; G. Scharf, *Geschichte der Arbeitszeitverkürzung*, Cologne: Bund-Verlag, 1987; G. Cross, *A Quest for Time: The Reduction of Work in Britain and in France, 1840–1940*, Berkeley: University of California Press, 1989; G. Cross, *Worktime and Industrialization: An International History*, Philadelphia: Temple University Press, 1988; J.L. Bodiguel, *La réduction du temps de travail, enjeu des luttes sociales*, Paris: Editions Ouvrières, 1969. For Italy, however, there is no comprehensive work on the subject. The collections of material from the First, Second and Third Internationals are, of course, of fundamental importance.

25. See Schor, *The Overworked American*, p. 7 (author's stress).

26. Ibid.

27. The two most important reflections on this 'category', qua sociological category, are to be found, from completely different perspectives, in A. Schutz, *The Phenomenology of the Social World*, trans. G. Walsh and F. Lehnert, Evanston IL:

Northwestern University Press, 1967, and *Collected Papers*, vols. I–III, The Hague: Nijhoff, 1971–73, and in H. Lefebvre, *Critique de la vie quotidienne*, Vols I–II, Paris: L'Arche, 1958–61, and *La vie quotidienne dans le monde moderne*, Paris: Gallimard, 1968.

28. See P.L. Berger and B. Berger, *Sociology: A Biographical Approach*, New York: Basic Books, 1972; quoted from the revised edition, Penguin Books, 1976, pp. 19, 17 (author's stress).

29. See even just the latest investigations of working conditions in Italy: L. Corradi, *Il tempo rovesciato. Quotidianità femminile e lavoro notturno alla Barilla*, 2nd edn, Milan: Angeli, 1994, chs 4–6 (on the Barilla plant at Castiglione delle Stiviere); D. Bubbico, 'Sata e il suo rovescio', *Finesecolo*, Nos. 3–4, December 1996, pp. 100 ff. (on the Fiat–Sata plant at Melfi); FIOM–CGIL, *Esplorare il lavoro. Indagine nazionale sul lavoro delle donne nelle fabbriche di Bologna, Palermo, Torino*, Bologna, March 1997; F. Anderlini, *Ristrutturazione aziendale e melanconia operaia. Il caso Zanussi–Electrolux di Susegana*, Milan: Angeli, 1993, pp. 76 ff.

30. See 'Spécial: Etats généraux de la santé au travail', *Santé et Travail*, no. 17, September/October 1996, p. 49.

31. This aspect is emphasized by A. Cavalli, 'Le trasformazioni del lavoro nelle società industriali avanzate', in A. De Lillo, ed., *Scuola e lavoro: nuovi problemi e nuove prospettive*, Bologna: Il Mulino, 1981. One must not forget, however, to relate the 'late entrance' into the workforce and the tendentially 'early exit' from it (pension 'reforms' notwithstanding) to the average life expectancy of the worker, which has doubled over the past century.

32. Once in a while we come across a study of labour questions that feels the need to abandon a 'Westernistic' vision of the problems for a 'more planetary' one (see the Prefatory Note to the book by A. Negri, *Il lavoro nel novecento*, Milan: Mondadori, 1988), but very rarely is this need translated into consequential lines of investigation.

33. See I. Wallerstein, *Historical Capitalism*, London: Verso, 1983, p. 101 (my stress). See, also, M. Sahlins's acute considerations on 'the original affluent society', in *Stone Age Economics*, ch. 1.

34. See R. Munck, *The New International Labour Studies: An Introduction*, London: Zed Books, 1988, p. 188 (my stress).

35. See A. Accornero, *Era il secolo del lavoro*, Bologna: Il Mulino, 1997, p. 46. Accornero recalls that *Business Week* warned the Southeast Asian countries of, among other things, the danger of rising wages.

36. See *Il sole 24 ore*, 24 June 1989.

37. See International Metalworkers' Federation, *I metalmeccanici e l'orario di lavoro nel mondo*, Geneva: IMF, 1997; *Il sole 24 ore*, 10 December 1997. Official annual hours (in Italy, the figure is 200 to 300 hours less than the real hours) are estimated for Brazil at 1,954 hours, for Egypt at 2,134, for Turkey at 2,151, for China at 1,953.

38. We note, nonetheless, that the figures for weekly hours that they do admit (and

here there are no four weeks of vacation: 'vacations' are, in general, limited to the occasional holiday) are not always trifling: 46.1 hours for Turkey, 48.9 for South Korea, 49.2 for Singapore, 53 for Sri Lanka, 56 for Egypt (see Bureau International du Travail, *Annuaire des Statistiques du travail*, Geneva, 1994). Following these figures, if workers in these countries worked the same number of weeks as in Europe, they would put in from 300 to 750 hours more than European workers per year; but if we take the lack of vacations into account, the difference rises to between 500 and 1000 annual hours, which means between 1½ and 3 hours more work *per day*. Actually, the gap can be even greater than this maximum level.

39. See Munck, *The New International Labour Studies*; R. Southall, ed., *Trade Unions and the New Industrialisation of the Third World*, London: Zed Books, 1988; H. Thomas, ed., *Globalization and Third World Trade Unions: The Challenge of Rapid Economic Change*, London: Zed Books, 1995.

40. Except for the case of China, where, moreover, it is now being drastically reduced, this sector is quite small. As regards the Indian subcontinent, L. Marcuccio, *Rapporto India. Le riforme economiche e il difficile rapporto fra centro e periferia* (Turin: Edizioni della Fondazione Agnelli, 1995), estimates that the 'organized sector' of private industry (the only one where the worker has some 'guarantee') in 1991 absorbed only 2.8 per cent of the labour force, down from the 3.1 per cent of 1981 (p. 36). In his report we read: 'Working conditions, even in the organized sector, are extremely distressing: India now ranks fourth in the world, after Pakistan, Kenya and South Korea, for the incidence of on-the-job deaths in industry with respect to the total number of employees in the sector' (p. 28). 'Recourse to child labour [another presumed archaeological find from the nineteenth century] is massive' (p. 36). These exploited young children work between 8 and 12 hours a day (see V. Dupont, 'Les mobiles du travail. Itinéraires de travailleurs de la petite industrie textile en Inde de l'Ouest', in G. Heuzé, ed., *Travailler en Inde*, Paris: Éditions de l'École des Hautes Études en Science Sociales, 1992, p. 91). The official average number of hours worked per person per year in India is 2,250 (see *Il sole 24 ore*, 29 February 1996).

41. See *Time*, 21 November 1994; B. Ellis, 'Widespread oppression of woman workers in Indonesia', *Green Left Weekly*, 19 November 1997; *L'Unità*, 16 May 1993; G. Bonazzi, *Lettera da Singapore, ovvero il terzo capitalismo*, Bologna: Il Mulino, 1996, p. 27; *Newsweek*, 9 May 1994. See also W. Galenson, *Labor and Economic Growth in Five Asian Countries: South Korea, Malaysia, Taiwan, Thailand, and the Philippines*, New York: Praeger, 1992, which affirms that the normal working week in those countries is 6 days, and working days of 9 hours are common. But there are other areas where things are certainly no better. In the thousands of Mexican *maquiladoras* people work as many as 63 hours a week. In Argentina as restructured by the IMF, legal daily working hours have been extended from 8 to 12 hours (*Internazionale*, 27 September 1996). In the Palestinian territories occupied by Israel, Arab entrepreneurs are themselves no slackers when it comes to imposing

long hours on their workers (the 'usual' 12-hour days, as reported by *Il sole 24 ore*, 24 April 1991). From A. Serhane, *Les enfants des rues étroits*, Paris: Editions du Seuil, 1986, we learn that in Morocco the average working day is between 10 and 11 hours – just one aspect of a social picture lacerated by devastating contradictions. In Tunisia, the official figure for annual hours in textile factories – suppliers and subsuppliers of Italian and French firms – is 2,307 (*Il sole 24 ore*, 23 October 1997).

42. See J.P. Béja, 'Quand les ouvriers doutent de la dictature du prolétariat', *Perspectives chinoises*, no. 28, March–April 1995, p. 29. This doubt about the real social nature of so-called 'market socialism' is quite well founded.

43. See *La lettre d'information*, no. 68, 15 January 1997, and no. 71, 1 March 1997.

44. See *Bulletin des travailleurs chinois*, no. 2, April 1997; the article has a significant (and ironic) title: 'Des ouvriers de "Grande Fortune" [Gaofu] pareils aux esclaves'; *Bulletin des travailleurs chinois*, no. 4, September–October 1997, the article 'Du "bonheur" apporté par les investissements internationaux aux travailleurs chinois.'

45. See A. Chan, 'L'agitation ouvrière derrière le "Made in China"', *Perspectives chinoises*, no. 24, July–August 1994, pp. 10 ff; R. Lew, 'Sur les flots agités du développement chinois', *Le Monde Diplomatique*, December 1994.

46. See *Change*, October 1997. The *China Labour Bulletin* of April 1996 gives a figure of 12 million children between the ages of six and fourteen working in factories. But the elderly, too, have serious problems: since 'there is as yet no social labour security system, those who should retire remain in their posts' (see Z. Zonghan, 'An analysis of the Cost of Industrial Products in China', *Social Sciences in China*, no. 2, 1994, p. 18).

47. See J.P. Béja, 'Les travailleurs itinérants, des immigrés de l'interieur', *Perspectives chinoises*, no. 21, January–February 1994; *Rapport de la Commission Indépendante Internationale de Syndicalistes (Shenyang, Dalian, Changchun, 25–30 April 1996)*, Hong Kong, May 1996; and the travel diary of the Commission itself, *Informations Ouvrières*, no. 230, May 1996.

48. See K. Ohmae, *The End of the Nation State*, New York: The Free Press, 1995, p. 85 (author's italics).

49. Ohmae, p. 87. The Italian duo Gianni De Michelis/Gad Lerner are also enthusiastic, with the latter writing of the former: 'In the air sooty with coal and drenched with construction dust, De Michelis savors the animal spirit of capitalism. He feels nothing but admiration before that human anthill, day and night, working around the clock, Saturdays and Sundays included, bunches of workers illuminated by the photoelectric cells on the bamboo scaffolding of the hundred-story buildings under construction, while window-cleaners dangle on a single rope outside the ones already built, and in just six months!' (*La Stampa*, 24 December 1996). A fine example of neocolonial prose.

50. As Lew puts it, in 'Sur les flots agités'.

51. See W. Yalin, 'A study of time allocation of city and town residents', *Social Sciences in China*, no. 2, 1992, p. 72.

52. As an expression of this concern see, for example, the records of the conference

on working hours organized by the European unions of the textile and clothing sector, one of the most highly internationalized, held in Milan on 30–31 May 1990, *Contrattare il tempo*, Rome: Datanews, 1991.

53. See S. Sassen, *Cities in a World Economy*, Thousand Oaks CA: Pine Forge Press, 1994, in particular ch. 4. For his part, H. Thomas, in *Globalization and Third World Trade Unions*, assumes the term 'industrialization' as inclusive also of the modern organizations in the services sector – transportation, banks and insurance companies, and some public services (p. 22).

54. See N. Luhmann, 'Il tempo scarso e il carattere vincolante della scadenza', in S. Tabboni, ed., *Tempo e società*, Milan: Angeli, 1987, p. 123. On the 'hunger for time' and the acceleration of all types of activity in contemporary society it produces, see S.B. Linder, *The Harried Leisure Class*, New York: Columbia University Press, 1970, pp. 77–109.

55. See Luhmann, 'Il tempo scarso', p. 129 (my stress).

56. One of the first to describe the profound transformation of office work was H. Braverman, *Labor and Monopoly Capital: The Degradation of Work in the Twentieth Century*, New York and London: Monthly Review Press, 1974. D. Taddei, 'Les temps de travail dans les services', *Futuribles*, no. 165–166, p. 205 ff., particularly emphasizes the 'trend towards the growing homogenization' of average weekly hours between industry and services, and the trend, also in services, towards a longer utilization time of plants, at least in the sectors most exposed to foreign competition.

57. See P. Levy, *Les technologies de l'intelligence*, Paris: La Découverte, 1990.

58. See Sassen, *Cities in a World Economy*, p. 123.

59. Ibid., p. 117. We find similar views in D. Harvey, *The Condition of Postmodernity: An Enquiry into the Origins of Cultural Change*, Oxford: Basil Blackwell, 1989, chs 9 and 10.

60. Sassen, *Cities in a World Economy*, p. 106.

61. European Foundation for the Improvement of Living and Working Conditions, *The Social Implications of Teleworking*, Dublin, n.d. [1997], pp. 1–7; my stress.

62. See L. Frey, 'Verso l'armonizzazione delle statistiche sul tempo di lavoro con altre informazioni economico-sociali comparabili nei paesi dell'Unione Europea', in L. Frey, ed., *Le statistiche sul lavoro in Europa* (*Quaderni di economia del lavoro*, no. 56, 1996), p. 42, tab. 5.

63. European Foundation for the Improvement of Living and Working Conditions, *Working Conditions in the European Union*, p. 1.

64. Ibid., p. 5.

65. See J.Y. Boulin, 'Les politiques du temps de travail en France: la perte du sens', *Futuribles*, no. 165–166, May–June 1992, pp. 41–62. Given certain premises, such an outcome was inevitable from the start. We must not forget that one highly influential French political party, Le Pen's National Front, has long proposed the return to a week of 45 hours worked and 40 paid, as well as the abolition of the fifth week of vacation.

66. In the programme of the CGT there was a demand for the reduction of working

hours, not for paid vacations: see A. Prost, 'Il primo maggio del Fronte popolare in provincia (1936–1939)', in A. Riosa, ed., *Le metamorfosi del primo maggio*, Padua: Marsilio, 1990, p. 13; see also M. Verret, *La culture ouvrière*, Paris and Montreal: L'Harmattan, 1988, p. 75, which emphasizes the aspect of the twelve vacation days granted as a 'concession from above.'

67. See European Foundation for the Improvement of Living and Working Conditions, *Statistics and News*, Dublin: BEST, no. 9, 1996, p. 8.

68. In the booklet by F. Giulietti, K. Gotnich and S. Palumbo, *Il castello infranto. Volkswagen: una risposta allo sviluppo senza lavoro*, Bari: Slimservice, 1996, we find all of the following: the 'splintering' effect of the Volkswagen agreement (156 varieties of working hours!); 'the problems of many workers due to company pressure to increase productivity' and to 'step up the work pace' (p. 56); 'the abolition and/or reduction of breaks' (p. 58); the increasing competition between co-workers (p. 60); the 'explicit, continual threat of individual dismissal in case of unproductiveness' (p. 58); the 'unfriendly' treatment of 'troublesome workers' (p. 55, a classic of company democracy); and, on the whole, an atmosphere of uncertainty such that 'the dominant feeling at Wolfsburg is fear, and you go to work even if you're sick or in precarious physical condition' (p. 55). This, then, is the 'different' European model?

69. See G. Bosch and S. Lehndorff, 'Working time and the Japanese challenge: the search for a European answer', *International Contributions to Labour Studies*, no. 5, 1995, p. 2.

70. See European Foundation for the Improvement of Living and Working Conditions, *Part-time Work*, Dublin: BEST, no. 8, 1995, p. 66 (my stress).

71. Ibid., p. 65.

72. See Bullock, *Women and Work*, pp. 21, 31; A. Bihr and R. Pfefferkorn, *Hommes/ femmes. L'introuvable egalité*, Paris: Les Editions de l'Atelier-Les Editions Ouvrières, 1996, pp. 69 ff.; D. Kergoat, 'Le donne e il lavoro a tempo parziale', in G. Gasparini, ed., *Tempo e orario di lavoro. Il dibattito in Francia*, Rome: Ed. Lavoro, 1985, pp. 237 ff.; B. Giacomini, 'Occupazione e "tempi" del lavoro femminile', in Istituto Gramsci–Sezione Veneta, ed. U. Curi, *L'orario di lavoro tra fabbrica e società*, Milan: Angeli, 1981, p. 91 ff.; G. Altieri, 'L'occupazione femminile', in M. Paci, ed., *Le dimensioni della disuguaglianza. Rapporto della Fondazione Cespe sulla disuguaglianza sociale in Italia*, Bologna: Il Mulino, 1993, pp. 115–17.

73. Bihr and Pfefferkorn, *Hommes/Femmes*, p. 74, point out that the largest age groups of part-time working women are the under-25s and the over-55s – that is, the ages when women are less burdened with domestic work.

74. With the great prevalence of female part-time work, the 'idea' that women's wages are nothing but a supplement to men's re-presents itself in a different form (C. Saraceno, *Dalla parte della donna*, Rome: De Donato, 1976, p. 146) – an 'idea' that had never disappeared, since the social relations that generated it have themselves by no means disappeared.

75. See Schor, *The Overworked American*, ch. 4; Roediger and Foner, *Our Own Time*,

pp. 276, 364 n. 89; Bihr and Pfefferkorn, *Hommes/Femmes*, pp. 113, 121–3; Corradi, *Il tempo rovesciato,* pp. 152 ff.; L.L. Sabbadini and R. Palomba, 'Differenze di genere e uso del tempo nella vita quotidiana', in Paci, ed., *Le dimensioni della disuguaglianza*, pp. 220 ff.

76. See European Foundation for the Improvement of Living and Working Conditions, *Part-time Work*, p. 25 ff.

77. See P. Concialdi, 'Les bas salaires en France (1983–1995)', *La Lettre de l'IRES*, no. 33/October 1997.

78. A doubt of this kind was raised by the McKinsey Global Institute: see A. Orioli, *Flessibilità*, Milan: Il Sole 24 Ore Libri, 1997, p. 16.

79. Both theses are put forward in the 'hors série' issue, dedicated to the 'Dutch model', of *Chronique Internationale de l'IRES*, October 1997.

80. See M. Wierink, 'Philips mène l'offensive contre la réduction de la durée du travail', *Chronique Internationale*, no. 41, July 1996, pp. 7 ff. Moreover, lest we forget, in the Netherlands, according to Confindustria estimates, average annual working hours in manufacturing as a whole amount to 1,792 hours per employee, 71 hours more than the figure for Italy (of 1,721 hours, according to the same estimates – in any case, far from true). Furthermore, hours are even longer in Great Britain, another country that vaunts no small percentage of part-time work (22.7 per cent of all employees, versus 28.3 per cent in the Netherlands).

81. Sylos Labini, *Nuove tecnologie*, p. 214.

82. See M.C. Belloni, ed., *L'aporia del tempo*, Milan: Angeli, 1986, p. 42.

83. See Rifkin, *The End of Work.* There are, of course, also psychical disorders due to the lack of work: see Rifkin and, in particular, E. Pugliese, *Sociologia della disoccupazione*, Bologna: Il Mulino, 1993, chs 2 and 4; and P. Crepet, *Le malattie della disoccupazione*, Rome: Edizioni Lavoro, 1991.

84. See P. Paoli, 'Les conditions de travail en Europe', in *Santé et Travail*, p. 12; R.C. Kessler, K.A. McGonagle, Sh. Zhao, C.B. Nelson, M. Hughes, S. Eshleman, H. Wittchen and K.S. Kendler, 'Lifetime and 12-month prevalence of DSM-III-R psychiatric disorders in the United States. Results from the National Comorbidity Survey', *Archives of General Psychiatry*, vol. 51, January 1994, p. 8 ff.; Schor, *The Overworked American*, pp. 11 ff. In Great Britain things are no better. A 1994 study ascertained that 44 per cent of British workers get home completely exhausted due to overwork; also in 1994, the British Medical Association reported a significant rise in health problems linked to work-related stress ('cared for', in 60 per cent of the cases, with alcoholic beverages).

85. See D. Cru and S. Volkoff, 'La difficile construction de la santé au travail', *La Revue de l'IRES*, no. 20, Winter 1996, pp. 47 ff.

86. See C. Dejours, *Travail usure mentale. Essai de psychopathologie du travail*, Paris: Bayard, re-edition 1993, p. 251 (my stress).

87. See B. Maggi, 'Sociologia, ergonomia e scienze bio-mediche', *Sociologia del lavoro*, no. 45, 1992, which ascribes the 'shift of interest' of these sciences 'from fatigue to adjustment' (i.e. from labour to capital) to the influence of structural

functionalism. A first 'shift' took place in the 1930s; and a second, even more totalitarian, in the 1980s.

88. We can see the backtracking of the official publications themselves by comparing the fairly good text (source: the ILO) by J. Carpentier and P. Cazamian, *Night Work*, Geneva, 1977, with what has been written (or not written) recently to justify the massive expansion of nightwork.

89. Dejours, *Travail usure mentale*, p. 29.

90. See the WHO document, *The Preparatory Committee of the International Health Conference*, 21 March 1946.

91. See M. Schneider, *Neurose und Klassenkampf*, Hamburg: Rowohlt Verlag, 1972.

92. See A. de Tocqueville, *Democracy in America* [1835–1840], vol. II, New York: Vintage Books, 1957, pp. 168–9.

Chapter 5

1. See S. Bologna, *Nazismo e classe operaia*, Rome: Manifestolibri, 1996 (with an important bibliographical note); T. Mason, 'The workers' opposition in Nazi Germany', *History Workshop*, no. 11, 1981, pp. 120–37, and *Arbeiterklasse und Volksgemeinschaft. Dokumente und Materialen zur deutschen Arbeiterpolitik*, Opladen: Westdeutscher Verlag, 1975; K.H. Roth, 'Arbeiterklasse und Arbeiterorganisationen – Deutschland 1890–1920', in E. Lucas, J. Wickham and K.H. Roth, *Arbeiterradikalismus und die andere Arbeiterbewegung*, Bochum, 1977, ch. 5; E. Collotti, *La Germania nazista*, Turin: Einaudi, 1962 (in particular ch. 9); and the series of *1999. Zeitschrift für Sozialgeschichte des 20. und 21. Jahrhunderts*, journal of the Hamburg Foundation for 20th and 21st Century Social Science. We should recall that in the course of World War II some 50,000 soldiers of the Wehrmacht were sentenced to be shot, as suspected communists, dissidents or unzealous executors of orders.

   We note that also the left and extreme left-wing European press – particularly so, in some respects – is imbued with a semi-racist feeling of preconceived hostility to everything German, which has profound repercussions on its attitude towards the German labour movement and proletariat, present and past.

2. On the farce of denazification in post-World War II Germany, see W. Abendroth, *Aufsteig und Krise der deutschen Sozialdemokratie*, Cologne: Pahl-Rugenstein Verlag, 1974.

3. See E. Collotti, *Storia delle due Germanie 1945–1968*, Turin: Einaudi, 1968; Istituto Gramsci–Sezione Emiliana, *Modello Germania. Strutture e problemi della realtà tedesco–occidentale*, Bologna: Zanichelli, 1978; K.H. Roth, *Die 'andere' Arbeiterbewegung und die Entwicklung der kapitalistischen Repression von 1880 bis zur Gegenwart*, Munich: Trikont Verlag, 1974; J. Agnoli, *Die Transformation der Demokratie*, Berlin: Voltaire Verlag GmbH, 1967; EMIM, ed., *Il sindacato tedesco tra cogestione e lotta di classe*, Rome: Coines, 1975. This full-fledged bombing of the rights of workers went

hand-in-hand with the carpet bombing of the war years, which the 'allies' concentrated on the working-class neighbourhoods of the German cities; a form of terrorism that was indiscriminate and discriminating at one and the same time, just as post-war authoritarianism was.

4. On the historical and theoretical roots of *Mitbestimmung*, see the essay by S.G. Alf, 'Conflitti sociali e sindacato dal dopoguerra a oggi', in Istituto Gramsci–Sezione Emiliana, *Modello Germania*, pp. 112 ff., and F. Naphtali, *Wirtschaftsdemokratie. Ihr Wesen, Weg und Zeil*, Frankfurt: Europaische Verlaganstalt, 1966.

5. See P. Kammerer, *Sviluppo del capitale ed emigrazione in Europa: la Germania federale*, Milan: Mazzotta, 1976, pp. 125 ff. On the discrimination against immigrant workers, see G. Wallraff, *Ganz Unten*, Cologne: Kiepenheuer & Witsch, 1985.

6. In my opinion *Chronique internationale de l'IRES*, which has taken up the question a number of times, with essays by U. Rehfeldt, A. Hege and others, tends to underestimate the effective heightening of tensions between capital and labour, and thus to see the overall picture of *Mitbestimmung* as essentially unchanged. We find the same underestimation in the joint study by the Bertelsmann Stiftung and the Hans-Bockler Stiftung, *Mitbestimmung und neue Unternehmenskulturen – Bilanz und Perspektiven. Bericht der Kommission Mitbestimmung*, Gutersloh: Bertelsmann Stiftung, 1998; the political reasons for it are not hard to understand.

7. P. Martin and H. Schumann, *Die Globalisierungsfalle. Der Angriff auf Demokratie und Wohlstand*, Hamburg: Rowohlt, 1996, p. 150.

8. See Eurostat, *Labour Force Survey: Results 1997*, Brussels and Luxembourg, p. 168, Table 73.

9. See IPRAS, 'Allemagne: la flexibilisation forcée du temps de travail. La semaine de 35 heures dans la pratique entrepreneuriale et syndicale', in Raisons d'agir sur le lieu de travail, ed., *Temps de travail. Temps modernes, horaires antiques*, Lausanne, 1999, p. 26. The survey carried out by IPRAS for IG Metall involved 2,388 metalworking companies, and ascertained that 'à la carte' working schedules were in place in 51.1 per cent of the companies with up to 299 employees, 78.7 per cent with up to 599 employees, 79.4 per cent with up to 999, and 90.9 per cent of the companies with over 1,000 employees.

10. Ibid., p. 25.

11. My discussion of *Zeitkonten* is based on an unpublished paper by G. Mandarino, 'Il lavoro "normale" nella Germania d'oggi' (1998), which examines a wide range of DGB documents. In some respects the 'réglementations des 13/18' may be considered a primordial form of *Zeitkonten*.

12. See the long interview with Oskar Negt in *il manifesto*, 15 November 1997.

13. Martin and Schumann, *Die Globalisierungsfalle*, p. 151.

14. See P. Hassenteufel, 'Allemagne: la mise en place de la troisième étape de la réforme de l'assurance maladie', *Chronique internationale de l'IRES*, no. 49, November 1997, pp. 17 ff. On the antecedents of these counter-reforms, see Hassenteufel, *Les médecins face à l'Etat: une comparaison européenne*, Paris: Presses de Sciences Po, 1997, pp. 297 ff., 330–40.

15. A. Hege writes: 'German workers, in 1997, had the lowest wage increases in forty years.... The recent evolution of wages prolongs a trend towards the fall in real wages that we have seen in the western Länder since 1990. The weak growth of nominal wages is not the sole cause. Workers have been subject to an increase in taxes and other social contributions and have had to accept reductions of certain benefits' ('Allemagne: décentralisation de la négociation collective: éléments d'un débat', *Chronique internationale de l'IRES*, no. 51, March 1998, p. 23).

16. See *Frankfurter Allgemeine Zeitung*, 3 June 1996; *Frankfurter Rundschau*, 2 December 1995; *La Stampa*, 12 August 1998. H. Doss, a Christian Democrat leader, came straight to the point, suggesting 'a collective return to the 40-hour week' with no rise in pay, because 'in Germany people *have to work more* [my stress] for our industry to regain competitiveness on the international markets and to improve the competitiveness of German products domestically with respect to imports.' Perfectly logical. A year earlier, it was the Social Democrat L. Ruschmeier who proposed a return to the 40-hour week for municipal employees (*Suddeutsche Zeitung*, 27 October 1997).

17. See I. Artus, 'A l'Est, un paysage contractuel fragile', *Chronique internationale de l'IRES*, no. 57, March 1999, pp. 14–15. We should recall that the first government body for industry that excluded union representatives was Treuhand, constituted in 1990 to dismantle the almost entirely state-owned east German industry and reorganize it from top to bottom. The first major formal rupture in *Mitbestimmung* took place, then, in a matter regarding the east but, obviously, not only the east. And in the east we also note the ultra-flexibility in the pilot agreement between the small Christian union CGB and the Association of metalworking and electrical industrialists of Saxony that permits the negotiation – in each plant, and without restriction – of an 'exchange' between wage reduction, flexibilization of working time, and maintenance of employment levels.

18. See M. Promberger, J. Rosducher, H. Seifert and R. Trinczek, *Weniger Geld, kurzere Arbeitszeit, sichere Jobs? Soziale und ökonomische Folgen beschaftigungssichernder Arbeitsverkurzungen*, Berlin: Sigma, 1997.

19. Ibid., pp. 152 ff.; K. Jurgens and K. Reinecke, *Zwischen Volks- und Kinderwagen. Auswirkungen der 28.8–Stunden-Woche bei der VW AG auf die familiale Lebensfuhrung von Industriearbeiten*, Berlin: Sigma, 1998, pp. 158 ff.; W. Scherer, 'Un modèle en trompe-l'oeil', *Page 2*, no. 3, July–August 1996, which also reports on significant union agitations in Hanover against the agreement.

20. See F. Giulietti, K. Gotnich and S. Palumbo, *Il castello infranto*, p. 55 (my stress).

21. Promberger et al., *Weniger Geld, kurzere Arbeitszeit, sichere Jobs?*, p. 39, Table 1.1. Overall, 49 per cent declare themselves satisfied or highly satisfied, 35 per cent partially satisfied, and 16 per cent dissatisfied.

22. Jurgens and Reinecke, *Zwischen Volks- und Kinderwagen*, passim; B. Kraatz, 'La fabbrica che respira', *il manifesto*, 14 February 1999.

23. See U. Jurgens, 'Il caso Volkswagen', in the trade-union publication *Strategie di prodotto, di globalizzazione e di fornitura delle grandi aziende automobilistiche: lo scenario*

internazionale, Turin, April 1997, pp. 34 ff.; Scherer, 'Un modèle en trompe-l'oeil', *Handelsblatt*, 1 December 1999.

24. For that matter, consider the fact that Article 3 of the new German law on working hours that came into force in July 1994 (replacing the 1938 decree signed by Goering) makes it possible to extend working hours to a maximum of 10 hours a day and 60 hours a week, with 'compensatory' days off within 6 months. If I'm not mistaken, with the 'revolutionary' method proposed by Hartz the very principle of 'compensation' goes out of the window.

25. See Eurostat, *Labour Force Survey: Results 1997*, p. 168, Table 73; 'Travailler au-delà de la durée habituelle', *Insee Première*, no. 591, June 1998.

26. See G. Filoche, *Le travail jetable non. Les 35 heures oui*, Paris: Ramsay, 1999, p. 16; chapters 1 ('Ils nous rallongent notre temps de travail…') and 2 of this book are of particular interest.

27. Ibid., p. 73.

28. The statement is in *Corriere della sera*, 6 March 2000.

29. Filoche, *Le travail jetable non*, pp. 21–2. D. Mothé writes: 'A law limiting the working week to 35 or 32 hours would have no possibility of being respected in small businesses if employers, workers and the surrounding population are not really committed to it' (*L'Utopie du temps libre*, Paris: Esprit, 1997, p. 81). But from what we have seen here, only the pressure and organization of workers could make small businesses 'really commit themselves' to respecting such a law – which is exactly what Mothé rules out. And since the matter can certainly not be resolved by the intervention of factory inspectors, who in France, moreover, are far less numerous than in northern Europe (see *Santé et travail*, no. 28, July 1999, p. 9), it is clear that Mothé's argument itself calls the bluff of a 35-hour week prescribed by law, which 'would have no possibility of being respected in small businesses', as is already the case with the 39-hour week.

30. See S. Beaud and M. Pialoux, *Retour sur la condition ouvrière*, Paris: Fayard, 1999, pp. 419–20; F. Caron, *Place et importance des PME dans le système productive française*, Lyon: Document Glysi, 1992; J. Bunel, 'Le patronat français', in J. Kergoat, J. Boutet, H. Jacot and D. Linhart, eds, *Le monde du travail*, Paris: La Découverte, 1998, pp. 401–2.

31. See G. Balbastre and S. Binhas, 'A production-line dictatorship', *Le Monde diplomatique* (English edition), January 2000. These researchers describe the Douai plant as a sort of total institution: 'The Renault Douai works would appear to be hermetically sealed, setting its own rules behind a wall of silence.'

32. See M. Gollac and S. Volkoff, 'Citius, altius, fortius, l'intensification du travail', *Actes de la recherche en sciences sociales*, no. 114, 1996; J. Hodeburg, 'L'évolution des conditions de travail', in Kergoat et al., eds, *Le monde du travail*, pp. 146 ff.; the entire Dossier *Travail et santé*, edited by Raisons d'agir sur le lieu de travail, Lausanne, November 1998; the Dossier 'Chiffrer la santé au travail' in *Santé et Travail*, no. 27, April 1999; and DARES, *Premières informations – Premières synthèses*, nos. 23 and 27, 1999, dedicated respectively to 'Les troubles du sommeil, l'âge

et le travail' and 'Travail et charge mentale'.

33. See Beaud and Pialoux, *Retour sur la condition ouvrière*, especially the introduction, the first part, and the conclusion. More than twenty years ago R. Linhart, in *L'établi*, Paris: Minuit, 1978, noted that 'fear is part of the factory; it is an essential cog'. C. Dejours, too, emphasizes how 'today, the first structural element for work is fear, the threat of dismissal, the threat of casualization' (interview in *Critique communiste*, no. 152, Summer 1998, p. 14). The capitalist factory, for capital the realm of freedom, is for wage labour the realm of despotism.

34. See M. Husson, 'Le temps de travail', in Kergoat et al., eds, *Le monde du travail*, p. 185.

35. See the interview with the ergonomist S. Prunier-Poulmaire in the dossier 'Repos et récupération', *Santé et travail*, no. 25, October 1998, pp. 22–4, on the working condition of cashiers in hypermarkets, a job 'where the constraints of the work pace are intense, the possibilities of rest are limited, and are often compromised by the way the stores are organized and managed'. The entire Dossier, also dealing with types of work not often the object of study, such as that of sea fishermen, is of interest.

36. For statistical data on the strikes, see J. Kergoat, 'Les conflits du travail', in Kergoat et al., eds, *Le monde du travail*, p. 380, Table 1.

37. See A. Touraine, F. Dubet, D. Lapeyronnie, F. Khosrokhavar and M. Wieviorka, *Le Grand Refus. Réflexions sur la grève de décembre 1995*, Paris: Fayard, 1996.

38. See C. Aguiton and D. Bensaid, *Le retour de la question sociale*, Lausanne: Page deux, 1997; and S. Beroud and R. Mouriaux, *Le souffle de décembre*, Paris: Syllepse, 1997.

39. See the interview with Martine Aubry in *Le Nouvel Observateur*, 9–15 October 1997.

40. See J. Decoster, 'Les 35 heures intensifient la course à la productivité', *La Tribune*, 22 June 1999.

41. See Filoche, *Le travail jetable*, p. 61.

42. Ibid.; see also L. Maurin, 'Comment mesurer le temps de travail?', *Alternatives économiques*, no. 164, November 1998, pp. 24–5. Even those who are most favourably disposed towards Aubry's mystifications know that 'the reduction of legal hours does not necessarily translate into a reduction of real hours' (E. Heyer and X. Timbeau, '35 heures: pas une seconde à perdre', *Lettre de l'OFCE*, no. 188, 19 July 1999, p. 4) – which, of course, does not mean they choose to look into the question further.

43. See G. Duval, '35 heures. Pourquoi ça marche mal, pourquoi il faut continuer', *Alternatives économiques*, no. 171, June 1999, p. 27.

44. L. Cremieux called the first Aubry law 'a formidable lever for the development of flexibility', for 'the generalization of flexibility', or, simply, 'the flexibility law' (see 'Loi Aubry: les travailleurs ne lui disent pas merci!', in Raisons d'agir sur le lieu du travail, ed., *Temps de travail*, pp. 28–30).

45. See C. Yerochewski, 'Intérim: la dérive', *Alternatives économiques*, no. 173, September

1999, p. 30. In her interview with *La Nouvel Observateur*, Aubry admits that 85 per cent of new hirings 'are for temporary jobs' – especially if it is the state that does the hiring!

46. On the second Aubry law, see M. Bulard, 'What price the 35-hour week?', *Le Monde Diplomatique* (English Edition), September 1999; P. Le Moal, 'Contenu et enjeu du second projet de loi des 35 heures', *Carré rouge*, no. 12, October 1999.

47. The events of 1936–38 ought to serve as a warning for the French proletariat. Then too, with the initiative of a 'good father' concerned about the well-being of his (presumed) worker children, the Blum government introduced a 40-hour week, obtaining for the state a sort of mandate for the improvement of the workers' conditions of existence. However, only two years later the Daladier government abolished the 40-hour law, and a labour movement larger than the one today but undermined by its own foolish trust in the neutrality of the state, if not by its good will towards the workers, was absolutely incapable of mounting any sort of opposition.

48. See M. Paci, 'Tempo, occupazione e benessere', *Sociologia del lavoro*, no. 54, 1994, pp. 11–12. Research on female labour carried out in Bologna, Palermo and Turin by FIOM, the Italian metalworking union, show that, even today, the amount of time woman workers have to devote to the work of family reproduction is enormous: if for 20.6 per cent the figure is 'only' 1 to 3 hours a day, for 36.2 per cent it is 4 to 5 hours, for 40.4 per cent it is over 6 hours, while for 15 per cent it is fully 7 to 8 hours (see FIOM–CGIL, *Esplorare il lavoro. Indagine nazionale sul lavoro delle donne nelle fabbriche di Bologna, Palermo, Torino*, Bologna, March 1997, p. 13).

49. See B. Ugolini, *I tempi di lavoro*, pp. 168–9; T. Treu, T. Geroldi and M. Maiello, 'Italy: Labour Relations', in J. Hartog and T. Theeuwes, eds., *Labour Market Contracts and Institutions*, London: Elsevier, 1993.

50. See P. Brusetta and E. Giovannini, eds, *Capire il sommerso*, Naples: Liguori, 1998. Statistics show that in Italy, in 1996, 47 per cent of workers were employed in firms with fewer than ten employees, and most job creation continues to take place in precisely these small or very small businesses (see Ministero del Lavoro e della Providenza sociale, *Piano d'azione nazionale per l'occupazione 1999*, Rome, 1999, pp. 22, 32).

51. N. Cacace, one of the very few researchers who has reconstructed historical statistics on working time, gives an estimate of average annual working time in Italy for 1994 of 1,800 hours, 100 hours more than the decades 1961–71 and 1981–91, and 150 more than the period 1971–81 (see his Table *107 anni di lavoro italiano 1891–1991*; 'Ridurre l'orario si può, anzi si deve', *L'Unità*, 5 May 1997; 'Riduzione di orario e occupazione', *Finesecolo*, no. 3–4, December 1996, p. 237). His estimate of the increase in hours in Italy is very close to Schor's estimate for the United States, set at 158 hours on average in the period 1969–89.

52. See I. Diamanti and D. Martini, 'Il Nordest: una società laburista', *Il Progetto*, second series, no. 12, November–December 1996, pp. 7–14. A. Bonomi (*Il*

capitalismo molecolare, Turin: Einaudi, 1996) sums up his view as follows: 'The northeast is booming, also as regards job creation, but this boom is built on intensive forms of exploitation and self-exploitation, of production decentralization, of unrestrained flexibility, of technological backwardness' (interview with *Corriere della sera*, 10 November 1997). With the exception of this last element, which may or – more often – may not be the case, these are the salient features of the production process of the 'age of flexibility'.

53. See P. Perulli, 'Sindacato, politiche degli orari e organizzazione del lavoro', in Istituto Gramsci–Sezione Veneta, ed. U. Curi, *L'orario di lavoro tra fabbrica e società*, Milan: Angeli, 1981, pp. 47–8 (my stress).

54. So child labour, too, is thus provided for in this agreement, between CISAL and ANILF, a small manufacturers' association. The agreement regards piecework.

55. See S. Bologna and A. Fumagalli, eds., *Il lavoro autonomo di seconda generazione*, Milan: Feltrinelli, 1997. For the working hours – also extremely long – of the 'officially' self-employed who are actually employees, see G. Polo, *Il mestiere di sopravvivere*, Rome: Editori Riuniti, 1999 and IRES – Ministero del Lavoro e della Previdenza Sociale, *Le nuove forme di lavoro: opportunità, caratteristiche e problemi regolativi del lavoro coordinato e continuativo*, Rome, 1998, pp. 143 ff.

56. See F. Belussi, ed., *Nuovi modelli d'impresa, gerarchie organizzative e imprese rete*, Milan: Angeli, 1992; F. Belussi and M. Festa, 'L'impresa rete del modello veneto: dal post-fordismo al toyotismo? Alcune note illustrative sulle strutture organizzative dell'indotto Benetton', *Oltre il Ponte*, no. 31, 1990. In many towns in the Veneto a half-day of work on Sunday mornings is the norm.

57. Interview in *Liberazione*, 11 February 1997.

58. See I. Zanchetta, 'Una fabbrica di sogno senza luce e libertà', in *Il nuovo macchinismo* [anthology], Rome: Datanews, 1992, pp. 53–4.

59. See M. Agostinelli, 'Le radici economiche della Lega', *Finesecolo*, no. 3–4, December 1996, pp. 281–4. An important study by the FIOM of Brescia, the results of which were presented on 5 November 1999, emphasized the glaring parodox facing the trade-union movement: 'We talk about reduction, and the fact is that we have lost control over hours. There is a rise in overtime, in shiftwork, there is total saturation: real hours have come to equal theoretical hours (98.97 per cent in 1997). These figures by themselves reveal a worsening of material conditions, starting with risks for the workers' very safety' (*il manifesto*, 22 October 1999).

60. See the report 'Viaggio nel tessile da Praia a Prato', *L'Unità*, 26 October 1997.

61. It would be hard to beat the Fiat plant at Melfi on that score; the latest survey conducted at Fiat Melfi and its ancillary industries reveals that 76 per cent of the workers consider their working conditions *very bad*, only 24 per cent consider them normal, while the percentage of workers that consider them good is *zero* (material received directly from the FIOM of Potenza).

62. See *Crescere insieme*, no. 20, November–December 1996 (the average rate of absenteeism is 5 per cent in Japan and 3.5 per cent in the United States). To say

nothing of the working conditions in the fields, where even today harvest days (transportation included) go from three in the morning to seven in the evening (see A. Leo, L. Limoccia and N. Piacente, *Vite bruciate di terra*, Potenza: Ega, 1997).

63. The Telecom 'Information' operators, for example, have to respond to each caller in no more than 44 seconds.

64. M. Ambrosini has emphasized how the growing use of immigrant labour in industry throughout the North is specifically due to the growing demand for 'atypical' work schedules that are particularly heavy and harmful to health: see Fondazione Cariplo–ISMU, *Primo rapporto sulle migrazioni in Italia*, Milan: Angeli, 1995, pp. 153–5, 163–4.

65. The very latest is the decision of Pininfarina, a firm in the auto sector, to lay off employees who are unfit to work – because of illnesses contracted on the job!

66. The deputy secretary of the FIOM–CGIL, Cerfeda, speaks of a 43- to 44-hour week for industry (*La Stampa*, 14 November 1997), an estimate that has been confirmed also by the national direction of the FIOM (*il manifesto*, 12 January 2000). Some directors of the Confindustria give 40 to 55 hours (*Corriere della sera*, 13 October 1997). A Datamedia survey gives 45.4 hours as the average for the economy as a whole (*Panorama*, 25 November 1999). A study by the CGIL of Turin, however, speaks of a working week that often exceeds 50 hours, while also denouncing the repetitiveness of work found in 70 per cent of the cases, and the rise in episodes of violence in the workplace (*il manifesto*, 5 April 2000).

Chapter 6

1. See W. Grossin, 'Gestione del tempo e tecnologia: la difficoltà delle scelte', in G. Gasparini, ed., *Tempo e orario di lavoro. Il dibattito in Francia*, Rome: Ed. Lavoro, 1985, p. 103. J. Gershuny, 'La répartition du temps dans les sociétés post-industrielles', *Futuribles*, no. 165–166, May–June 1992, p. 220, claims that the prime beneficiary of the creation of leisure time has been none other than the 'people of the working class.'

2. See P.A. Samuelson, *Economics*, New York: McGraw-Hill, 1973, p. 1.

3. On the fact that Chile, and Latin America as a whole, were the first field of experimentation for neoliberal policies, see *Page 2*, no. 5, October 1996, in the dossier 'La fabrique sociale', with articles by P. Anderson and Ch.A. Udry.

4. See A. Cuevas, *Sindacato e potere nell'America latina. Modelli e tendenze nel sindacalismo latinoamericano*, Rome: Ed. Lavoro, 1985, p. 125.

5. Naturalizing, naturalizing, Milton Friedman has even discovered the 'natural[!] rate of unemployment'. Yes, it is true that this is made to depend on specific non-natural economic conditions. At the same time, however, the term says a great deal, in light of the fact that this school of economics has paid extremely

close attention to keeping unemployment from dipping below a certain level, which on average is twice that of the 1950s and 1960s, in order to discourage the growth of wages 'naturally'. And discouraging the growth of wages is one of the best 'natural' incentives to long working hours. (See M. Friedman, *Monetarist Economics*, Oxford: Basil Blackwell, 1991, pp. 94 ff., which contains a formulation of monetarist policies that is still rather prudent and indirect; the text is Friedman's 1976 Nobel Prize acceptance speech.)

For Friedman and his followers any 'unpleasant' aspect of capitalist society, such as unemployment or poverty, or, at the other extreme, speculation and the like, is attributed to 'nature'. The capitalist social order itself is seen as a 'natural order' of relations between human beings. If truth be told, this self-proclaimed 'naturalistic' economy is nothing but a cookbook of fast-food recipes to satisfy the appetite of the nonworking classes, taken as the peak of human nature, for other people's work. It goes without saying that such an *ideology* presents itself as a rigorously 'value-neutral' theory, Weberianly free of presuppositions 'of value' (Friedman, *Monetarist Economics*, pp. 88–9).

6. 'I want these people to be beaten at all costs', Alfred Marshall wrote in 1897 on the occasion of a strike by engineering workers, adding: 'The complete destruction of unionism would be as heavy a price as it is possible to conceive, but I think it is not too high a price' (see G. Therborn, *Science, Class and Society*, London: New Left Books, 1976, p. 94). F.A. Hayek is not less violent than Marshall in attacking a unionism that, moreover, has become far more institutional and 'compatibilist' than the one that was fighting for an 8-hour day at the end of the nineteenth century (see *Economic Freedom*, Oxford: Basil Blackwell, 1991, ch. 8).

7. The documents regarding the exchange of views between Luigi Einaudi and Giovanni Agnelli are in L. Villari, *Il capitalismo italiano del novecento*, Bari: Laterza, 1972, pp. 256 ff.

8. See J.M. Keynes, *Essays in Persuasion*, London: Macmillan, 1931, p. xviii.

9. Ibid., pp. 321 ff. In the ambit of classical political economy, it was above all John Stuart Mill who foresaw the shortening of working time as a 'legitimate effect' of the development of industry (see *Principles of Political Economy*, 1848).

10. Samuelson, *Economics*, p. 576. Note that this is the most widely read introductory economics textbook in the world today, at least in the West.

11. See R. Sue, *Temps et ordre social*, Paris: PUF, 1995, p. 8, and in particular chs VII and VIII; Sue, 'Tra il lavoro ed il tempo libero: l'emergenza di un tempo di utilità sociale', *Sociologia del lavoro*, no. 56, 1994, pp. 63 ff.

12. See J.B. Schor, *The Overworked American: The Unexpected Decline of Leisure*, New York: Basic Books, 1991, p. 164. 'A 1989 letter to three hundred business leaders advocating a shorter workweek failed to yield a single favorable response' (p. 152). But in another survey, carried out in the same year, fully 80 per cent of the workers interviewed 'declared that they would sacrifice career advancement in order to spend more time with their families' (p. 132). Two opposite points of view.

13. Ibid., p. 157.

14. See I. Cipoletta, 'Le 35 ore anti-storiche', *Il sole 24 ore*, 5 December 1997 (my stress).

15. See International Metalworkers' Federation, *I metalmeccanici e l'orario di lavoro nel mondo*, Geneva: IMF, 1997, pp. 54–57; A. Orioli, *Flessibilità*, Milan: Il Sole 24 Ore Libri, 1997, p. 33.

16. See, for example, C.P. Kindleberger, *Economic Law and Economic History*, Cambridge: Press Syndicate of the University of Cambridge, 1989.

17. *Verwertung*: 'valorization', realization, expansion, creation of surplus value [trans.].

18. K. Marx, *Capital*, Volume 1, trans. S. Moore and E. Aveling, ed. F. Engels, Moscow: Progress Publishers, 1965, part IV, ch. XIII, pp. 322 ff.

19. K. Marx, *Grundrisse: Introduction to the Critique of Political Economy* [1857–58], trans. M. Nicolaus, London: Penguin Books, 1993, pp. 584–90.

20. See R. Luxemburg, *The Accumulation of Capital* (1913), trans. A. Schwarzschild, London: Routledge & Kegan Paul, 1951, p. 39. Rosa Luxemburg refers, with greater precision, to surplus value instead of profit. To avoid complicating the treatment of the issue further, I prefer to prescind from the distinction between surplus value (or surplus labour) and profit, and thus from the subdivision of surplus value into profit, rent and interest.

21. J.M. Keynes, in his essay 'The End of Laissez-faire' (1926) (in *Essays in Persuasion*, p. 293), makes a particularly blunt statement about 'the essential characteristic of capitalism, namely the dependence upon an intense appeal to the money-making and money-loving instincts of individuals as the main motive force of the economic machine.' He then goes on, however, to drown his remark in an incredible series of 'propensions', individual natural 'instincts', and other forms of incongruous subjectivization of 'the impersonal forces of the market', whose effect is to annul its meaning.

22. 'Time is the root of human development. A man who has no free time to dispose of, whose whole lifetime, apart from the mere physical interruptions by sleep, meals, and so forth, is absorbed by his labour for the capitalist, is less than a beast of burden. He is a mere machine for producing Foreign Wealth, broken in body and brutalized in mind' (K. Marx, *Wages, Prices, and Profit* [1865], in vol. 20, *Collected Works*, London: Lawrence & Wishart, p. 142).

23. Marx, *Capital*, unpublished draft of Volume I, ch. VI, in *Collected Works*, vol. 34, London: Lawrence & Wishart, p. 399.

24. In saying this, I prescind from three forms of exchange in which surplus value may in fact be created: exchange between a capitalist economy and a natural economy, exchange between a dominant capitalist economy and a dependent capitalist economy, or exchange between superdeveloped and concentrated industry and agriculture still based on small-scale production.

25. For those who intend to study 'what Marx really said' on the subject, it is indispensable to tackle *Capital*, especially parts III, IV and V of Volume I; part II of Volume II; parts II and III of Volume III. Not less important, for the questions dealt with in this book, are the so-called 'Fragment on Machinery' in *Grundrisse*,

pp. 690–706, and the analysis in *Theories of Surplus Value*, (1861–1863), Volume 2, of the theories of Ricardo and of Barton on the influence of machinery on the situation of the working class (*Collected Works*, Lawrence & Wishart, vol. 32, pp. 177–208).

26. This relation between wage labour and the 'other' – capital – that grounds every other intersubjective relation has slightly different characteristics from the ones theorized for the encounter with the 'other' by Levinas or Habermas. In fact, the 'face-to-face' relation between capital and labour is a relation between neither equal nor free subjects. And the face of the 'other' – capital – does indeed look towards 'the infinite', except that this infinite is the infinite of its self-valorization, which is realized with the crushing, with the devalorization, of the 'interlocutor' – that is, of the worker and of his humanity.

27. See J. Fallot, *Marx et le machinisme*, Paris: Cujas, 1966. In this text, the part on the 'Marxist definitions' of science is substantially valid and useful; I am not in agreement, however, with the opening chapters and the concluding section. Marx is a critic of the capitalist *use* of science and mechanization, not of science and mechanization as such. On the contrary, for Marx the development and socialization of the forces of production, even with the imprint of capitalism, are to be considered the indispensable presupposition, both technically and socially, of the communist organization of society.

28. See A. Ure, *The Philosophy of Manufactures: or an Exposition of the Scientific, Moral and Commercial Economy of the Factory System of Great Britain*, London: C. Knight, 1835, p. 368.

29. See W. Grossin, 'Gestione del tempo e tecnologia', pp. 106–7 (my stress).

30. Grossin, p. 107.

31. In urging workers and foremen to make technical suggestions aimed at improving the methods and instruments of production, Toyotaism demonstrates its awareness that even in this age of extreme polarization between intellectual and manual labour, workers can make a valuable contribution to the progress of technology, and even of science.

32. Quoted in M. Rubel, *Karl Marx. Essai de biographie intellectuelle*, Paris: Rivière, 1971, p. 437.

33. *Grundrisse*, p. 706 (Marx's stress).

34. See P. Manacorda, *Lavoro e intelligenza nell'età micro-elettronica*, Milan: Feltrinelli, 1984, p. 88.

35. Marx, *Capital*, Volume I, part IV, ch. XV, sec. 3, p. 403.

36. Indeed, for several decades the United States and the West in general have been acquiring scientists, technologists and highly skilled workers from the dominated countries of the Third World at extremely low cost (it is a sort of expropriation): see L. Potts, *The World Labour Market: A History of Migration*, London: Zed Books, 1990, pp. 160–161; T. Coutrot and M. Husson, *Les destins du Tiers Monde*, Luçon: Nathan, 1993, p. 64. Evidently, the capitalist tendency to lower the value of labour power knows no exceptions.

37. This frank but perfectly accurate expression was used by Andrew Ure, who, in the passage cited in note 11, writes: 'When capital enlists science in her service, the refractory hand of labour will always be taught docility.' In our day, on the subject of science such frankness of judgement and intent has been lost. What now prevails is the mystifying 'divinization' of science and technology as autonomous powers that dominate the *entire* life of society, and that therefore rise above even the capitalist class itself. For the more sophisticated forms of such 'divinization' (for the more cultured reader), see Jünger (in a 'metaphysical' vein) or Heidegger (in a 'romantic' one). As for second- and third-rate mystifications (for the general public), there is an astoundingly vast assortment.

38. By organic composition of capital is meant the relation between the elements that constitute fixed capital (raw materials, plants, machinery, etc.) and the elements that constitute variable capital (human labour power, wages). The composition is low when variable capital prevails over fixed capital. It is a relation of *value*, whose foundation is the 'technical' relation between a given quantity of labour power and the quantity of machinery, means of production, raw materials, and so on, which this labour power sets in motion and controls in the production process. Here I am speaking of it *in general*, prescinding from the fact that both these relations vary considerably from one sector to another, from one country to another, and even from one moment of the cycle to another.

39. Note how also in the nineteenth century the key dates for the reduction of the working day coincide with the moments of most heated class struggle (1847–48, the years in which British and French workers obtained the 10-hour day), or with the most significant moments of the organization of the working class into a political party (1864–66, respectively the year of the birth of the First International and the year of the International Congress in Geneva, which marked the beginning of the struggle for the 8-hour day).

40. Marx, *Capital*, Volume I, part IV, ch. XV, sec. 3, p. 409. Marx notes that the shortening of the working day (compared to a previous phase of its unlimited lengthening) 'increases to a wonderful degree the regularity, uniformity, order, continuity, and energy of the labour' (pp. 410–11).

41. Marx, *Grundrisse*, p. 340 (translation modified).

42. We shall not discuss here how the 'taking' of working time by the state is to be considered.

43. Marx, *Grundrisse*, pp. 333 ff.

44. For data of the period 1900–1973, see E. Pugno and S. Garavini, *Gli anni duri alla Fiat*, Turin: Einaudi, 1974, pp. 230–31; for subsequent years I have used figures from the trade-union or financial press. Note that the figures refer to *all* the Fiat employees, which means that, for example, in 1997 the output per production worker is considerably more than 500 million lire per year, perhaps close to 600 million.

45. To this end, W. Lepenies ('Il declino del lavoro', *Reset*, January 1994, pp. 58–60) calls for the adoption of a 'new system of values' in which work and 'nonwork'

are values that are equally acceptable. It takes 'imagination', he tells us. But his 'imagination' (moulded like wax by the imperatives of the market) boils down to calling employed workers 'privileged', and the unemployed 'nonworking'. Come on now, we can do better than that! How about calling the overworked 'do-nothings'; then, for the night shift, we can do away with that horrible expression 'graveyard shift' and try calling it 'tiptoe through the tulips'; and even for the 'assembly line' (do you find that a pleasant name?) we can come up with something much much nicer. It just takes imagination! A changed name, a changed life.

46. See O. Negt, *Lebendige Arbeit, Enteignete Zeit*, Frankfurt am Main: Campus Verlag, 1984, pp. 44 ff.

47. Marx, *Grundrisse*, pp. 707 ff.

48. Adam Smith, in his *An Inquiry into the Nature and Causes of the Wealth of Nations* (1776), vol. 1, Oxford: Clarendon Press, 1976, pp. 330–31, minces no words in his list of 'menial servants' and 'unproductive labourers', headed by 'the sovereign with all the officers both of justice and war ... servants of the public, and maintained by a part of the annual produce of the industry of other people', and going on to include 'churchmen, lawyers, physicians, men of letters of all kinds; players, buffoons, musicians, opera-singers, opera-dancers, &c'. Saint-Simon in his 'Parable' was no less scathing (see C. de Saint-Simon, *Oeuvres*, vol. II/2, Paris: Anthropos, 1966, pp. 17–26).

 Also today many of the exalted and untouchable figures in our society are indeed 'unproductive labourers', but who will dare to make such a list? Headed by the sovereigns of finance, of the stock exchange, of industry, of war, of disinformation, with all their 'officers both of justice and war', their lawyers who break the law, their churchmen with or without the cloth, their players without art, their buffoons without wit – the list goes on and on.

49. If the sea of vagabonds was the most visible 'epiphenomenon' of the dissolution of feudalism, the ocean of migrants and of urban outcasts is the most visible epiphenomenon of the dissolution of societies on the 'periphery' of the world market. But can the dissolution of the 'periphery' ever be an autonomous process?

50. Always, of course, within the limits of the guarantee of maximum profitability for their own companies.

51. 'The consumer is no freer than the producer. His judgement depends on his means and his needs. Both of these are determined by his social position, which itself depends on the whole social organization' (K. Marx, *The Poverty of Philosophy* (1847), New York: International Publishers, 1963, p. 41).

52. Penetrating remarks on mass consumerism have been made, from differing viewpoints (and different from 'mine'), by Guy Debord, by Pier Paolo Pasolini (in *Scritti corsari*), and by Christopher Lasch. If working time and the worker who provides it are commodities, then 'free' time cannot in fact be time that is free for the full realization of the 'humanity of human beings'.

53. See F. Block, R.A. Cloward, B. Ehrenreich and F. Fox Piven, *The Mean Season:*

The Attack on the Welfare State, New York: Pantheon Books, 1987; K. Newman, *Falling from Grace*, New York: The Free Press, 1988; F. Strobel, *Upward Dreams, Downward Mobility: The Economic Decline of the American Middle Class*, Lanham: Rowman & Littlefield, 1993.

54. Let me remark, parenthetically, that Cipoletta categorically denies the axiom that technical–scientific progress has, of necessity, to translate into reduced working hours.

55. K. Marx, *Capital*, Volume 3, trans. D. Fernbach, London: Penguin Books, 1981, ch. 20, p. 450, and ch. 27, p. 573.

56. See K. Marx and F. Engels, *India Cina Russia* (1850–1894), published in Italian, ed. B. Maffi, Milan: Il Saggiatore, 1970; A. Bordiga, *I fattori di razza e nazione nella teoria marxista*, Milan: Iskra, 1976, Part III.

57. To say nothing of all its financial, state, diplomatic, and military means of oppression–expropriation.

58. It is the contradiction between the *universal* social character of the capitalist development of the productive forces of labour and their *national* appropriation; between the creation of a unitary worldwide process of production and labour and the 'private' competition between companies and nation-states to garner its fruits.

59. Marx discusses the relation between two working days of different length and intensity on a number of occasions; see, for example, *Capital*, Volume 3, ch. 13, pp. 321–2.

60. See F. Chesnais, 'Mondialisation du capital & régime d'accumulation a dominance financière', *Agone*, no. 16, 1996, p. 24. By the same author, see also *La mondialisation du capital*, Paris: Syros, 1994 (2nd enlarged edn, 1997), one of the most lucid and complete discussions of the issue; and the collected writings, edited by Chesnais, *La mondialisation financière*, Paris: Syros, 1997.

61. More and more European and US-American corporations are decentralizing their accounting services to Third World countries. The decentralization of services is snowballing in all spheres. Just one example: in airports in Germany Lufthansa utilizes companies in California to transmit its night-time announcements to passengers, saving on costs.

62. See P. Basso, 'Mondialisation et temps de travail', *Page 2*, no. 11, May 1997, p. 49.

63. See the statement by M. Videt, a leader of the French textile, garment and leather-goods union, in *Contrattare il tempo*, Rome: Datanews, 1991, p. 67. The statement by the Portuguese unionist M.A. Teixeira De Freitas is even more scathing: 'The majority [of the Portuguese textile and garment working women] work from 14 to 16 hours a day [including domestic work]; they do not have weekends free and they do not have time for the necessary cultural, social and political activities' (*Contrattare il tempo*, p. 42).

64. See *International Herald Tribune*, 20 November 1996.

65. On the central role of outsourcing in so-called 'flexible accumulation', see D.

Harvey, *The Condition of Postmodernity: An Enquiry into the Origins of Cultural Change*, Oxford: Basil Blackwell, 1989, p. 141 ff. It has been estimated that at the beginning of the 1990s General Motors was outsourcing 57 per cent of its work, Ford 62 per cent and Chrysler 66 per cent. The aim is clear: to cut production costs. The by-products are clear: low wages, long hours, zero union rights. Globalized postmodern paradises.

66. See Bureau International du Travail, *Annuaire des statistiques du travail 1957*, Geneva, 1957, p. 189, and *Annuaire des statistiques du travail 1991*, Geneva, 1991, p. 729.

67. I say this with no nostalgia for any of these past political regimes, which paved the way for the present ones, and with no support for new 'closures' or 'closed national economies', but rather to record the effects upon workers of the 'opening' of these societies to the totalitarian demands of the world market.

68. See the study by M. Chossudovsky, *The Globalisation of Poverty: Impacts of IMF and World Bank Reforms*, London: Zed Books, 1997 (and its bibliography).

69. See World Bank, *China 2020: Development Challenges in the New Century*, Washington DC: World Bank, 1997, and *Viet Nam, Transition to Market Economy*, Washington DC: World Bank, 1993.

Index